What We See

What We See

ADVANCING
THE OBSERVATIONS
OF JANE JACOBS

Edited by
Stephen A. Goldsmith & Lynne Elizabeth

NEW VILLAGE PRESS • OAKLAND, CA

Published in the United States by
New Village Press
P.O. Box 3049, Oakland, CA 94609
(510) 420-1361
bookorders@newvillagepress.net
www.newvillagepress.net

New Village Press is a public-benefit, not-for-profit publishing venture of
Architects/Designers/Planners for Social Responsibility. www.adpsr.org.

"The Intelligence of Informality" by Nabeel Hamdi contains adapted
content from *Small Change*, 2004, reprinted with permission of Earthscan, Ltd.

"The Needs of Children in Contemporary Cities" by Clare Cooper Marcus
contains adapted content from *Biophilic Design*, 2008, reprinted with
permission of John Wiley & Sons, Inc.

Grateful acknowledgment is made to funders of this publication:
The Rockefeller Foundation, Furthermore: a program of the J. M. Kaplan Fund,
The Nathan Cummings Foundation, The Zeidler Family, Greg O'Connell,
Martha Jean Shuttleworth, and The Newburgh Institute.

In support of the Greenpress Initiative, New Village Press is committed
to preserving endangered forests globally and advancing best practices
within the book and paper industries. The printing papers used in this book
are acid-free and have been certified with both the Forest Stewardship
Council (FSC) and the Sustainable Forestry Initiative (SFI).

ISBN-13 978-0-9815593-1-5
Publication Date: May 2010

Library of Congress Cataloging-in-Publication Data

What we see : advancing the observations of Jane Jacobs /
edited by Stephen A. Goldsmith and Lynne Elizabeth. — 1st ed.
p.   cm.
Includes bibliographical references and index.
ISBN 978-0-9815593-1-5 (hardcover : alk. paper)
1. City planning. 2. Urban renewal. 3. Community development. 4. Urban policy.
5. Jacobs, Jane, 1916-2006. I. Goldsmith, Stephen Arthur, 1954– II. Elizabeth, Lynne
HT166.W483 2010
307.1'216—dc22   2010012266

Interior design and composition by Leigh McLellan Design
Illustrations of Jane Jacobs and her spectacles by Robert Cowan

CONTENTS

SECTION 4

THE ORGANIZED COMPLEXITY
OF PLANNING

SECTION 5

DESIGN FOR NATURE,
DESIGN FOR PEOPLE

SECTION 6

ECONOMIC INSTINCTS

...ONE THING I *do know, or think I do, is that it is most important to look at the real world, not at what somebody has said is right—and that includes me! So be skeptical and critical in considering what I say, but not because of what somebody else says. Rather, because of what real life informs you.*

—Jane Jacobs letter to Hidenori Tamagawa, November 29, 1990

For Jane Jacobs (1916–2006)

JANE'S SPECTACLES

Michael Sorkin

JANE JACOBS SAW the city through corrective lenses. In her case, these were held in cat's eye frames. The contrast with the canonical glasses of her conceptual nemesis, Le Corbusier, is clear. His were rationalist spectacles, circular and dour, and emblematically male. Jane's were not simply more cheerful, more feminized, more biological than mathematical in their inspiration: they were more timely in their fashionability. And so it was with her view of the city: her gaze took in both the feral and the cooperative, a way of looking that saw urbanity not in the reduction of its order to the regularity of clockwork but in its vivid spontaneity and expansive, ever-transforming difference.

We all wear cat's eye glasses now. Too many of us, though, wear them to be seen rather than to see. One of the most succinctly trivial news items during the debate about the design of Ground Zero was a squib in the *Times* about the eyewear of the architects who were up for the job. All were studied and expensive and included at least one pair of the Corb/Johnson/Pei wannabe classics, parcel of starchitecture's most elemental displacement—the idea that the style and celebrity of the author were more than certification enough for the architecture to come.

Jane Jacobs' celebrity was more substantial, not the result of whom she knew or how she looked, but of what she did and how she thought. Like any great activist, her reputation shaded into notoriety and was voluminous enough to encompass many versions of her persona, from the economic thinker of depth, originality, and elegance, to the woman ready to climb on the table to be heard or to snatch a stenographer's notes to redirect a bureaucracy's remorselessness, to the door-to-door organizer of neighborhood will. Her stomping ground was the White Horse Tavern (just down the block from her legendary Hudson Street pad), not the Four Seasons or the Century Club, with their refined rituals of exclusion. Jane preferred a spot where crowds gathered cheek by jowl, grew convivial, and poured out onto the sidewalk.

Such sociability was and is a primary transaction of the way-of-seeing so expansively elaborated by Jane Jacobs. She was acutely sensitive to the membranes and thresholds— both visible and invisible—that structure the gradations from private to public, from the interior to the extroverted life. These shadings, in their richness and specificity, characterize the life of the city. Part of Jacobs' greatness as an urbanist was her simultaneously fearless and measured power of extrapolation. She had a unique ability to move from the particularities of the local interaction of incident and morphology to the larger patterns of urban life, as well as a keen understanding of the way in which the economies of life and exchange are embedded in what can only be inadequately described as "lifestyle."

I am continuously impressed by both the scalability and the translatability of Jacobs' fundamental insights about urban form, and have long used her specs to see cities more clearly. For many years, I have lived and worked within the ambit of Jacobs' Greenwich Village and, in both its excellences and deficits, the place remains a wonderful laboratory for urban observation. Like Jacobs, I have been accused of myopia, as critics contended that the Village is simply too exceptional, that the rising price of admission is exclusionary, and that there are insuperable issues in translating the virtues of a thickly developed and historical set of ecologies into the tasks of building the new. As the planet adds a million people to the urban population every week, however, it is both impossible and dangerous simply to expand existing cities, creating the urbanism of megacities, slums, and sprawl without end. Calling Jane's analysis irrelevant to this project is a strange critique, one that purges aspiration and memory from the necessary pursuit of the new.

Here is where Jacobs is especially vital, and it is crucial that her message be received in its authentic context. Jacobs is plagued by misappropriation and reductionism. While the prosody of her urban proposition—the short blocks, the multiple uses, the mix of building types and ages—is timelessly relevant, there is always a risk that formalization (as in the monochrome, mock-urban suburbs that often claim her imprimatur) will rob Jacobs' vision of its social core, of its politics: her message is not reducible to form. In seeing the city not only as artifact but as habitat, Jane Jacobs was not simply offering a riposte to the sterile, disciplinary order of modernist planning: she was anticipating a refreshed urbanity, capable of merging the social, environmental, and constructed environments into a single discourse. This is at the core of her innovation and its center of relevance today.

Henri Lefebvre, another great urbanist and rough contemporary of Jacobs, shared many of her principles, if expressing them in a somewhat different theoretical register. His argument for a shared "right to the city" is crucial to their common reading of the urban. Lefebvre understood this right only in a simple, instrumental way, as a defense of the public realm and a critique of the city of compounded discrimination and stratification. But, more importantly, he also insisted that this right must include the empowerment of citizens to work toward the city of their own dreams and fantasies, the right to multiplicity, the right to a city in which contention is permanent and negotiation unending.

For Jacobs, the negotiation was not simply cultural but economic, and this came to be more and more at the center of her work. Jacobs was ahead of the curve both in her command of the intricate, balletic ecology of urban economies and in her insistence on the relationship between the physical city, exchanges of every variety, and the defense and expansion of individual liberty. She argued that in economic systems—as in natural ones—diversity founds resiliency, and she examined and exalted cities as diversity's most secure habitat. Her arguments for import substitution as a driver of urban development (indeed, as foundational for cities) brought the question home to both the personal and the political. It was not simply economies that were expanding but choices, potentials, and freedoms.

The lenses in those glasses were multifocals, allowing Jacobs to see the city with unrivaled richness and nuance, and the ballet she saw was complex and rich with the beauties of everyday transactions. But it was a ballet in which the choreographic role was ceded to every individual. Rejecting the "ballet mechanique" of modernism as an autocratic dance akin to the maniacal, dehumanizing North Korean "mass games" (as well as the more elegant but equally prescriptive constraints of *Giselle*), she saw the decisive beauty and democracy in the ineffable yet concrete intercourse of the conventional and the creative. She recognized that the city can only be the crucible of dreams if it offers a stimulating home to every dreamer.

So much to see through those cat's eyed frames!

ACKNOWLEDGMENTS

ASSEMBLING THIS VOLUME could not have happened without the receptive ear of Joan Shigekawa at The Rockefeller Foundation. When we approached her with the concept of *What We See*, Ms. Shigekawa understood immediately the potential of bringing together the international voices of those whose work had been touched by the ideas of Jane Jacobs. She also shared our goal to advance new ideas rather than revisit old ones. To Ms. Shigekawa, along with Edwin Torres and Donald Roeseke-Dupree of The Rockefeller Foundation, we express our sincere gratitude.

The wisdom of Max Allen, Jane Jacobs' friend and the author of *Ideas That Matter: The Worlds of Jane Jacobs*, illuminated a path to avoid with this book, namely that it not be a book *about* Jane Jacobs. Over Chinese food in Toronto, one evening before Jacobs passed away, he told a few of us, "everything needing to be written about Jane has already been written." His support was catalytic in framing this project.

Early guidance from William S. Moody at Rockefeller Brothers Fund, followed by funding and assistance from Ben Rodriguez-Cubenas, allowed us to begin our voyage, while The Center for the Living City was still docked at Purchase College. Welcomed early on by Thomas J. Schwarz, the college's president, these men offered both a lifeline and a mooring. Without these two trusting friends and colleagues, the Center and this volume would not exist.

Critical support came also from Canada, especially from the Zeidler Family and Martha Jean Shuttleworth, who sustained the effort at a time when the world's economy imploded. Their gifts, along with Joan Davidson's assistance at Furthermore, a program of the J.M. Kaplan Fund, and Brandon Fragg's advocacy for funding from the Newburgh Institute, kept this project alive. Thanks to Claudine Brown and the Nathan Cummings Foundation for supporting New Village Press in the realization of this book and related civic engagement programs. To Greg O'Connell, whose Brooklyn-based redevelopment efforts are indicators of Jacobs' influence, and to all of these generous contributors, we express our gratitude.

When the time came to put hands on deck and move the project forward, the dedicated efforts of Maya Borgenicht were invaluable. To her and Brandy Brooks, BreAnne McConkie, and Roger Borgenicht our sincere appreciation. Our brilliant, high-spirited staff editor Stefania De Petris was a priceless gift to *What We See*. We owe much to her deft abilities to organize and her precision with language and style.

Our gratitude is also huge to the Jane's Walk teams, especially Jane Farrow, Nathaniel Currey, and Paige Pitcher for enlivening neighborhoods, honoring Jane, and bringing *What We See* to the streets. Similarly we thank the publicity team of New Village Press—Julie Miller, Laura Stumpf, and Janice Sapigao—for presenting *What We See* to the world in so many creative ways.

Special thanks to the Municipal Art Society of New York for hosting our advisory committee meetings and for their dedication to honoring the spirit of Jane Jacobs. To the board of the Center for the Living City—Ron Shiffman, Margie Zeidler, Mary Rowe, Richard Rabinowitz, Samina Quraeshi, and Rosanne Haggerty—our sincere thanks for their enthusiasm. Roberta Brandes Gratz, the board's president, provided essential guidance, and remained on call seven days a week for queries large and small. Mary Rowe's wisdom, guidance, and knowledge were indispensable.

Finally, the editors wish to thank their families and friends for their generous patience, understanding, and good humor.

EYES WIDE OPEN

Stephen A. Goldsmith & Lynne Elizabeth

To see is to forget the name of the thing one sees.
—Paul Valéry

OBSERVATION CAN TELL more about the observer than about the environment being observed. It reflects the values, beliefs, and worldview of the witness. We see through the lens of our interests and understanding. We recognize patterns that match what we have seen before. Hiking with a birdwatcher is quite a different experience from hiking with a geologist—one points out the flicking wings of a Ruby-crowned Kinglet, the other notes the lavender glint of Lepidolite mica. Neither may notice the changing cloud formations that spell tomorrow's snow. Taking an eye to the city, sociologists will track interactions among people, traffic planners will watch the flow of vehicles, and architects will scan the structure and façade of the buildings. What we see is largely who we are and what we have learned to see. There is no such thing as an objective observer.

All the same, philosophers, monks, and judges have sought for millennia the elusive skill of observing what *is*, without influence of their personal opinions. The open mind, the beginner's mind, and the blindfolded eyes of justice remained their ideal. Scientists, too, strived to measure the physical world without bias. Failing that, they learned to state their bias as hypothesis, and set to prove or disprove it by experiment. The veracity of neutrality in science was already conundrum enough, when quantum physicists came running in to declare the most startling observation to date—that the very act of observing affects the state of reality being observed. They had seen that observers become participants in their observation, whatever that observation might be.

Looking with a clear mind, unswayed by internal or external prejudice and unfettered by popular beliefs, was an abiding aspiration of Jane Jacobs. Jacobs was determined to see the truth. She held a bright torch to everything she observed, and that brilliant light revealed obscure details, hidden corners, and new interpretations that transformed our consciousness. That her observations have played a role in the state of the world she observed is, like the principle of quantum mechanics, something to be reckoned with. Among the most illustrative phrases she coined was "ballet of the street," an eye-opening idiom of grand proportion. This renaming of an everyday experience shifted our perspective, influencing the way we would experience sidewalks forever after.

Although she had no academic pedigree, Jane Jacobs respected scientific investigation, choosing useful, "fruitful questions," as she called them, and framing and reframing potential answers to test. She took delight in the unexpected questions and unexplored paths that arise through the act of investigation itself. Jacobs was concerned about the demise of scientific process and outraged at society's failure to heed the valuable truths science had already revealed. She was particularly irked by blatant political blindness to common sense and by slavery to formulaic thinking. Jacobs aimed to break through those stonewalls of ignorance with the force of fresh evidence, evidence she presented fearlessly in her writing and activism.

Perhaps less rigorous than intuitive in her looking, she looked nonetheless with a keen and imaginative eye, tracking, her whole nearly ninety-year life, an insatiable curiosity, finding insights galore that she shared with the glee of a child turning over rocks in the woods to see what wiggles underneath.

As an original thinker, Jacobs continued to stretch the boundaries of what we know—her views flew in the face of common dogma. As a practical, grounded thinker, she made her purpose to uncover how cities work and explain the mechanisms that bring health to urban areas, vitality to abandoned places, and economic growth where there is stagnation. She is remembered as a champion of neighborhoods and a formidable opponent of urban renewal models, with their bulldoze-and-modernize credo. *Not a single person—not a single sparrow—shall be displaced* was the rallying cry she inspired to protect New York City's Greenwich Village housing from the wrecking ball. Jacobs had a profound effect on the entire field of urban planning and economics through her ability to use examples from the street to inform her elegant philosophies.

Jacobs favored insertion of the good and warned against damage caused in excising the bad: "It's not so much a matter of taking out bad things as sensitively adding in good things." She exhorted city fathers not to study the causes of poverty, but rather to apply their minds to the causes of prosperity, poverty being simply the absence of prosperity, as darkness is the absence of light—"To seek the causes of poverty is to enter an intellectual dead end." Her work presaged the shift within the community development field from a focus on the pathologies of low-income neighborhoods to a focus on neighborhood assets. Jacobs loved the cities she lived in with fierceness and tenderness. Among her many gifts was her ability to see the inherent rhythm and melody of casual urban encounters and to treasure things as mundane as the tomatoes grown on her roof.

She saw cities as the cauldrons of inventiveness and industry; cities as centers of creativity, self-organization, and synthesis; cities as the womb of wealth. Jacobs believed it was possible to understand the world by looking deeply at the city. "Cities… they're the crux of so many different subjects, so many different puzzles… There's almost nothing you can think of that cities don't provide some insight into." Jane Jacobs' observations empowered us to trust what we see as the point of departure for new inquiry. This open way of looking is her most lasting gift.

To observe Jane Jacobs' influence during these early years of the twenty-first century, one only needs to set a Google Alert with her name. An early adopter of the concept of "web-thinking," as she called it long before the internet was a daily part of our lives, we wonder what her reaction might be in seeing her name pop up every morning in a Google Alert, attached to a blog, a news story, a keynote speech, a city council meeting, or a public celebration. Just as "Google" went from a brand name to a verb, "Jane Jacobs" has evolved from a proper noun to an adjective and an adverb. By now, even streets, awards, and fellowships are named after her.

Evidence of Jacobs' influence is also heard when her ideas are referred to as "Jacobsian," as if one could freeze and isolate her thinking in a discrete system of thought. Close friends and colleagues agree that they could never suppose what Jacobs was about to think or say at any given moment. She was full of surprises and was averse to any dogmatic fixation of her views. Therefore, if there is anything *Jacobsian* for us to emulate, it is to open our minds as observers, to see the continually evolving processes that operate in our world at every scale.

Perhaps Jacobs' invitation to trust our eyes helps explain why an August 2009 *Planetizen* survey affirmed her place in history as the most influential urban thinker of all time. Finding her at the very top of a list of one hundred people, ahead of the likes of Lewis Mumford, Daniel Burnham, Vitruvius, and Baron Georges-Eugene Haussmann, is made even more striking by the wide margin of her acclamation. Jacobs received 1,147 votes, compared to the 791 votes of the closest runner-up. Out of these top one hundred urbanists, only nine are women. And significantly, of the eight other women who made the list, three are contributors to this book—Janette Sadik-Khan, Roberta Brandes Gratz, and Saskia Sassen.

The idea to assemble *What We See* began with conversations among people whose lives had been woven in Jacobs' broad community for many years. During the last years of her profoundly engaged life, she encouraged the establishment of The Center for the Living City, an organization dedicated to exploring the complexity of contemporary urban life. Shortly after her death in 2006, a month before her ninetieth birthday, a small band of activists, writers, journalists, and community organizers imagined producing a book celebrating the breadth of her influence on the interrelated fields of economics, urban life, and ethics. *What We See* is that book, and one of the Center's first major projects.

Advancing knowledge, whether by debunking old ideas or allowing them to flourish in new directions, is the taproot of this book. New ideas are always built upon old ones. The biblical pronouncement that there is nothing new under the sun might as well read, "There are only things newer under the sun." The development of *What We See* has been a humble attempt to look back at Jacobs' contributions in order to push new observations forward. During the assembly of this book we've tried to hold onto the idea that the book's posture carry a forward lean, and each essayist has held to this expectation.

The responsibility of selecting our essayists was an enormous challenge. We knew from the beginning that we could only present a few prime examples of those whose lives, ideas, and work were influenced by Jane Jacobs and, in several instances, whose work she admired. To illuminate what might have been a dark path ahead, we assembled an advisory committee of people who had either worked with Jacobs or knew firsthand the interdisciplinary, international impact of her contributions. The committee included Susan Witt, Sanford Ikeda, James Stockard, and Mary Rowe. Also by our side offering guidance during this selection process was Margie Zeidler, winner of the Jacobs Prize in 2003 and a family friend of Jacobs. This group's indispensable insights helped plant the first seed of what would become the volume in your hands.

The selected essays pay tribute to Jacobs not out of a desire to bow before the altar of her legacy, but as an attempt to take her legacy of disciplined inquiry to new heights. Although Jane Jacobs is most widely known for her discussions about cities, one objective of this book is to expand the acknowledgment of her influence beyond the physical and social aspects of urban life. This volume is an interdisciplinary effort and collects contributions from a broad range of fields, including economics, sociology, psychiatry, journalism, playwriting, social activism, politics, urban planning, biology, and architecture.

Some of the authors never met or spoke with Jane Jacobs. Some are working on economic theories that affect people worldwide, such as Saskia Sassen, Pierre Desrochers, Samuli Leppälä, and Sanford Ikeda; others are devoted to specific neighborhoods or regions, such as Jacobs Medal winner Alexie Torres-Fleming. Some of our authors have engaged in urban planning at local and regional levels such as Jaime Lerner; practitioners such as Ron Shiffman have developed community-based planning models that have affected national policy; and others such as Mindy Fullilove have worked to reveal how insensitive urban development practices have displaced people and decimated neighborhoods. But in every case the threads from Jacobs' broad loom, her tapestry of connections and web thinking, are what bind together the pages of *What We See*.

The book's six sections are divided into porous themes. We open the book with a look at what Jane Jacobs loved the most: the bustling vitality of neighborhoods, their organized complexity and self-organization, gritty as it has to be. Section 2 suggests ways to look at this spectacle with the same wonder and appreciation that characterized Jacobs' relentless gaze. In Section 3 we apply these new tools and lenses to the exploration of cities, villages, and streets in their most authentic forms, raising questions and exposing nuances of how we move through time and space.

Once we have identified what works in a city and what could be improved, we examine in Section 4 innovative ways to address the complex problems of planning, exploring hardscrabble edges, public engagement processes in cities around the world, and stories that encourage next steps toward environmental, economic, and social justice. Observing new ways of addressing environmental challenges and social vulnerabilities is the subject of Section 5. Finally, Section 6 expands some of Jane Jacobs' most inspiring (and less famous) economic intuitions. Here, fresh perspectives on urban creativity and alternative practices endow us with palpable possibilities for the future.

We believe this book presents ideas that would have engaged Jane Jacobs in passionate conversations. To be *Jane's Cup of Tea*, the title of her friend Mary Rowe's epilogue, is what we imagined for this book. What we envision for you, Dear Reader, is that you will join us as we work together to build more resilient cities and more responsive communities. To that end, we have included a study guide, to encourage conversations about ideas and opportunities that matter to you. Using our essayists' thoughtful contributions as points of departure, we invite you to continue exploring our world with the open-eyed spirit of one of the most extraordinary, courageous thinkers of our time.

What We See

SECTION I

Vitality of the Neighborhood

BETWEEN UTOPIAS

Deanne Taylor*

U TOPIA IS A DESTINATION so beautiful and beneficial for all, quite a few must be hideously sacrificed en route. The city of Toronto does not dream of such perfection. Its civic imagination is shaped by generations of immigrants unfit for utopias around the world: people who fled Divine Monarchs, Great Oarsmen, Beloved Leaders, Infallible Clerics, Infamous Tyrants and Obscure Social Engineers, war, reservation, pogrom, gulag, holocaust, apartheid, genocide, slavery, conscription, torture, and endless utopian techniques of great evil for a Greater Good. Toronto's collective anthem or civic prayer might be "No megalomania, please, we're *between* utopias."

Between -Isms, between Ideals, between Paradise and Hell, Torontonians are free from the weight of a purely racial, religious or ideological destiny—relieved by the relative lightness of being Canadian. Thanks to centuries of creative resistance by Aboriginals and *les Canadiens français,*

---

*From the time Jane Jacobs arrived in my hometown of Toronto she began to alter the very terms of our planning debate and made us see our habitat through new eyes. She showed us how buildings and byways either nurture or strangle economic and social life; she championed the public realm and public interest; she blew away weasel words like "growth" and gave us language to apprehend the vital dynamics of city life. The following essay began as a brief speech I gave in honor of Jane Jacobs, was then expanded for a Toronto-focused anthology, and is revised for this book so that it might entertain a wider audience. Although it is a portrait of Toronto, others may recognize their own city's glories and follies.

Canada's nationality is not based on the simple solidarities of ethnicity but on shared political ideas like liberty, justice, and enfranchisement—complex principles and instruments that evolve with use. Once acquired, these legalistic entitlements may not fire the blood, wet the eye, set armies marching, or unleash collective passions as flags, martyrs, myths and hymns can do, but that's the idea. Citizens are free to be as English or Irish, as American or Iraqi, as Indian or Pakistani as they can, as long as they don't blow up each other's discos.

Toronto's messianic potential is tempered not only by a cool nationality but by an even cooler climate. The city's natural antidote to old crusades and new insurrections is winter, when all Torontonians are created equal and made peaceful by wearing parkas. Shivering in slush, reaching home before frostbite, thawing out, ensuring supply lines: the tyranny of winter demands alliances with neighbors and co-workers on the ecumenical and apolitical basis of a war against cold. The city unites in puffy coats and runny noses; newcomers are woven into the ancient rhythm of shoveling snow for people who threw their backs out while shoveling snow; all are linked for survival in mitt-borrowing and boot-lending without regard for race or creed. In spring, Torontonians are filled with gratitude for the return of light and warmth and are not the fodder of grandiose missions, but more inclined to cultivate their own gardens, water their neighbors' yards while they're away, and pick up litter in the local park.

Toronto is a young metropolis whose taxation and planning powers are firmly in the parental grip of a provincial government. Whenever the city threatens to mature, it is restructured or vastly expanded, arresting its sense of city-hood. Now comprised of 640 square kilometers, a hundred languages and ten centuries of custom, Toronto is almost unknowable. In the outlying areas, dispersed suburban tracts, high-rise slums, and expressways conspire to stunt social and economic life; but in the older and densely residential core, the city's scale and cultural dissonance are moderated by hundreds of village-like neighborhoods, which socialize and civilize their inhabitants with human-scale buildings and byways created and recreated since the nineteenth century. Few neighborhoods are monocultural, or homogenously rich or poor; most embrace residents of many mother cultures and means, and feature modest homes, decent schools, safe parks, community centers, snow removal, tree doctors, wildlife rescuers, and a billion dollars worth of policing to discourage sociopaths and illegal parking.

Most vitally, at the physical centers of these neighborhoods are low-rise, fine-grain, mixed-use mainstreets where the social, entrepreneurial, and recreational energies of the community gather, recombine, and evolve. Blessed with laws, humbled by climate, unburdened by history or destiny, Torontonians remake the world in their small communities, adding yoga, sweat lodge, dim sum or donuts to their lives. Neighbors meet easily and frequently in local stores, schoolyards, parks; they transcend private beliefs to share common aspirations—healthy children, peaceful streets, stable work, helpful neighbors, mutual respect. Toronto's genius for hyper-local improvisation and collaboration sustains social peace and economic stability in hundreds of organically grown neighborhoods. Here, Toronto fashions small miracles of civilization: multiple urban ecosystems of social and entrepreneurial imagination, the DNA of civic life.

There is a quality even meaner than outright ugliness or disorder, and this meaner quality is the dishonest mask of pretended order, achieved by ignoring or suppressing the real order that is struggling to exist and to be served.
　　　—Jane Jacobs, *The Death and Life of Great American Cities*

To live in Toronto is to live in two cities at once, one real, one virtual. For most residents the real city is a few neighborhoods, the familiar places of home, work and play, experienced with feet on the pavement, hand on a tree, eye on a sunrise, ear to the street, nose in the bakery. Beyond the body's intimate knowledge is a virtual city of words and images, a post-colonial city built with shards of history and avalanches of media, a city of myths, brands, and megaplans. Those who create the virtual Toronto, who spin virtu-topian stories of its gifts and possibilities, who frame the city's history and therefore its future, are always those who own the biggest microphones. Toronto's most amplified mythmakers are the oracles of media, business, politics, and city planning.

In the mirror of the local mass media, Toronto glimpses its cutest, saddest, proudest, most horrifying features, and wherever a little is magnified, much is hidden. Some journalists seek to reflect the city's true character, but most publishers and broadcasters are faithful to Toronto's colonial tradition of emulating or importing rather than creating, and derive the bulk of their advertising and content from the American infotainment empire. So complete is the local habit of self-effacement, many broadcasters, editors and reporters are proud to call Toronto "Hollywood North"—to honor the city's branch-plant film industry. "Hollywood North" and "Broadway North" are the simu-topian dreams of those who see Toronto as a sequel to a really successful utopia. Industriously, they shape the city as a local backdrop for the foreign celebrities of mass-market TV, movies, music, sports, and fashion, and much profit is made without risk by those with no need to invent, develop, produce and distribute original goods.

Imported vision is the preference not only of the media but of all the higher echelons of Toronto's corporate class. In the boardrooms and conference rooms of big business, the ideal city is a franchise, based on the magic formulae, branding and investment of a mightier power: this is The City That Goes Ka-Ching. For these corporate utopians, Toronto is real estate and ad space, where citizens are consumers, City Hall is a business facilitator, and politics is an extension of deal-making. To make their dreams come true, corporate leaders and lobbyists groom political candidates, finance and run election campaigns, write and promote public policy for private profit, and show an enthusiasm for civic politics that literally knows no bounds. With the passion of soothsayers, they urge Torontonians not to hoard public property as their grandparents did; not to pass on to their children the natural infrastructure of the city, the waterfront, greenspace, sky, sunlight, vistas; not to bequeath public space, public services, public institutions, but rather to unload these assets quickly to stave off the virtual bankruptcy of the virtual city.

The ideal Toronto conjured by the media and big business is well represented at City Hall, where few challenge the basic models of Hollywood North or The City That Goes Ka-Ching. Indeed, the better to serve such visions, City Hall has largely replaced the old language of the public interest with the shiny new ad-speak of profit and promotion. The idea of taxation as a collective investment in social harmony has been succeeded by tax phobia, a disorder accompanied by the wasting disease "downloading" in which expenses rise and tax revenues shrink until local government is all stick and no puck. Understaffed and under-financed, the public service often depends on private studies and statistics, on private development or purchase of public assets, on privately underpaid workers and the "lower costs" they are said to ensure. With think tanks and summits, with Power Point spiels and adbuys, with job offers and junkets, with campaign-financing and editorial endorsements, Toronto's most powerful private interests engage the minds and gild the tongues of public servants. And City Hall, grappling with hundreds of thousands of micro-decisions, is all too grateful for utopian metaphors and slogans, language that orders the chaos of democracy, language that conjures the common good while justifying particular evils.

The vernacular spirit of Toronto is informal, ingenious, quite romantic and full of fun... The official spirit of Toronto is... impressed with mediocrity if it's very very big and expensive.
—Jane Jacobs, Canadian Broadcasting Corporation

Constructed of hype, branding, polls, and other rumours, the virtual Toronto is a comforting home filled with flattering portraits of the leading citizens, a glamorous home adorned by celebrity architects and visiting superstars, a wealthy home that desires only an Olympian bankruptcy to cap its ambitions. Through years of practice Toronto residents manage to ignore the contradictions between the virtual city and their own tangible neighborhoods; that is, until the two collide—and in the oldest parts of the city collisions are constant. Though already marred by decades of ugly "renewal" and mall-aping "transition," the civility and creativity of residents and entrepreneurs make the area vitally attractive, and the let's-make-a-deal zoning offered by City Hall has made the area speculatively priceless. Every day on someone's block the megadreams of developers and planners crash into the treasured equilibrium of a neighborhood ecosystem, demanding the sacrifice of a precious aspect—a sunny sidewalk or window, a fine-grain block of main street, a lakefront, a vista of natural or architectural grace. At City Hall, where dreams become bylaws, where abstractions become all too concrete, Virtu-topia meets the Neighborhood in a contest of urban vision.

This contest plays out continuously for stakes great and small. On one side are corporate lobbyists and strategists, paid by the year, friendly with politicians and bureaucrats, fluent in laws and loopholes, and armed with the civic goods of Progress, Development, Investment, Intensification, or Tourism. On the other side of the contest is the volunteer neighborhood group, funded by bake sales, composed of a few veterans and raw recruits, and armed with the civic goods of Stability, Harmony, Beauty, Heritage, Local Innovation. Some call this no contest, some call it the tough love of democracy.

In every neighborhood battle lost or won, residents and small business owners grow new civic muscles. For every condo tower eclipsing the sun, for every threat of an expressway, airport, incinerator or megaproject, new political energy gathers in quiescent neighborhoods. As long as planners, developers and politicians blueprint perfect cities, real communities resist.

When citizens have activism thrust upon them, they discover there is honor in being a member of the unofficial government of the verifiable Toronto, but the price of voluntary participation in politics is dear—thousands of life-hours for meetings and mailings, for studies and bylaws opaque in their specialized idioms, years of deputations to inattentive City Councillors, and lifelong status as Nimbys (Not In My Back Yarders), or Selfish Interests, or A Few Malcontents Standing In The Way Of Market Forces and Other Inevitabilities. In any development skirmish, neighborhood residents are not in the right until proven wrong, but immediately charged as Enemies of the Common Good, and forced to defend what Arundhati Roy calls the Greater Common Good, the officially unrecognized Good that does not sacrifice the small, real and irreplaceable treasures of nature and culture.

I hate the government for making my life absurd.
—Jane Jacobs on activism. Interview with
the journal *Government Technology*.

Such citizen-governors stand in the path of the utopian bulldozers and cranes that would plunder the land and sky and diminish community wealth for the benefit of a few, all in the name of "growth." As victories are usually temporary and losses usually unjust, many inspired or irate citizens do not return to an apolitical state, but rather are propelled deeper into the mysteries of electing city politicians, providing them with evidence and direction, cultivating a neighborhood meeting by meeting, voter by voter. Yet most of these battles are so local and idiosyncratic they have yet to snowball into a citywide movement for better planning—most planners and even most politicians seem to prefer it that way. For decades, the left wing of council has joined the right wing in support of large developments and grotesque rezoning. No doubt some councillors truly love these towering, big-boxing, block-busting edifices, but just as surely almost all are addicted to the crack cocaine of city planning—large dollops of cash from developers for the councillors' pet projects, officially known as "public benefits."

The pork-barrel planning decisions of individual councillors fit well with the long-term aspirations of the virtual Toronto. Utopian lingo and greasy loopholes are entrenched in City bylaws, budgets, processes, and plans. The current Official Plan posits an imminent Torontopia that is comelier, greener, neighborhood-ier, and simultaneously the opposite: a bigger and cheaper tax base, a magical stretchy city where half a million new ratepayers ("or even more") can be acquired for free by wedging them into the existing public infrastructure on Toronto's main street grid. Developers, who helped the city's tax-starved bureaucrats design this policy of rapid intensification, are maximizing the windfall by stuffing cheap condo towers and their associated megastores into modest-scale mainstreets across the city; there is no process to ensure that new buildings fit their profile and profits to the long-term interests of these successful neighborhoods. While the iconic heritage-scapes of the city are assaulted by development that evicts successful small businesses for global franchises, wrecks architectural scale, and steals public goods, City Hall keeps on tax-farming in the sky.

Toronto's oldest buildings and neighborhoods nurture the oldest civic DNA *and* incubate the newest mutations, as Jane Jacobs first observed in New York. It was in the mature neighborhoods of Toronto's core where official "multiculturalism" began to fuse into a true local culture, where the tribes mixed in street markets and music clubs and saw that it was good, where the world came to enjoy the harmonious polyrhythms of this urban jam. Just as each successful neighborhood depends on an energy-transforming main street, Toronto-at-large has always needed this thumping heart at its center—neighborhoods where inventors and newcomers can afford to live, collaborate, and provide a market for the new. The urbane downtown has been shaped and defined by heritage buildings, sociable streets, views of the sky's endless dance—non-renewable public resources now being ravished by developers. Like farmland and wildland threatened by lateral sprawl and its attendant pollutions and extinctions, Toronto's urban ecosystem is a fragile mix of nature and culture, endangered by vertical sprawl and the destruction of rare urban life-forms. In the next decade, the city will decide whether it wants a heart or a mall, whether to protect the older downtown neighborhoods for their priceless sociocultural value, or tear them down as sacrifices to the latest one-size utopia.

In the venerable Cameron House Tavern on Queen West hangs a simple sign made by sculptor Tom Dean: it reads THIS IS PARADISE. Most of Toronto's residents know that in their comfortable neighborhoods they have found the sweet spot, found as perfect a 'topia as possible under the circumstances so far. They enjoy and renew the city's heritage of built forms and social values, shaping the prosperity and harmony of their communities and the city-at-large. The same cannot be said of Toronto's leaders who are blinded by utopias from another place and time, and cannot see the golden neighborhoods for the glittering towers. Toronto can only aspire to be great by deciding to be itself—by cherishing its own heritage and values, its own thinkers and artists, its own small-business owners and residents, its own funky sky-lines and safe streets, its own live-and-let-live/all-in-the-same-canoe ethos. Perhaps one day the city's leaders will tear themselves from their simu-topian fantasies, fall deeply in love with the real Toronto, and help to cultivate the true-topia no one could have dreamed.

POSTSCRIPT

Any culture that jettisons the values that have given it com-petence, adaptability, and identity becomes weak and hollow. A culture can avoid that hazard only by tenaciously retaining the underlying values responsible for the culture's nature and success. That is the framework into which adaptations must be assimilated. —Jane Jacobs, *Dark Age Ahead*

In instances of apparent inconsistency between existing and planned contexts when interpreting the built form policies as they relate to height and density, the planned context will prevail. *Toronto's Official Plan* (3.7)

In a city where so many politicians and planners claim to be influenced by Jane Jacobs, it's remarkable how rarely they act to preserve, sustain, or genuinely enhance with new development the main streets and neigh-borhoods that define Toronto's civic character. At a downtown corner where I've lived and worked for thirty years, I've watched the buildings and pavements channel the creative energy of perhaps the most cultur-ally and economically diverse community anywhere—and watched as careless "planning" eroded that energy one entrepreneur or family at a time. Jacobs and others strove for decades to celebrate and nurture the old city's modest and well-distributed treasures, but the purveyors of "very very big mediocrities" have never backed down except to regroup.

Indeed the earliest and most astonishing successes of Jacobs and her cohort of reformers in the 1970s—stopping a city-center expressway from destroying lively neighborhoods, limiting building heights, electing a visionary mayor—produced a fierce backlash: Toronto's top burghers formed a fundraising coalition that enthroned for twenty years a series of megaproject-loving mayors. By the turn of the century, these prophets of private-sector ingenuity and accountability had crazy-glued Toronto to four suburban boroughs and created a sprawling metropolis: in utopia-speak, "a global player" wildly attractive to investors and tourists; in truth, starved of resources for schools, transit, housing, and street-cleaning, bursting at its welfare-seams, and prey at the highest levels of public service to multi-million-dollar boondoggles and conflicts of interest. Real estate prices soared, services shrank, condos boomed, big box stores devoured mainstreets, every corner featured beggars or squeegee-kids; between out-of-control profiteering and out-of-control poverty, average citizens felt powerless to act. The new urban-suburban government was so large and culturally conflicted it managed to discourage all but veteran activists for many years.

Unchallenged and unaccountable, the regime finally self-destructed with revelations of scandal, graft, and incompetence. In the 2003 election the political machine that had fabricated the virtually unworkable "megacity" lost its mojo and many of its loyal hacks. The young councillor who improbably won the mayoralty lauded neighborhood values and diverse communities, as all Toronto pols must, but stood out from blander opponents for his vision of the city-at-large. He spoke of beauty and civility, he promised to sweep the lobbyists from the corridors of city hall and to defend the public interest over narrow private interests. Emblematically, he opposed a waterfront jetport and the Tourism Utopia promised by its powerful boosters; he restored the lakeshore to the public imagination as a neighborhood for walking and talking and pushing the baby carriage, a public realm where jet-fueled profit had no place. His message was brave, unusual and resonant; in a fever of hope, Toronto's multitude of activists briefly gave up realism, and imagined that such a mayor might understand and accomplish almost anything.

Following the election the airport briefly cooled its jets, but like all truly bad ideas was refitted for a new attack and further expansion, protected by federal fiat. Public space and neighborhoods continue to be gutted by disfiguring development; and despite new rules, lobbyists adeptly manipulate them, assisted by a provincial municipal board with still unchecked power to overturn City Council decisions. The young mayor in his second term has successes to his credit on all the big-picture items: transit, waste, housing, poverty, gun control, infrastructure, and so on. But regarding the finer details of street life, the mayor has been disappointingly blinkered: blind to the city microcosms where councillors trade rezoning for slush funds; focused instead on bidding for the Pan Am Games ("Your moment is Here"), and projecting the rewards of intensification ("Smart Growth"). Having lost sight of neighborhood ecosystems, the mayor also lost the voice that once articulated the city's modest un-utopian dreams, and finally lost the will to run for re-election. His untimely exit produced a leadership vacuum, instantly filled by one-trick councillors and bored or failed provincial politicians, all certain they were qualified to cut the ribbon at the Pan Am Games.

Given political leadership and sanction, the civic energy of Toronto's neighborhoods would be used to create local plans that allow for benign growth; in the absence of political leadership for such a process, each block must field its own out-matched volunteers to fight mainly unwinnable battles—a terrible diversion of neighborly time. Despite the indifference of City Hall and the burnout of a generation or two of activists, Jane Jacobs' troops are everywhere, falling in love with their city, shaping and being shaped by its character. Some residents' groups are working to pre-empt careless rezoning by drawing up local plans for medium-rise, mixed-use intensification with floor-plate limits; there are young advocates for public space, for cycling, for pedestrians, for billboard control, for car-free market days, for a jet-free lakeshore, for guerilla gardening, and so on. Neighbors build a public oven in a local park; a community theater company leads a gorgeous carnival in the slushy December streets; mom-and-pop entrepreneurs work twice as hard to afford their rising rents; musicians and writers and painters search the city's soul and apartment listings.

The older city tenaciously holds on as her charms are bartered away. Many hands made these buildings, many generations collaborated in forming a cityscape where private life and the public life of work and play are dynamically integrated: the remains of this coherent habitat continue to generate cultural and economic bounty. But it's not difficult to imagine that global players with sweatshop products, and local developers with shoebox condos, will succeed in transforming downtown Toronto into a sky-scraping, mall-ified, youth-fleecing faux-topia: where rents rise 500 percent and keep rising; where whole blocks tumble to branded boxes, and other blocks are cast into shade from October to March; where fine-grain variety turns to slabs of sameness, pedestrians take other routes, old owners cash in, innovators and young families move out, schools close, huge clubs open, and drunken louts from the hinterland rampage through the streets three nights a week. In fact, it's unnecessary to imagine this degeneration, because it is already deforming my neighborhood, and its symptoms are diagnosable across the old city.

Jane Jacobs' last book, *Dark Age Ahead*, was written no doubt with her beloved American cities in mind, but also with Toronto in her face—a city in perpetual conflict between the "official spirit" and the "vernacular spirit" she identified forty years ago. Official Toronto is still losing memory of its own heritage and pursuing novelty, gimmicks, and brands, still dismantling cultural stabilisers and erecting faux-topian built-forms known to be fatal to living cities. Vernacular Toronto is still reanimating old buildings and cherishing sunny sidewalks, hugging trees and returning lost wallets, keeping the city's heart beating and the city's eyes on the humble streets. Even Jane Jacobs could not predict the future, but plainly saw that in the contests between cultural amnesia and memory, between fanciful and functioning economies, between civic alienation and harmony, the winners will be. . . almost no one, or almost everyone.

JANE JACOBS AND THE "BATTLE FOR THE STREET"

Ray Suarez

AMERICANS HAVE HAD a long and ambivalent relationship with the street. Since the days when America's great cities were in their infancy and huddled along the eastern seaboard, the custodians of propriety wished to shoo people indoors, away from the grime, chaos, temptations, and sheer randomness of social life carried out in the public way.

Take a look at the fading photographs of daily life in late nineteenth-century cities. The sidewalks were filled with open-air shops, performance spaces, debating societies, restaurants, and miniature factories. From their crowded and sweltering flats people poured onto the pavement to catch a little air, run into friends, and simply take in the distraction and novelty of the passing parade. There was crime, but also the social enforcement of decent behavior by countless eyes on the street. At the same time as home folks kept an eye out for you, the urban street also offered the gift of anonymity. Not far from your own street, your "village," was a block where you could reinvent yourself, unbound for a little while by the constraints of family, heritage, religion, and status.

For all the centuries of tut-tutting and hand-wringing in the salons and drawing rooms of our country, the street hung in: we simply were not wealthy enough to hustle young America's masses off to the presumed safety, cleanliness and social uplift of somewhere else.

When we finally were wealthy enough, we gave it a shot. The hugger-mugger of the sidewalk was going to be reformed, improved, sanitized. Although from the earliest days of the earliest cities people the world over had established the joys of urban life, the country that had rewritten rules for everything else was going to show Europeans, Asians, and Africans just how wrong they could be. From the 1920s to the final days of the twentieth century we engaged in an economically destructive and socially corrosive assault on the street that was doomed to failure.

Jane Jacobs understood what was going on. Her monumental ur-text, *The Death and Life of Great American Cities*, was a long paean to the humanizing, secure, child-friendly, and economically coherent nature of the urban street. Again and again, she raked the idea that sidewalks were places of disorder and danger, and used devastating examples of how much more dangerous places became when people were made strangers to each other by the forcible pursuit of utopian fantasies.

> That the sight of people attracts still other people is something that city planners and city architectural designers seem to find incomprehensible. They operate on the premise that city people seek the sight of emptiness, obvious order and quiet. Nothing could be less true. People's love of watching activity and other people is constantly evident in cities everywhere. (Jacobs 1961, 47)

To remember just how countercultural *Death and Life* really was, you have to cast your mind back to 1961, when the book first appeared. After World War II, millions of returning service people and hundreds of thousands of internal sojourners were heading back to metropolitan areas with minuscule vacancy rates for antiquated rental housing. Millions of couples were going to have postponed weddings and, eventually, millions of postponed babies. After the dislocation of the Great Depression and the war, family formation was undergoing an explosion, and the standing bricks and mortar in America's cities were simply unequal to the task of housing everyone who needed it. The vacancy rate in Chicago and New York hovered around one percent, as extended families doubled up to stretch crimped wartime household budgets.

It was a time of great potential, and America chose fantasies over planning, dreams over design, caprice over care. We built thousands of new places in corn and potato fields, and imagined that when we discarded the multiple dwelling and the streetcar, we could also throw out everything that went with it: schools a fourth-grader could walk to, stores an elderly person could reach without a car, and the great stage on which the daily drama of centuries of urban life in America had been played, the sidewalk.

Just over the city line, a thousand sons of Ebenezer Howard got busy creating idealized garden cities, a riotous and isolating mishmash of circular drives, cul-de-sacs, and sidewalkless streets. Closer to the urban core, cut-rate Corbusiers tried their best to kill whole flocks of birds with one stone: thousands of old residential blocks that had given birth to and raised the working class that had just won the war were razed and replaced by Radiant City developments sorted by class and race. Old was bad. New was good. Public was bad since by definition it belonged to everyone. Private was good because those with money could make the rules. Suddenly you could choose your neighbors, choose the children your own little ones would meet at school, and climb into the private, insulating world of the automobile to carry you along publicly financed roads to work.

Jane Jacobs set her face to the gale-force winds of change destroying the urban core of older American cities, as the newest cities were built from scratch according to the deadening dictates of the automobile. For so many cities, a perfect storm brought together regional planners, editorial pages, federal legislation, veterans' subsidies, suburban developers, and politicians prepared to throttle the spatial aspirations of their black (and increasingly brown) residents. The sidewalk didn't have a chance.

Jacobs warned that tampering with or handicapping the organic and delicately calibrated web of relationships existing on the urban street would set a powerfully self-reinforcing downward spiral into motion. From the 1950s onwards, a fast-growing metropolitan middle and upper-middle class could demonize the urban street until its lurid fantasies of what it was like there finally came true.

Commercial strips that allowed an after-work stroll to assemble the ingredients for dinner from the offerings of several different stores were abandoned in favor of the auto-imperative strip mall. The neighborhoods that blended commercial space seamlessly and unremarkably into residential areas were tagged as undesirable for both business and daily life. Those with means were expected, and often required by the devastation of urban renewal, to leave for greener pastures, suburban monocultures where home and shop were kept well apart for the happiness and well-being of both.

I wish I could report, more than sixty years after the end of the last world war, that accumulated wisdom, economic rationality, and care for human beings dictated our planning and building decisions. Alas, design decisions tend to follow the rigorous planning process that brought us the Nehru jacket, miniskirts, maxiskirts, and Mohawks. It was fashion and convenience, not utility and success, that drove the shape of the communities built in the thousands from the 1960s on. After all these years, politicians and planners might be feeling a little walleyed, keeping one eye on the means and desires of their wealthiest customers, and controlling the poor and near-poor who still outnumber them even after decades of breakneck economic growth.

The dreams for sidewalkless America never panned out. The neighborhoods millions of Americans fled to "for the children" still held dangers and fears, and over time required more adult oversight, not less. Empty streets turned out to be scarier and more dangerous than streets crowded with a mix of neighbors and strangers. And the new *homo suburbaniensis* was still afraid of blacks and Latinos, even after having successfully engineered a new order where all residents were in their place. Paradoxically, scrubbing the environment of outsiders heightened stranger anxiety rather than alleviating it.

Sadly, Jane Jacobs did not live in America, or on earth, long enough to see the full rebirth of the street in American life. Suburban-raised and college-educated young adults are flocking to once moribund neighborhoods in large and mid-sized cities to continue their journey to adulthood. The folly of moving to remote communities "for the children," only to sentence yourself to endless hours behind the wheel, has been dawning on tens of thousands of adults. Most important of all, new subdivisions are rising around suburban America trying to bring humane scale to the world where millions of children and elderly, our citizens

18

least able to negotiate every aspect of commercial transactions and social intercourse, live strapped into a two-and-a-half ton vehicle.

We are engaged in a massive rethink. Street life is not only once again encouraged in the urban core, but the suburbs are hoping the new frameworks built for social life—walkable streets, accessible shopping, and natural places for people to pool up—will see people live their way into the new space... the way a birdhouse stuck on a pole in the backyard will eventually have birds in it.

What's remarkable from a reread of *The Death and Life of Great American Cities'* chapters on street life is the extent, a half century after the book first appeared, that Jacobs' observations of the mechanics of metropolitan life might profitably serve as a design protocol today. Granted, she could sometimes be a little hard on the suburbs, and could romanticize the disorder of urban life with precious little sympathy for the millions who wanted something better after the war. However, attention must be paid: *Death and Life* was a prophetic text to a degree this country may never concede.

A culture that equated the presence of minorities, especially minority men, with danger and disorder, acted as a particularly cruel self-fulfilling prophecy. Add to that the dangerous mixture of control, capital, privilege, and widening gaps between rich and poor, and the hand we have to play in metropolitan America as we enter the second decade of the twenty-first century looks more complicated than Jane Jacobs could have imagined in 1961. Her warnings about social isolation, the way poor people would live in enormous housing projects, and the loss of economic vitality that would accompany the degradation of the street all came painfully true, and what we do today must be soberly conscious of the last half century's mistakes.

Sociologist Ray Oldenburg, in his *The Great Good Place*, understood completely what had been lost in the tidying up of American street life, the engineering-out of places where people naturally pool up and have a chance to talk. Oldenburg saw how many Americans had been hustled into a work-to-home and home-to-work routine that left them little time or opportunity to pleasurably, and cheaply, take a break from the demands of both.

Totally unlike Main Street, the shopping mall is populated by *strangers*. As people circulate about in the constant, monotonous flow of mall pedestrian traffic, their eyes do not cast about for familiar faces, for the chance of seeing one is small. That is not part of what one expects there. The reason is simple. The mall is centrally located to serve the multitudes from a number of outlying developments within its region. There is little acquaintance between these developments and not much more within them. Most of them lack focal points or core settings and, as a result, people are not widely known to one another, even in their own neighborhoods, and their neighborhood is only a minority portion of the mall's clientele. (Oldenburg 1999, p. 119)

One of the most remarkable changes in metropolitan life in recent decades has been the creeping privatization of the public way. In many newly built places, the "street" created for mass enjoyment resembles the old urban street championed by Jacobs only as much as a tree farm resembles a forest. In an attempt to engineer a "responsible" good time, communities have tried the new Potemkin Main Street, where privately employed, liveried street-sweepers comb the sidewalks for the smallest pieces of garbage. Try to hand out political handbills and a private security guard will escort you to the edge of the property. The mania for safety in a country with a plummeting crime rate has taken the logic of the enclosed shopping mall and turned it inside out, making it look something like a street again. Mixed use is valued, *sort of*. Any use that does not ring cash registers and reach the target number of dollars-per-square foot is explained as an illustration of the selfless generosity of private developers, rather than a reflection of any understanding of what makes public spaces great.

We seem to be remembering, at long last, what Jacobs did not want us to forget: that people like being around each other; that there is nothing desirable or safe about empty places, whether they're made of bricks and mortar or covered in banal green grass; that being allowed to organize themselves and their own play makes children self-reliant and confident, while children who need adults to navigate every social transaction often end up being quite the opposite. At the end of her long life, Jane

Jacobs could be grateful to have never needed to utter those two dreaded words: "play date."

Granted, it is a bad idea to lay the problems of being an American child in the twenty-first century at the doorstep of bad design. What might be more defensible is understanding the much-lamented loss of young people's independence as a symptom of the same spirit that sought to defend children from the endless threats imagined by urban self-exiles. The idea that growing children might develop habits of self-mastery by managing their own time is not entertained. We imagined we would protect them from everything... and then recoiled in shock and surprise when their childhood extended deep into their twenties. Only then we disgorged them into American society, fully grown and sometimes helpless naifs. Wealthier parents were more fearful, not more secure.

> Sidewalks, their bordering uses, and their users, are active partici-
> pants in the drama of civilization versus barbarism in cities. To keep
> the city safe is a fundamental task of a city's streets and its sidewalks.
> (Jacobs 1961, 37–38)

Along with spaces that enable rather than thwart our social desires, we need to have well-exercised muscles for social engagement. The happy coincidence of plummeting violent crime in center cities allowed millions to rediscover the delights of the urban street on their own terms. The old default assumption that all cities are by their nature more dangerous than all suburbs is dying a delayed and well-deserved death. Reshaping the metropolitan map we carry around in our heads to keep up with reality turns out to be a "lagging indicator." A place must be safe and inviting for a long time before people finally believe things have really changed. (Or maybe not: during a 2009 U.S. Senate debate over the relationship between the Second Amendment and individual state gun-possession laws, Sen. John Thune (D-SD) brought up his desire that his daughter be armed while in New York's Central Park. The good senator was not aware—or perhaps reluctant to let go of the hoary cliché of urban danger—that Central Park, though used by millions every year, is statistically much safer than South Dakota's small cities.)

It is far too soon to declare victory and head to the stoop for a celebration party. The desires of Americans are too diverse and pushed and pulled by too many factors to simply agree with the phrase uttered by politicians for decades, "people everywhere want the same things." It turns out they really don't. To reach a new rationality in the tug-of-war between modes of metropolitan life, a key thing had to happen: there had to be enough supply of various forms in the marketplace to satisfy the desires of different consumers.

At least the twenty-first century won't offer families a take-it or leave-it proposition. Dense urban environments are beckoning families that never would have expected to make homes in them. At the same time, urban families whipsawed by a narrower-than-expected set of choices in the center city are heading out for a little space and bringing a hunger for density and diversion with them. The marketplace, finally comprehending the many varieties of desire, is rising to meet a more stratified and interesting set of buyers.

Recent decades have brought a new influx of immigrants, this time from the rest of the world and not just Europe, who come from places where street life is an important part of all life. Sociologists can stay busy for the next fifty years, as we approach "majority-minority" status, to see if the new immigrants help us remember what was valuable about the sidewalk, or if we succeed in teaching them to forget.

Head to Washington Heights, at the other end of Manhattan from Jacobs' beloved West Village, or to Pilsen on Chicago's Southwest Side, or even to new immigrant enclaves in the less pedestrian-friendly Northern Virginia suburbs across the Potomac from Washington, DC: there you'll find people walking, shopping, and having casual encounters in comfort and safety. The strollers are both newcomers from Latin America and Asia and native-born Americans who just want to get out on two feet, shop, and people-watch.

The hostility to the urban street is not gone. Many of the bad design ideas that misunderstand commerce and basic human yearnings are still with us. But today, the street heads into battle with more allies at its side and more successful models of what a better place to live might look like. Jane Jacobs was wrong about a few things, but she was right about many more. Her faith in the vitality of the street as a necessary precondition to civilization is finally, and durably, getting its due.

REFERENCES

Jacobs, Jane. 1961. *The Death and Life of Great American Cities*. Modern Library Edition. New York: Random House.

Oldenburg, Ray. 1999. *The Great Good Place: Cafes, Coffee Shops, Bookstores, Bars, Hair Salons, and Other Hangouts at the Heart of a Community*. New York: Marlowe & Company.

THE MIRAGE OF
THE EFFICIENT CITY

Sanford Ikeda

I do not mean that cities are economically valuable in spite of
their inefficiency and impracticality but rather because they
are inefficient and impractical.

—Jane Jacobs, *The Economy of Cities*

FROM A DISTANCE, large-scale, planned urban landscapes of both
yesterday and today look rational and efficient. How could it be
otherwise? Planning implies rationality and the efficient choice of means
to a consciously chosen end. But as the scale of the planner's ambition
grows from a single building to districts to entire cities, rationality and
efficiency transform from useful benchmarks for decision making into
weapons of mass destruction. Any attempt to impose a particular vision
of rationality on urban life, whether inspired by the car and Euclidean
geometry or the pedestrian and the ethos of early-twentieth-century New
England, will confront this problem. That is why architects tend to make
bad urban planners.

THE NATURE OF THE CITY

A city is not a man-made thing. Its complex markets, intricate social
networks, dizzying traffic, and rich culture do not spring complete from
an overarching plan, but arise from the unpredictable yet orderly interactions of its inhabitants. Under the right conditions or "rules of the
game," these things are born, adapt, and die in ways that are vital, radi-

cally uncertain, and profitable. Such a living city—self-regulating and self-sustaining—is the result of human action but not of human design.[1]

This holds as well for the so-called "built environment" of a city. Of course, the street grid, mass transit, bridges, tunnels, and the overall physical infrastructure of the city are initially the product of deliberate planning. But exactly how this infrastructure adapts over time to unexpected changes in social, political, and particularly economic circumstances, is not. The creativity and determination of the architects and designers responsible for its buildings, plazas, parks, and malls, however important, do not account for how these diverse elements fit together to create over time, for better or worse, the look and tactility of a city and its districts—in spite of their having been constructed in different eras by different people with different knowledge and ethos. Like language and other evolved social institutions, a living city is an "emergent phenomenon" (Johnson 2001) and a "spontaneous order" (Hayek 1967).

This is not to deny that certain kinds of urban planning may contribute indirectly to the evolution of a spontaneous order. It is possible for careful planning to nudge parts of this emergent order in a way that promotes urban dynamism and creativity. Paris may have become "The City of Light" as a direct result of Baron Haussmann's massive and brutal urban renewal projects of the mid-nineteenth century. In more recent times, urban planning has produced street grids and other infrastructure (e.g., aquaducts, sewers, power and communication lines, transport tunnels and bridges, and street lighting) without which modern urban life would be difficult to imagine. These are not always successful, however.

(Some of Haussmann's interventions may have been successful while many of Robert Moses' [see below], at least by some estimates [Caro 1975], were far less so. In any case, we need not assume that the provision of something as vital to a city as major streets requires a central authority. London, which had no central government until 1855, managed

---

1. I borrow the term "living city" from Roberta Brandes Gratz (1989) and use it in the sense of Jane Jacobs' concept of a "city" as "a settlement that consistently generates its economic growth from its own local economy" (Jacobs 1969, 262). This usage is also consistent with that of the sociologist Max Weber (1958) and the historian Henri Pirenne (1952).

to have realized by 1825 the first major boulevard in a European city, Regent Street, decades before Haussmann [Wilson 2004, 90]. Regent Street twists and turns through central London—compare it with Haussmann's arrow-straight boulevards—because the various local-governance bodies would not permit the builder, John Nash, to significantly impinge on their property rights. Though administered by very different models of governance, Paris and London were at mid-century the two greatest cities in the Western world.)

The point here is that even the visible infrastructure of a city evolves in ways that its designers could not have foreseen. For example, the original designers of the New York City subway system or the London Underground could not have foreseen how their systems would change over time, much less the diverse patterns of usage that we see today. We also know that not all the consequences of such interventions, even the successful ones, are either intended or desirable, due to the inherent limits of the human mind and the complexity of the social world.

MACHINES FOR LIVING?

A city, in this sense, is not a "machine for living," to borrow a phrase from Le Corbusier, who used it to describe the austere skyscrapers that tower over his grand, hyper-rational Radiant City (Le Corbusier 1929). Indeed, Le Corbusier was one of the first to demand that great cities be rational and efficient, and conform to the principles of what James C. Scott calls "high modernism," the doctrine holding that improving the human condition requires a sweeping, rational engineering of all aspects of social life (Scott 1998, 88). In this sense Le Corbusier, no less than Friedrich Engels (1844), viewed the unplanned, unregulated city as a chaotic, market-driven horror.

Still, the machine is the appropriate metaphor for Le Corbusier's Radiant City, as well as for the great twentieth-century urban planner, Robert Moses.[2] A machine has a specific purpose. It is constructed from

---

2. The standard reference for Moses is Caro (1975), but for a more sympathetic treatment see Ballon and Jackson (2007).

a detailed plan and operates according to articulable, often quantifiable, principles to achieve a definite end, to which all of its separate parts are subordinate. A single wrong part can jeopardize its operation.

The complexity of any machine, however, is necessarily limited by the mind or minds that designed it.[3] By contrast, the living city can achieve a level of complexity, and promote an array of individual ends, that far surpasses any designed construction, whether physical or social, precisely because cities are the emergent, collective expression of many individual minds interacting day after day. This is why a city, as a spontaneous order, is far "smarter" than any person or any group obeying central direction. Compared to the problem-solving power of dynamic social processes, such as those we find in markets and cities, the human mind is surprisingly limited. No one, for example, no matter how brilliant, could alone make something even as simple as a common lead pencil (Read 1958). The required technical and, more importantly, local knowledge of "the particular circumstances of time and place" (Hayek 1945) go far beyond any person's cognitive ability.

But this also means that a living city has no particular purpose or serves no particular end. Thus, while the machine analogy may indeed be apt for a given building, consciously designed and deliberately constructed, it is utterly the wrong way to view the living city. (However, a city that is not self-sustaining and creative and survives by parasitically drawing its wealth from more creative settlements, as religious or political centers typically do, tends to be more machine-like and ends-oriented than a spontaneous order. Compare, for example, renaissance Rome to Florence, or present-day Washington, DC to New York City.) On the contrary, the living city enables its inhabitants to promote their own ends and pursue their own plans, based on their own local knowledge.

That is, what a great city manages to do is enable the better part of its inhabitants to be free to pursue their own diverse interests in the context of personal freedom (*Stadtluft macht Frei*, after all), which means they are free

---

3. Johnson (2001) describes computer programs that have emergent qualities, such as those found on many internet sites that automatically update the reliability of users; however, these programs too utilize the information that many separate minds unintentionally provide.

to take chances and, because of the wealth from trade that cities typically generate, have the wherewithal to do so (i.e., the cost of failure is lower and the benefits of success higher). So, if we want to say that a living city has a "purpose," it is to enable any given inhabitant, chosen at random, to pursue his or her own plans, dreams, and ambitions with the maximum likelihood of success. People flock to cities, risking the possibility of suffering as well as inflicting deep disappointments on themselves and on others, because this is where their individual plans are most likely to be fulfilled.

Ignoring this fact—that people often have radically conflicting ideas and goals, and that it is within the social networks of the urban environment that these are most effectively resolved—gives rise to the mirage of the efficient city.

THE VIRTUE OF "INEFFICIENCY"

Efficiency, in the economic sense of the term, presupposes an overarching plan that links various means to a given end, against which measured outcomes can be evaluated.[4] It is a measure of the ratio of the value of an output to the value of the inputs employed to produce it. Thus, because a living city is itself unplanned, it cannot be efficient *qua* city. But neither can it be inefficient, because that too presupposes a system-wide plan. In other words, both efficiency and inefficiency presume that we know all the possible outcomes of a given action so that we can determine how things ought to be and clearly recognize success and failure. This is impossible in the spontaneous dynamic of cities.

Of course, the complexity of the emergent social world and the brute fact of our cognitive limitations do generate unpleasant outcomes.

---

4. I am not addressing here the concept of "energy efficiency," which in a broad sense refers to minimizing the quantity of inputs used (e.g., oil) to achieve a given output (e.g., human comfort). Indeed, this is what Jane Jacobs seems to have meant by efficiency, "the ratio of work accomplished to energy supplied" (1969, 89). Economic efficiency, by contrast, is a *value* concept and refers to minimizing the cost of achieving a given level of benefit for a particular person. They are not the same thing. However, nothing in this essay should be construed as a critique of energy efficiency *per se*, unless the latter is used as a measure of the efficiency of a city *qua* city.

Concerned citizens often yearn for "efficiency" and call for policies that purportedly will achieve it. This loose usage of the language of efficiency, however, can mean at least two things.

First, it can refer to how city government operates—e.g., how it spends its budget on police, fire control, education, sanitation, and infrastructure. The concept of efficiency in the technical sense of maximizing an output for a given set of inputs may be appropriate with respect to city government, which functions like a machine (no pejorative intended) in the sense that public authorities may spend resources to achieve specific political objectives. Even here, however, measuring the outcome of a government policy is problematic: witness the difficulty of evaluating the success or failure of public schools or the police by using only statistical measures (Wilson and Kelling 1982).

Could we say that a government is economically efficient if the city it governs prospers materially? I think not. For one thing, again, statistical measures of prosperity, such as gross metropolitan product, are crude indices of genuine prosperity. Certainly a city that is close to destitution, whose inhabitants lack sufficient water, food, and shelter, is unlikely to be prosperous (although a community of ascetics might live happily under such conditions). So, while a broad correlation between measured material wealth and genuine prosperity likely exists, it is insufficiently close in most cases to be an accurate measure of efficiency. More importantly, however, it is unlikely that all the citizens of a city agree that material prosperity should be the paramount objective—some may believe that social justice or some other goal is more important. Without a universally agreed-upon ranking of priorities among the citizens, which would enable public authorities to plan rationally, economic efficiency would not be possible. In any case, such unanimity of opinion may be quite undesirable in a society that cherishes freedom of thought and meaningful ideological diversity.

Second, the demand for efficiency may be a response to the apparent chaos of daily urban life. Living cities have been described as "inefficient" in the sense that duplication, trial and error, failure and disappointment, and unpredictable explosive growth happen as a matter of course. People often use the word "inefficient" as a shorthand for "things that I don't like," such as crime, pollution, congestion, and disease. However, some amount of each of these things may actually be consistent with economic efficiency—it all depends on whether the benefit of reducing them is greater than the cost of doing so. If it is, reduction is efficient; if not, it is not.

If the concepts of economic efficiency and inefficiency are inappropriate, what normative standard might apply?

In *Delirious New York*, Rem Koolhaas writes that "the dark side of metropolis" is where "an astronomical increase in the potential for disaster [is] only just exceeded by an equally astronomical increase in the ability to avert it" (1994, 56, 59). Success barely stays ahead of failure. Though a good thing, this is probably not a state of affairs that a reasonable person would aim for. Even more importantly, it is not a state of affairs that anyone could deliberately achieve. Genuine inefficiency cannot be planned for in this way any more than one can make a mistake on purpose.

Instead of invoking efficiency, borrowing from ecology (and certain heterodox schools of economic thought),[5] we might say that a living city is a "dynamically stable" process, in which the forces of positive and negative feedbacks, as well as sudden mutations, combine under the right conditions to generate order.[6] This process involves trial and error, surpluses and shortages, apparently useless duplication, conflict and disappointment, trust and opportunism, and discovery and radical change. These are in the nature of the living city. Normatively, then, since we cannot accurately predict outcomes, we should focus on the "rules of the game" that generate dynamic stability.

For example, the designer-jeans industry seems to have re-emerged in downtown Los Angeles.[7] Outsourcing to Asia by major manufacturers threatened the local businesses that had previously done the specialized work of stone-washing, sand-blasting, sewing, laundering, packaging, and even inspecting and repairing for those same companies. The inefficiency of this economic strategy, however, later turned into an opportunity for new entrepreneurs, who found not only the needed infrastructure in place,

---

5. See for example the work of Israel M. Kirzner (1992).
6. See in particular Jacobs (2000).
7. "Reborn in the U.S.A.," *The New York Times*, 26 September 2007.

but also the tastes of local Hollywood celebrities to buy and tout their product.

While it was not by sheer accident that these small, diverse operators were located close to one another, no one planned it having in mind that years later alert entrepreneurs could more effectively revitalize the industry in downtown L.A. The designer-jeans industry was cobbled together from the remnants of earlier investments and errors. The dynamics of the global entrepreneurial-competitive process generate commercial and industrial "slums" of this kind all the time, but like residential slums, they are not all alike. Under the right conditions, they can be the source of future endogenous economic growth. This kind of entrepreneurship arises from overlooked opportunities hidden in the detritus of earlier experiments.

What are the conditions, the rules of the game, that make this possible? Certainly, as the designer-jeans industry exemplifies, a diversity of land uses and local tastes, combined with a dense population, is vital. But this would generate little discovery and economic development without the economic freedom to pursue opportunities where no one else imagined them to be, and to develop urban space in ways sometimes radically different from the past and from the expectations of urban planners. In the context of economic freedom, density, and diversity, then, the essential "social infrastructure" made of norms of reciprocity and networks of trust can emerge and promote lasting prosperity.[8] These relations, indeed, form the essential matrix within which the actions of individuals interact to form complex, dynamic, and coherent social orders. They are the foundation of the living city.

None of this has to do with static notions of economic efficiency or strict rationality.

THE LIMITS OF PLANNING

From a distance, many of today's "sprawl" communities and mall-centered "edge cities" look ugly and chaotic. Some of them may indeed appear

---

8. Jane Jacobs pioneered the concept of social networks. She coined the modern term "social capital" (1961, 188) common today among sociologists and economists.

placeless and devoid of culture, but certainly not all of them are or will eventually be (Garreau 1991). Historically, economic development has taken place on the fringes of traditional cities, in the "faubourg," "suburbium," or "portus" (Pirenne 1952, 142). Such unregulated growth seldom conforms to the planners' ideas of what is "smart."[9] But in any living city, intricacy and order are things that must be experienced up close. Meanwhile, nearer to the heart of the city, other political forces earnestly but vainly attempt to choose which districts are worthy of preservation and which are not, hoping to consciously direct its evolution.

The lesson here is that a living city is always becoming. It is a process that issues both breathtaking advances and deep disappointments. As such, a city cannot be perfect or efficient or ideal—or preservable, because you cannot preserve something that is still alive. If you try hard enough, you will end up killing it or, which is the same thing, stifling its spontaneity. At most you can alter the direction of its becoming—and then hope, because there is really no telling where it will go from there.

REFERENCES

Ballon, Hilary and Kenneth T. Jackson. 2007. *Robert Moses and the Modern City: The Transformation of New York*. New York: W.W. Norton.

Caro, Robert. 1975. *The Power Broker: Robert Moses and the Fall of New York*. New York: Vintage.

Engels, Friedrich. 1844. "The Great Towns." Abridged in LeGates and Stout (2003).

Garreau, Joel. 1991. *Edge City: Life on the New Frontier*. New York: Anchor.

Gratz, Roberta Brandes. 1989. *The Living City: How America's Cities Are Being Revitalized by Thinking Small in a Big Way*. New York: John Wiley & Sons.

Hayek, Friedrich August. 1945. "The Use of Knowledge in Society." In *Individualism and Economic Order*. Chicago: University of Chicago Press.

---

9. Government-initiated community participation has softened the edges of urban renewal and planning, but "communities" are never really heard. Given the limits of time and cognitive ability, only a few have a voice, and only a subset of their preferences can ever be reflected in policy. On this issue see Pennington (2004).

———. 1967. "The Result of Human Action but not of Human Design." In *Studies in Philosophy, Politics, and Economics*. Chicago: University of Chicago Press.

Jacobs, Jane. 1961. *The Death and Life of Great American Cities*. New York: Vintage.

———. 1969. *The Economy of Cities*. New York: Vintage Books.

———. 2000. *The Nature of Economies*. New York: Modern Library.

Johnson, Steven. 2002. *Emergence: The Connected Lives of Ants, Brains, Cities, and Software*. New York: Simon & Schuster.

Kirzner, Israel M. 1992. *The Meaning of Market Process: Essays in the Development of Modern Austrian Economics*. New York: Routledge.

Koolhaas, Rem. 1994. *Delirious New York*. New York: Monacelli Press.

Le Corbusier. 1929. "A Contemporary City." Abridged in LeGates and Stout (2003).

LeGates, Richard T. and Frederic Stout, eds. 2003. *The City Reader*. 3rd ed. New York: Routledge.

Pennington, Mark. 2004. "Citizen Participation, the 'Knowledge Problem,' and Urban Land Use Planning: An Austrian Perspective on Institutional Choice." *The Review of Austrian Economics* 17, no. 2:213-31.

Pirenne, Henri. 1952. *Medieval Cities: Their Origin and the Revival of Trade*. Princeton: Princeton University Press.

Read, Leonard E. 1958. *I, Pencil*. Irvington-on-Hudson, NY: Foundation for Economic Education.

Scott, James C. 1998. *Seeing Like a State: How Certain Schemes to Improve the Human Condition Have Failed*. New Haven: Yale University Press.

Weber, Max. 1958. *The City*. New York: Free Press.

Wilson, A.N. 2004. *London: A History*. New York: Modern Library.

Wilson, James Q. and George L. Kelling. 1982. "Broken Windows." In LeGates and Stout (2003).

THE INTELLIGENCE
OF INFORMALITY

Nabeel Hamdi*

IN MY PROFESSIONAL and academic career over the years I have come to understand practice as a strategic and not just a practical or problem-solving activity. Practice is a process whose purpose is to build an architecture of opportunity—an architecture of invitation—disciplined as much by ethics and our sense of justice and moral purpose as by standards of efficiency and cost-effectiveness. It is a process designed to enable rather than disable the creativity and inventiveness latent in the everyday to which Jane Jacobs has often referred in her writings. Responsible planning of this kind liberates the resourcefulness of people and of street life.

In his book *Emergence*, Steven Johnson (2004) describes the process by which small individual elements self-organize and form a collective in response to need. These collectives are grassroots, creative and flexible, and capable of changing and evolving if not interrupted. The ability to organize and become sophisticated—to move from one kind of order to a higher level of order—is what scientists call "emergence." In the language of emergence, "it is better to build a densely interconnected system with simple elements and let the more sophisticated behavior trickle up" (Johnson 2004, 78). These are what Zohar calls "quantum systems," in that their individual cells have

---

* This chapter is based in part on the introduction to Nabeel Hamdi, *Small Change: About the Art of Practice and the Limits of Planning in Cities*. London: Earthscan 2004, xv-xxvi. Reproduced with permission of Earthscan Ltd. (www.earthscan.co.uk).

no fully fixed identity until they are in relationship. This gives the quantum system maximum flexibility to define itself as it goes along. It co-creates with its environment. All of nature's complex systems are at their most creative when they are delicately poised between fixedness and unfixedness—poised at the edge of chaos. (Zohar 1997, 50)

The same pattern can be observed in informal cities: here problems are solved by drawing on a variety of information and support from many small relatively simple and local organizations, rather than from some power elite.

Sociologists have their own way of describing the yin and the yang of "I" and "We." In his discussion on sociability, Georg Simmel, an innovator in contemporary sociology, put it this way:

The individual has to fit himself into a whole system and live for it: that, however, out of this system values and enhancement must flow back to him, that the life of the individual is but a means for the ends of the whole, the life of the whole but an instrument for the purpose of the individual. (Simmel 1971, 137)

Most cities in the developing world include informally planned areas in which emergent characteristics are common. Small organizations are everywhere providing goods and services, managing utilities, collecting garbage, and so on. Intricate and complex, formal and informal partnerships emerge for recycling waste, exerting political influence, pirating services, and securing employment, among other things.

Through the struggles with eviction, the crisis of resettlement, the daily uncertainty of risk from fire, flood or poor sanitation, we see the informal, progressive and spontaneous emergence of new and even original ways of solving problems, and of a whole new order. As this capacity to organize into collectives and networks wins broader recognition and commitment, we see these same collectives become community: they develop their own rituals, meanings and rules of conduct around work, and a common purpose or ideal. As they begin to achieve their purpose, however small or local, they win respect and dignity and a place in the governance of cities. They develop a series of connections and a sophisticated form of organization. These street-level enterprises can become integral to citywide programs involving local and even national level organizations—the city public works department, the university and its various departments, health care providers, and so on. Later, new and novel policy initiatives might emerge for contracting communities and creating new forms of partnership and governance based on networks and not hierarchies, where "enterprise is governed and run by and for its members" through mutual cooperation (Mayo and Moore 2001). It's an inside-out organization where the whole is held together by the bits, where design and emergence are balanced.

Experience everywhere confirms how all these small beginnings, this seemingly ad-hoc and makeshift landscape of loose parts and organizations give cities an ordered complexity which is at once flexible, durable and, as we have seen, infinitely resourceful. They offer fast and ingenious shortcuts to goods and services, "a vitality of energy and social interaction that depends critically upon diversity, intricacy and the capacity to handle the unexpected in controlled but creative ways" (Harvey 1990, 73). Practice and practitioners "using the power of [their] authority to empower others " (Capra 2002, 106) can nurture this process—or sometimes disable it. Skillful practice can trigger the emergence of novelty and organization, help rediscover community, build networks, and form stronger organizations and new partnerships. This strategy enables people to find new ways of doing, thinking, and relating in response to everyday problems that are usually taken for granted. These are all qualities of leadership in practice and opportunities for development—a new openness for dialogue and learning.

Informal or emergent processes and organizations are intelligent, resourceful and full of inventive surprise, although formal planning often fails to recognize it. They are resourceful because they are fast, ingenious, and made up of organized rather than disorganized complexity (Capra 2002). Jane Jacobs referred to these processes as "the essence of city organization and life... Once one thinks about city process it follows that one must think of catalysts of this process." (Jacobs 1961, 575).

Neighborhood planning, however, also needs designed structures—physical, spatial, legal, institutional, and more—with standards, routines, and rituals that provide continuity and stability, a common meaning and purpose, a shared sense of place and belonging. It is to these structures, said Isaiah Berlin, that we "give up some of our liberty in order to protect the rest" (Berlin 1958, 11). The question, therefore, is: how much structure will be needed before the structure itself inhibits personal freedom, gets in the way of progress, destroys the very system which it is designed to serve, and becomes self-serving? At what point does it disable the natural process of emergence with all its novelty and creativity?

This shifting balance between the freedom of individuals and the order of collective responsibility, between large scale organizations and small ones, between public life (we) and private life (I), continues to preoccupy social scientists, architects, planners, and economists. Securing this balance is today at the heart of a new activism that can revitalize practice with a new purpose: it offers new roles and responsibilities to practitioners, and enables us to cultivate afresh the ideals of community, participation, and governance, and to reconceptualize the planning process itself.

In his book, *The Oregon Experiment* (1975), Christopher Alexander put it this way:

> Many of the most wonderful places in the world now avidly photographed by architects were not designed by architects but by lay people. But of course in order to create order, not chaos, people must have some shared principles. Nothing would be worse than an environment in which each square foot was designed according to entirely different principles. This would be chaos indeed.

He went on to develop his pattern language and talked of patterns that

> give the user a solid base for their design decisions. Each person or group of people would be able to make unique places, but always within the morphological framework created by the patterns. (Alexander 1975, 45-47)

It was Ebenezer Howard in 1898 who sought to reconcile freedom and order in his garden cities to

dispense the minimum of organization that would secure the benefits of planning while leaving to individuals the greatest possible control over their own lives. [Howard] hated bureaucratic paternalism...
[and] realized planning must stay within self imposed limits. (Fishman
1982, 51)

Driving it all is a simple and still challenging premise: intelligent
practice builds on the collective wisdom of people and organizations
on the ground—those who think locally and act locally—and recasts it
in ways which make a difference globally. It follows, therefore, that in
order to do something big, to think globally and act globally, one starts
with something small and relevant. Practice, then, is about making the
ordinary special, and the special more widely accessible—expanding
the boundaries of understanding and possibility with vision and common sense. It is about building densely interconnected networks, craft-
ing linkages between unlikely partners and organizations, making plans
without the usual preponderance of planning. It is about getting it right
for now and at the same time being tactical and strategic about later.
This is not about forecasting, nor about making decisions about the
future, but is about the long range. It is about being politically connected
and grounded, about disturbing the order of things in cultural practices,
urban governance, and environmental management in the interests of
change.

Practice disturbs. It can and does promote one set of truths, belief
systems, values, norms, rituals, powers, and gender relations in place of
others. It can impose habits, routines, and technologies that may lead
to new and unfamiliar ways of thinking, doing, and organizing locally,
nationally, even globally. It may do this intentionally because existing
structures have become malignant, or because they could work more
effectively if they were to change, or because there is no order, no so-
phistication where one is needed. It may also do so in the interests of
a power elite to induce a new international order. In all these respects,
practice—that skillful art of making things happen, of making informed

choices and creating opportunities for change in a messy and unequal world—is a form of activism and demands entrepreneurship.

Practice sparks the process by which small organizations, events and activities can be scaled up. This can happen in various ways: quantitatively, when programs get bigger geographically and financially; functionally, through integration with other programs and organizations; politically, when programs and communities wield power and become part of the governance of cities; organizationally, when the capacity to be effective increases, becoming sophisticated and influential—when it becomes a higher order of organization (see Gillespie 2004). Emergence and going to scale are, therefore, complementary processes: practice is a catalyst to both.

This philosophy of offering impulses rather than instructions, of cultivating an environment for change from within, starts on the ground and often with small beginnings that have an emergent potential—a bus stop, a pickle jar, a composting bin, a standpipe.

From practical objectives, such as improving housing, health, and education, emerges an agenda of policy reforms, legal frameworks, and standards that help to build social capital, promote social integration and gender equality, reduce dependency, unlock resources, and build livelihoods: "Shared ownership of the development agenda is seen as the key to its sustainability... Public, private and civic roles are being reconceptualized and reshaped, in both economics and social policy; the best route to problem solving lies through partnership" (Edwards 2001, 3).

Problem seeking and problem solving in these settings demand that we think at once serially, associatively, and holistically. Danah Zohar calls these three kinds of thinking the brain's intellect, heart, and spirit. With the intellect we define goals, set tasks, evaluate the evidence, collect facts, search for precedent, and search for logic. Then there is the brain's heart—parallel thinking, finding association between things, events, people, structures, tapping experience, and learning by trial and error. And finally there is the brain's spirit: imaginative, intuitive, insightful, creative, unwilling to accept old paradigms as given, and holistic.

In planning a professional intervention, imagination is as important as knowledge or skill. "Begin with imagination," said The Nobel Prize winning author José Saramago, "but from then on let reason prevail."[1] If we picture ourselves walking down any street in any of the informal settlements or slums of any major city in the South, it takes imagination to seed the idea of community around bus stops and water points, and craft these as centers of community life; to spot in someone else's garbage opportunities for enterprise, entrepreneurship and new forms of partnership to manage waste and conserve energy; to adopt a local cricket club as a partner to promote social development in an otherwise divided community; to spot a jar on someone's doorstep with pickles for sale and expand the source of produce through a community garden, managed by the elderly and involving children as partners for promoting healthy living. It takes imagination to turn a rickshaw into a school bus contracted by the local authority that offers services and security for children in a settlement otherwise inaccessible to services, generating employment and creating more partnerships, both public and private. As we continue our imaginary street walk, we observe an electricity pylon with its tangle of wires informally connected. Later we find out that people would pay a local electrician a small fee to make the connection and that, in time, a cooperative would emerge for managing the service that would become a legal partner to the council.

It takes imagination to see the pirating of electricity as an opportunity for privatizing a utility around a single pylon, or a standpipe with its intermittent supply of water as means of generating income, creating a community fund out of surplus tariff revenue, empowering women and promoting health awareness. And it takes even more imagination to convince the municipal authorities to seek new partnerships with these by now established and sophisticated community organizations, to change the legal structure of rights so that other communities who lack entitlement can benefit as well. In time, we might encourage a new horizontal structure of water management networks that may become an integral part of the way cities manage their supply—a new institutional arrange-

---

1. Quoted in *The Guardian Review*, 20 December 2002.

ment that everyone recognizes as useful and profitable. Drop in to "The Sustainable Barbershop" to get a pragmatic definition of sustainability: "I cut enough hair to satisfy my customers for now, but not too much so that they come back sooner rather than later. That way I keep my business going," said the barber.

It takes imagination to convince a multinational to partner with a community organization to fight fire in a slum inaccessible to the city fire trucks and to reduce the risk of man-made or natural hazards and disasters; or to negotiate a debt conversion agreement between governments that shares the benefits of debt relief with disenfranchised community groups, advancing a new global alliance designed to reduce poverty, promote social justice, and save the environment.

In all these ways, we recognize in practice the important dialectic between top-down planning, with its formal laws and structures, and all the bottom-up self-organizing collectivism, those "quantum and emergent systems" that, as Jane Jacobs argued long ago, give cities their life and order. We have come to learn that skillful and creative practice in these interdependent settings hinges on our capacity to handle the unexpected in controlled but creative ways, on chance encounters and chance learning, on the ability to improvise as we stumble upon good ideas and unpredicted problems, on upside-down thinking, on making mistakes and being reflective.

This kind of practice is less normative, less easy to standardize in fixed routines and procedures, less tolerant of data-hungry study, less reliant on statistics or systems analysis. Consistency, we now know, is the "hobgoblin of simple minds," rather than a measure of professional competency. There are few sacred prototypes to follow, no best practices to export, no brand names that guarantee quality. Instead, approximation and serendipity are the norm—the search for scientific precision is displaced in favor of informed improvisations, practical wisdom, integrated thinking, and good judgment based on a shared understanding of justice and equity, and on common sense.

These competencies, combined with a good measure of idealism and pragmatism, enable practitioners to move easily and creatively from the high ground of global issues into the swamp of the everyday, from the strategic setting of national policy development to the boardrooms of development banks and multinationals—seeking inspiration from all levels, following the moral imperative to solve problems and change minds, and making a difference. Finally, and by way of summary, I offer a code of conduct based on my own experience and the experience and advice of others, which I hope can provoke discussion among colleagues.

> *Ignorance is liberating*
> *Start where you can: never say can't*
> *Imagine first: reason later*
> *Be reflective: waste time*
> *Embrace serendipity: get muddled*
> *Play games, serious games*
> *Challenge consensus*
> *Look for multipliers*
> *Work backwards: move forwards*
> *Feel good.*

REFERENCES

Alexander, Christopher. 1975. *The Oregon Experiment.* New York: Oxford University Press.

Berlin, Isaiah. 1958. *Two Concepts of Liberty: An Inaugural Lecture Delivered Before the University of Oxford, 31 October 1958.* Oxford: The Clarion Press.

Capra, Fritjof. 2002. *The Hidden Connection: A Science for Sustainable Living.* London: Harper Collins.

Edwards, Michael and John Gavenita, eds. 2001. *Global Citizen Action.* Boulder, CO: Lynne Rienner Publishers.

Fishman, Robert. 1982. *Urban Utopias in the Twentieth Century: Ebenezer Howard, Frank Lloyd Wright, Le Corbusier.* Cambridge, MA: MIT Press.

Gillespie, Stuart. 2004. *Scaling Up Community Driven Development: A Synthesis of Experience.* Washington, DC: International Food Policy Research Institute.

Harvey, David. 1990. *The Condition of Postmodernity.* Oxford: Basil Blackwell.

Jacobs, Jane. 1961. *The Death and Life of Great American Cities.* New York: Random House.

Johnson, Steven. 2001. *Emergence: The Connected Lives of Ants, Brains, Cities and Software*. London: The Penguin Press.

Mayo, Ed and Henrietta Moore. 2001. *The Mutual State*. London: The New Economics Foundation.

Simmel, George. 1971. *On Individuality and Social Forms*. Chicago: The University of Chicago Press.

Zohar, Danah. 1997. *Rewiring the Corporate Brain*. San Francisco: Barrett/Koehler.

1.5

THE TAO OF URBANISM:

INTEGRATING OBSERVATION
WITH ACTION

Nan Ellin

ARTISANS, ARTISTS, DESIGNERS, choreographers, and other creators shape their work from what is at hand: materials, dancers, money, land, and other given resources. If they devoted their time and energy to bemoaning what they lacked, they would never bring forth anything of value into the world. In similar fashion, when we build upon our gifts rather than dwell upon our inadequacies, our strengths grow stronger. Some Native Americans call these intrinsic gifts our "original medicine" and say that when we are "in our medicine," we are at our best and we serve the world in the most optimal way. The Taoist tradition, hailing from the fifth-century BCE China, maintains that awareness and trust of our own Inner Nature allows us to know who we are and avoid manipulation by others. These and other wisdom traditions exhort us to honor this rich source of authenticity.

Likewise, when we identify the assets of a place, these too may flourish. When considering how best to improve the places in which we live, then, what if we focused on what we value rather than what we can't stand? What if we honed in on what works, rather than what doesn't work? Our goal would not be fault-finding, but gift-finding, just as truffle-sniffing pigs unearth delicacies for all to enjoy.

This does not mean ignoring what we may not like, for awareness of deficits surely helps us improve, and our survival imperative helps us scan the horizon for potential threats to our well-being. It is important to address these threats appropriately, but equally important to move on. For dwelling upon what is lacking is demoralizing and can engender a scarcity mentality that only spurs unhealthy competition, suppresses creative problem-solving, and may even prove paralyzing.

Conversely, focusing on strengths builds confidence and morale, spilling over into other arenas and inspiring positive transformation. As we begin identifying gifts, these multiply. In the process, our greatest weaknesses may become our greatest strengths, and our greatest problems may become our greatest solutions. This is partly because valuing what exists and building upon it empowers, while assigning blame undermines our efforts because it engages us in denial, deflection, and distraction, contributing to an abnegation of responsibility. Robert Kennedy famously evoked this attitude, saying: "There are those who look at things the way they are, and ask why... I dream of things that never were and ask, why not?"

Jane Jacobs was a paragon in this regard. An astute chronicler of urban life, she squarely addressed issues, eloquently showcased what worked, and advanced proposals for improving our cities. In doing so, she exemplified the tenets laid out by Joseph Pulitzer: "Put it before them briefly so they will read it, clearly so they will appreciate it, picturesquely so they will remember it and, above all, accurately so they will be guided by its light." Jacobs demonstrated through her craft—writing combined with advocacy—what she intuitively understood to work:

> Dull, inert cities, it's true, do contain the seeds of their own destruction and little else. But vital cities have marvelous innate abilities for understanding, communicating, contriving, and inventing what is required to combat their difficulties... Lively, diverse, intense cities contain the seeds of their own regeneration, with energy enough to carry over for problems and needs outside themselves. (Jacobs 1961, 585)

Indeed, Jacobs' insights and activism have provided multiple seeds for urban regeneration by inspiring urban professionals and dwellers alike.

Learning from and extending Jacobs' approach toward writing about the city, I suggest those of us who "construe construction"—we translators of the built environment—formulate positive as opposed to negative theses. As English composition professor George Brosi advises his students,

> Be sure your thesis is always positive. It may be tempting to use a negative thesis, but a positive thesis always represents a dramatic improvement. For example, instead of writing around the thesis that children should be removed from an abusive home, write around your particular alternative to the home environment. Sure it is more difficult to solve a problem than point out that another solution is inadequate, but the positive thesis is much more worthwhile.[1]

In writing about the city, the positive thesis aims to provide an understanding of the current scene and what led to it, identify strengths and opportunities, share relevant best current practices as well as worthy precedents, galvanize and empower others to contribute from their strengths, convene people to envision a better future, capture the imagination of others, advocate for and build support to realize the vision, and carve out specific proposals around which people can rally and act as stewards and watchdogs. In sum, this approach toward writing about the city would *aspire to inspire* by considering what was, what is, and what could be through valuing, visioning, and ad-vocating.

The ability to envision better futures relies upon another kind of vision: the ability to see clearly what is happening. This kind of vision is acquired by listening to self, others, and places. It is acquired by having meaningful conversations, noting assets—what John Kretzman calls "hope stories"—along with weaknesses and obstacles. Rather than being "problems," however, the latter contribute to building on assets, similar to the way childcare experts recommend "redirecting" children's energies.[2]

---

1. George Brosi, "The Research Paper Thesis," www.english.eku.edu/services/comp102/hand12.htm.
2. Charles Landry is an exemplary practitioner of this approach: see Landry and Bianchini (1995), and Landry (2006).

THE TAO OF URBANISM

We use the words "love" and "hate" a lot when we talk about places, probably even more than we use them for people. Indeed, we get very emotional about our places. What makes a place "lovable"? Usually, we feel connected when we're there: to ourselves, others, the place, nature, a higher being, the past, perhaps the future. We feel a sense of meaning, harmony, purpose, interest, and excitement.[3] Of safety and security. Of civility, respect, and generosity of spirit. We tend to describe these places as "authentic."

We prefer authenticity in a place just as we'd rather slip between pure cotton rather than polyester blend sheets at night. And, as current sheet trends suggest, the higher the thread count the better. Just as higher thread count improves the comfort and quality of our sheets, so higher urban thread count—that fine-grained as opposed to coarse-grained fabric—improves the comfort and quality of our cities.

Efforts to achieve authenticity backfire, however, when something that may work in another place or time is "dragged and dropped" onto the here and now. The goal of authenticity may also prove elusive when branders are commissioned to endow a place with identity by inventing catchy slogans. These various efforts to achieve distinction usually render it elusive, ironically generating similar results and producing only greater homogeneity. For an identity crisis is not resolved by adopting another persona or having someone tell you who you are or should be; it is resolved from within by finding and honoring the "Inner Nature" of a place.

After many decades of spiraling down, we have been making great strides in recent years towards creating authenti-cities. Indeed, over the last two decades a quiet revolution has been taking place that I have called "integral urbanism" (Ellis 2006). Integral urbanism aims to create adjacencies of uses and people and to allow relationships among them to develop and flourish. Rather than distill, separate, and control—the ethos of modern urbanism—this approach works toward integration, inclusion, and dynamism. Bringing together functions the twentieth-century city

---

3. Psychologist Mihaly Csikszentmihalyi (1990) famously describes this as being "in flow."

separated (living, working, circulating, creating, and recreating), integral urbanism offers a new model that integrates buildings with nature, center with periphery, local character with global forces, and connects the various professions involved with urban growth and development and people of different ethnicities, incomes, ages, and abilities. Aiming to heal the wounds inflicted upon the landscape by the modern and postmodern eras, integral urbanism engages in a range of restorative efforts incorporating five qualities: hybridity, connectivity, porosity, authenticity, and vulnerability.

Hybridity and *connectivity* bring activities and people together at all scales. While modern urbanism espoused the separation of functions, integral urbanism reaffirms their symbiotic nature by combining and linking them. These various integrations can be accomplished through cross-programming buildings and regional plans—spatially (plan and section) as well as temporally. Examples of cross-programming include the office building with basketball court and day-care center, intergenerational community buildings (combining day care, teenage community center, adult education, and senior center), public school/community centers, integrated parking structures (into office buildings and retail centers), restaurants, and the urban plaza by day/movie theater at night.

Transposing this concept onto the larger scale can increase density of activity without necessarily increasing building density. This translates into reduced commuting, greater convenience, preservation of the natural environment, increase in quality public space, and greater social interaction. The outcome is new hybrid typologies and morphologies that pool human and natural resources for the benefit of all. This approach activates places by creating thresholds, or places of intensity, where diversity thrives. By increasing density of activity and perhaps building mass, these thresholds weave connections between places, people, and experiences.[4]

---

4. An early advocate of hybridity, in *The Death and Life of Great American Cities* Jane Jacobs prescribed diversity for urban health and well-being, saying: "In our American Cities, we need all kinds of diversity, intricately mingled in mutual support. We need this so city life can work decently and constructively, and so the people of cities can sustain (and further develop) their society and civilization. Public and quasi-public bodies are responsible for

Porosity preserves the integrity of what is brought together while allowing mutual access through permeable membranes, as opposed to the modernist attempt to dismantle boundaries or postmodernist forti-fication. *Authenticity* involves actively engaging and drawing inspiration from actual social and physical conditions with an ethic of care, respect, and honesty. Like all healthy organisms, the "authenti-city" is always growing and evolving according to new needs, thanks to a self-adjusting feedback loop that measures and monitors success and failure. Finally, *vulnerability* calls upon us to relinquish control, listen deeply, value pro-cess as well as product, and reintegrate space with time.

Just as a good manager builds on existing strengths of an organi-zation, and good writing about places recognizes their capacities, so good urbanism builds upon given assets as well as exemplary practices elsewhere from which we can learn. Rather than neglect, abandon, or erase our urban heritage, integral urbanism *preserves* valuable buildings, neighborhoods, cultural institutions, creative and intellectual capital, and natural landscapes; *rehabilitates, reclaims, restores,* or *renovates* what is underperforming; and *adds* what we do not have yet but would like, as informed by effective community involvement. And it does so in that order. Consequently, the new builds upon existing assets and is deeply influenced by this "DNA" of a place, allowing for unique and meaningful expressions to unfold and for problems to generate solutions.

Conventional urban intervention has proceeded in the reverse order, considering first what is needed, but too often at the expense of what is valued. In many instances over the last century, urban interventions have even opted to begin with a *tabula rasa*, or clean slate, by razing what was already there or finding pristine land upon which to build. On this

---

some of the enterprises that help make up city diversity—for instance, parks, museums, schools, most auditoriums, hospitals, some offices, some dwellings. However, most city diversity is the creation of incredible numbers of different people and different private organizations, with vastly differing ideas and purposes, planning and contriving outside the formal framework of public action. The main responsibility of city planning and design should be to develop—insofar as public policy and action can do so—cities that are congenial places for this great range of unofficial plans, ideas and opportunities to flourish, along with the flourishing of the public enterprises." (Jacobs 1961, 315)

clean slate, conventional urban intervention has aspired to a master plan. Integral urbanism veers away from the clean slate as well as the master plan that, in its focus on determining the totality, ironically tends to generate fragmented cities without soul or character.

Instead, integral urbanism determines where there is energy, both physical and social, in the larger system, and where it is lacking. It can thus perform "urban acupuncture," skillfully inserting interventions into the urban organism that clear blockages and liberate energy to catalyze additional growth and change.[5] Setting the self-adjusting feedback mechanism into place, this process activates underutilized resources and *attracts new ones*. In Phoenix, for instance, the "problem" of too much sun could be an opportunity to become a global leader in solar energy. Similarly, the city's "problem" of low water supply might offer an opportunity to demonstrate innovative water management strategies, in the tradition of its early inhabitants who built hundreds of miles of canals with stone hoes. The common graffiti "problem" could engage youth in creating ever-changing "art walls," converting "vandals" into budding artists recognized for work that graces the urban landscape. And so forth.

Integral urbanism seeks to restore the connections that have been severed over the last century between body and soul, people and nature, and among people. While not forming a "school" of thought, since the expressions vary widely, this approach emphasizes reintegration (functional, social, disciplinary, and professional), porous membranes or permeable boundaries, and design with movement in mind, movement through space (circulation) as well as time (access to the past as well as dynamism and flexibility).

Although integral urbanism pertains specifically to urban design, its five qualities might effectively apply to governance, homeland security, management, business, education, mediation, technology, the arts, and other realms. Applied generally, these qualities translate into regarding organizations as dynamic networks with built-in feedback mechanisms;

---

5. Many have been applying the term "urban acupuncture." It is the title of a book by Jaime Lerner (in Portuguese). I advocated for urban acupuncture in *Integral Urbanism* (2006), acknowledging its use by Kenneth Frampton and Ignasi de Sola-Morales.

acknowledging the primacy of relationships and processes over products; bringing human and other resources together to achieve efficiencies (optimization); and maintaining an ethic of care and respect for self, others, and the environment. Incorporating these qualities in any given realm brings a profound shift from competition to synergism, the kind of collaboration that yields outcomes larger than the sum of its parts.

Modeling both asset building and community engagement, Jane Jacobs was a premier public intellectual, and her books have been read by millions, influencing planners, politicians, and communities around the world to this day. In addition, her advocacy has had wide-ranging impacts on public policy and urban design, particularly in her own communities. In contrast, scholarly journal articles, the basis upon which academics tend to be rewarded and promoted, are generally read by a handful of like-minded colleagues, with little to no actual impact on places.

Though not an academic herself, Jacobs' work epitomizes contemporary aspirations of many institutions of higher education. A national consortium of more than eighty colleges and universities recently released a report documenting a significant shift towards "scholarship in public." This report maintains that when the academy considers community engagement irrelevant, it renders itself irrelevant. To prevent such irrelevancy, it recommends academic institutions encourage and reward public scholarship by recognizing it as scholarship in tenure and promotion policies, not as "community service."[6] A front-runner of this movement, President Michael Crow of Arizona State University, advocates "socially embedded" and "outcome-oriented" research, declaring:

> We must no longer allow our universities to remain aloof from their communities... It is time for universities to recognize their moral responsibilities, both for the knowledge they produce and to the communities in which they exist... We must encourage intellectual fusion

---

6. "Scholarship in Public: A Resource on Promotion and Tenure in the Arts, Humanities, and Design," by Imagining America's Tenure Team Initiative on Public Scholarship, chaired by Chancellor and President Nancy Cantor of Syracuse University and President Steven Lavine of the California Institute of the Arts, 2008.

and create transdisciplinary knowledge that solves real-world problems, and not simply isolate ourselves to produce knowledge for the sake of knowledge itself. (Crow 2007)

This groundswell of support for engaged scholarship is long overdue and welcome; nonetheless, restoring health and well-being to our places extends beyond the purview of urbanists to everyone. One of the reasons we have abdicated responsibility to "experts" is that it can be hard to take care of the places we live in if we have not been taken care of ourselves. When parents, communities, and places are not able to provide adequate support, it may be hard to be good parents, citizens, and stewards. And the downward spiral continues. How to reverse it, or meet it with an upward spiral?

Everyone can practice integral urbanism, not only planners and urban designers. It entails discovering what is integral to a place—its DNA, unique qualities, gifts—and honoring them. As psychologist James Hillman maintains:

That flowing imagination which founded the city in the first place can be re-found. It is planted in our midst always ready to flower—if we begin, not with the "problem" of what needs to be changed, or moved, or built, or demolished, but begin with what already is here, still stands and sings of its soul, still holds the sparks of the mind that initiated it. (Hillman 2003, 18)

Once these gifts are identified, we can connect the dots to strengthen them and engage in urban acupuncture to liberate the life force of a city, allowing it and us to truly thrive. This process brings urban and economic revitalization, health, and well-being to places and people. Along the path, the city becomes integrated—functionally and socially—and its denizens empowered to take care of it on an ongoing basis.[7]

---

7. By assuming responsibility instead of ascribing blame, we shift from what Peter Block describes as the "retributive society" to a "restorative society": see Block (2008).

Focusing our attention on what we lack or don't want only demoralizes and erodes prosperity, rather than building it. For instance, fear leads to gates, which lead to more fear, more gates, and so forth. Alternatively, when focusing on what we value, we build upon these strengths and spiral up. The virtuous cycle replaces the vicious one.

Rather than cope with poor quality of places through denial, deflection, or distraction, we need *two kinds of vision:* the ability to see things clearly, and a vision for a better future. This entails listening to oneself to grow in awareness; listening to others and places to identify their assets and build relationships; engaging in conversations that paint a vision of what could be while energizing people to implement the vision; and what Otto Scharmer calls "co-creating," or "enacting prototypes of the future… through the guidance of fast-cycle feedback from all stakeholders in real time" (Scharmer 2007, 464). Rather than "see, hear, and speak no evil," an admonition encouraging us to dull our awareness, we might practice "urban dharma" by finding our voice, expressing it effectively, and having the courage of our convictions.

We can leverage our individual and collective strengths to build upon the assets of our places so that they will, in turn, support us. When we set authentic transformation into motion, we sustain—rather than strain—life by maintaining healthy bodies, relationships, communities, and places. As we take care of our places, Hillman maintains, "we restore soul."[8] The price we have paid for not doing this, for selling our souls, has been too high.

We have all benefited from Jane Jacobs' enduring legacy of restoring soul to the places we live. For me, Jacobs modeled a way of seeing as well as shaping, communicating, and applying ideas towards enhancing urbanism. From her skill and wisdom, I have learned. In her professional and creative boundary-pushing, clarity of vision, and forbearance, I find a source of continuous inspiration and deep gratitude.

---

8. Hillman (1987, 106). Thomas Moore elaborates upon Hillman's recommendation that we learn from the Renaissance doctrine of "anima mundi"—bringing soul back into the world—in *Care of the Soul* (1992).

REFERENCES

Block, Peter. 2008. *Community: The Structure of Belonging*. San Francisco: Berrett-Koehler.

Crow, Michael. 2007. "American Research Universities during the Long Twilight of the Stone Age." Remarks made at the Rocky Mountain Sustainability Summit, University of Colorado, Boulder, February 21.

Csikszentmihalyi, Mihaly. 1990. *Flow: The Psychology of Optimal Experience*. New York: Harper & Row.

Ellin, Nan. 2006. *Integral Urbanism*. New York: Routledge.

Hillman, James. 1987. "Power and Gemeinschaftsgefuhl". In *City and Soul*. New York: Spring Publications, 2006.

——. 2003. "City". In *City and Soul*. New York: Spring Publications, 2006.

Jacobs, Jane. 1961. *The Death and Life of Great American Cities*. New York: Random House.

Landry, Charles and Franco Bianchini. 1995. *The Creative City*. London: Demos.

Landry, Charles. 2006. *The Art of City Making*. London: Earthscan.

Moore, Thomas. 1992. *Care of the Soul: A Guide for Cultivating Depth and Sacredness in Everyday Life*. New York: Harper Collins.

Scharmer, Otto C. 2007. *Theory U: Leading from the Future as it Emerges*. Cambridge, MA: The Society for Organizational Learning.

SECTION 2

The Virtues of Seeing

2 . 1

NINE WAYS OF
LOOKING AT OURSELVES
(LOOKING AT CITIES)

Arlene Goldbard

IN 2001 I CO-EDITED *Community, Culture and Globalization,* an international anthology of community cultural development. Community artists from fifteen nations contributed chapters about their own work—making meaning and beauty in collaboration with people creating community. Members of the international editorial team met in New York City just two months after 9/11. It took some persuading to get people there. It wasn't so much the aftermath of terrorism as all the commercial TV programming preceding it, portraying life on the streets of New York as nasty, brutish, and short. It was a little surreal to walk in a pack through a landscape festooned with larger-than-life American flags. We all felt dislocated, but not to the same degree. I learned something about looking without preconception from a colleague from India who, pointing to metal fire escapes retracted to the second stories of apartment buildings, asked if those were the only egress the residents possessed. With eyes gazing out from a beginner's mind, what would you or I see on a street corner in Chicago or San Francisco?

Perception is a partnership between the manifest world and the observer. People whose work focuses on the cultivation of community, as mine does, tend to emphasize intervention: what we see is valued primarily as an aid to conceiving the actions that can improve the picture. That is one truth: what we perceive and understand when we look at the world—the stories we tell ourselves to explain what we see—is what shapes our actions.

In tribute to Jane Jacobs, I write here not about *what* we see, but about *how* we see, taking my inspiration from *The Death and Life of Great American Cities*. Jacobs' hungry gaze absorbed the world in its infinite textures and varieties, tasting everything, refusing (almost) nothing. We relish her perceptions for their own sake, even as they create an appetite for the prescriptions that follow. Perhaps it came naturally to Jacobs, but for most of us, seeing that deeply and fully is a skill that must be—should be—cultivated. If our interventions can only be as good as our perceptions, what can we do to grind the lens of awareness and nurture the habits of mind that make us better—truer, clearer, deeper—perceivers of cities, and therefore better creators and tellers of the stories that ultimately shape them? Nine lenses, then, for looking at ourselves, looking at cities.

A WIDE LENS

In asserting what should be, we separate good from bad, loved from unloved. Jacobs loved the bustling dance of the urban core. In the half century since she published *The Death and Life*, we've seen people abandon the city in droves for suburban and exurban communities, trading density for space and mildness. More recently, many cities have experienced repopulation of a rapidly gentrifying urban core, returning empty nesters mixing with students, artists, and office workers. Large conurbations sprawl for miles, city eliding into town into village, trading inhabitants in a perpetual peristalsis. Each living situation answers some individual and cultural need. From my neighborhood, I can see skyscrapers in the distance, but the things I love and crave are close at hand: light on water, quiet, plenty of elbow room.

What if we drop the distinctions and think of the whole conurbation as the city, not just the urban core? What if the parts Jacobs and her descendents valorize—the density, the interchange, the speed and excitement—rely on the whole ecology the way *Sequoia sempervirens* relies on the vast forest floor? Do judgments and snobberies fall away? Or new ones arise?

I live in a part of Richmond, California, that was home to the Kaiser Shipyards, where World War II Liberty ships were made. The availability of good-paying factory jobs brought countless migrants here from the deep South and Southwest, changing a town of twenty thousand mostly white residents into a diverse city of a hundred thousand with a street life fed by blues clubs and busy restaurants. My apartment is a block from the Bay, on former factory land remediated by a developer in exchange for the right to build. Something has been lost, and something new is emerging. Nearby, an old Ford assembly plant is being converted into a conference center, and green enterprises are being offered incentives to occupy other disused industrial space. But downtown has become a ghost town as the factory workers' grandchildren drive around it on their way to other shopping destinations. Nearly half my neighbors speak English as a second language. I take my daily walk through a salt marsh inhabited by a lively population of avocets, curlews, and even herons. I must drive to the grocery store in a more densely populated area, crossing paths with urban neighbors who drive out here to walk. I do not think we inhabit two distinct places, city and not-city. I think we make the city together.

THE LENS OF
THE UNCOLONIZED MIND

Jacobs was a member of The Auto Club, the entirely unorganized society of autodidacts whose self-education is driven not by some normative notion of credential or curriculum, but solely by curiosity, desire, and need. I love the way Jacobs' perceptions illuminate the uncolonized mind, the consciousness untouched by the narrowing process that may follow submission to a too rigid or otherwise overdetermined formal education.

The chief handicap of the colonized mind is the habit of approaching any subject with readymade ideas of what is worth noticing and knowing. The fence enclosing worthy knowledge can be staked in varied terrain, but it always constrains. What types of information have been valorized by those in authority, or those in fashion? What types of information are unworthy because they cannot be weighed and measured by the instruments our numbers-crazy culture deems accurate? What is considered subjective, what objective, and how is the difference made to matter?

When we observe human beings in the shared habitat of cities, nothing is irrelevant. The challenge is to hold as much information in awareness as possible, allowing patterns to emerge rather than imposing them. As I began writing this chapter, scientists "discovered" a vegetarian spider. It is not that *Bagheera kiplingi* had never been identified before Christopher J. Meehan observed it during his fieldwork in Mexico. But as the spider's preferred home was a species of acacia typically swarming with ants—and as all previous spiders had been carnivores—investigators prior to Meehan simply concluded the spider had chosen the plant as a likely place to find a succulent ant dinner. Meehan paid open-eyed attention long enough to notice *Bagheera kiplingi* opting at mealtime for leaf tips rather than ant flesh. A thirsty mind freed from normative ideas of knowledge is the most fertile learning environment of all.

THE LENS OF COMMON FATE

Planners and policy makers commonly prescribe measures for others they would find intolerable in their own lives, such as the wholesale practice of relocation, which Jacobs calls "slum shifting" and "slum duplicating." Faced with the multiple discontents of a low-income housing project, planners "build a duplicate of the first failure and move the people from the first failure into its expensive duplicate, so the first failure can be salvaged" (Jacobs 1961, 512). I try to imagine the fantasies of the public housing authority director who devised such a scheme: that the bleak uniformity, cheap construction and non-existent amenities of a housing project would magically add up to a decent place to live, if only they were made new and fresh?

In considering the many recommendations made for improvement in our cities, I have found a simple thought experiment unfailingly useful. Would those who make these decisions live under their strictures for a meaningful stretch of time? Consider how unthinkable it is that policy makers' families might have to make do with the medical care they prescribe for users of the public health system; that their children might attend the poorest of the schools their policies shape;

that they might sleep night after night amidst the sounds, smells, and other sensations of public housing. That this common-sense question is almost never asked—and earns a huge laugh on the few occasions when it is—is the true absurdity.

THE LENS OF MOTIVE

The vistas of colonized thought resemble the Radiant City: stretches of ground-level landscape punctuated by the repetition of identical protuberances. Instead of tower blocks, these are questions severed from their reasons to exist. Almost every time I talk about community cultural development—the collaboration of artists and other community members—someone is sure to ask, "But is it art or social work?" Generally, the question comes just after I've described a public art project. It might be a participatory mural portraying a local story that contributes to a neighborhood's distinct character, or a project in which dancers or theater artists help the residents of a particular community share their stories and turn them into an occasion of public memory, such as a performance marking the toll of gun violence and putting forward a basis for greater conviviality.

The tendency to use the category "art" as a knife to pare the worthy and valued from the rest is so embedded in conventional thinking that when I respond to such questions with another—"Why do you ask?"—the reply is almost always a sputter or silence. Such questions have no independent meaning or value: whether one calls something art or not is a matter of indifference, unless some practical distinction or privilege attaches to the answer. The issue emerges when people are deciding which projects to fund, to respect, or to admire. On one such occasion, the director of a red-carpet theater described the belief that generated his question. "The major institutions," he said, "are about artistic excellence, and the smaller community-based groups are about participation." In truth, each is about both excellence and participation, each defining these aims in its own way, and each, given the crooked timber of humanity, achieving them only part of the time. Questions are essential to clear sight, but it is also necessary to know why they are asked.

THE LENS OF LANGUAGE

How we write about cities is as important as what we write. Too often, experts contradict themselves by proposing a vital, permeable, self-developing community using language that telegraphs specialization and exclusion. What Jane Jacobs says, and how she says it, are the same. Formal and casual arguments are stirred together to make a rich and satisfying stew. The observations of Mrs. Penny Kostritsky are presented with as much dignity and given as much consideration as the pronouncements of the Regional Plan Association of New York, and seem to the reader to bear more relationship to lived experience, and therefore carry more authority.

Strolling through no-nonsense descriptions and analyses of urban experience in *The Death and Life*, you come across Paul Bunyan's vest, a "head of withered lettuce," a "pipsqueak," a "wigwag," or a "bosky." When this happens, it is like finding a new penny or a red marble on the sidewalk: everything brightens. Jacobs' diction is calm, even when it crackles with underlying anger, but it is not moderate. She is not engaged with an invisible antagonist who requires that her words be scrubbed of anything that might give offense to those who, after all, have offended her by their indifference or stupidity. What she has to say is driven by a powerful, positive vision of possibility, and not by her disappointment, however potent, in those whose failures obscure it.

I crave such voices: forthright, slicing through a thick crust of blather with the satisfying inevitability of a hot knife through butter. Reading prose that demonstrates in its very tone, form, and vocabulary the points it has been deployed to argue, a sense of possibility awakens.

Jacobs' voice reminds me so often of Paul Goodman's, who brought the same open-eyed gaze, the same blending of the lofty and pedestrian, the same confiding tone to his writing on so many subjects. More than a decade before *The Death and Life* was published, Goodman wrote of the peril of leaving democracy to the experts:

> The idea of Jeffersonian democracy is to educate its people to govern by giving them initiative to run things, by multiplying sources of responsibility, by encouraging dissent. This has the beautiful moral

advantage that a man can be excellent in his own way without feeling special, can rule without ambition and follow without inferiority. Through the decades, it should have been the effort of our institutions to adapt this idea to ever-changing technical and social conditions. Instead, as if by dark design, our present institutions conspire to make people inexpert, mystified, and slavish.

One is astounded at the general slavishness. The journalists at the President's press conference never ask a probing question, they have agreed, it seems, not to "rock the boat." Correspondingly, the *New York Times* does not print the news, because it is a "responsible newspaper." Recently, the Commissioner of Education of the State of New York spoke of the need for young people to learn to "handle constructively their problems of adjustment to authority"—a remarkable expression for doing what you're told. (Goodman 1962, xvi-xvii)

The malady Jacobs and Goodman diagnosed half a century ago, the confusion that so easily accepts the substitution of authoritative nonsense for the evidence of our own bodies and minds, has its roots in the gradual disappearance of the democrat's voice in favor of the expert's or the demagogue's. It was a social ill when they wrote; now it is epidemic, and every one of us holds the cure.

THE LENS OF INDIVIDUAL INITIATIVE

Whether on the scale of a single life or a whole city, much conventional planning is merely superstition, pretending that our own wishes rather than the unpredictable interaction of events and energies will determine the future. Given the starring role randomness has already played in shaping the early twenty-first century, it is striking how strongly lodged in orthodox thinking is belief in the value of a type of planning analogous to drawing up blueprints. Imagine this place in five years, planners say, or ten, and then they write up the results, which are shelved along with other plans. Vast quantities of money and energy are wasted on this pretense, most of which could reasonably be invested instead in readiness, in developing nimbleness and resourcefulness, in improving our ability to recognize opportunity. Jacobs asserts individuals' right to have their own plans—to take the initiative, to be enterprising—as against the big plans imposed by believers in this superstition. When we look through this lens, we are looking for the signs of the elbow room needed to work out a *modus vivendi* despite our very real differences.

THE LENS OF EMBEDDED BELIEFS

The usual argument against investing needed public resources in livable cities is cost. In the decades since Jacobs published *The Death and Life*, our attraction to punishment has expanded almost beyond reckoning. As I write this, over seven million people are in prison, on parole or probation, with total state spending of around $52 billion, by far the highest incarceration rate and the largest prison population on the planet (Pew Center on the States 2009, 11). While U.S. population has increased by nearly half since Jacobs' book came out, the prison population has grown by well over 1,000 percent. Beyond our borders, the National Priorities Project[1] calculates that we have spent over $970 billion on wars since 2001, an average cost of $315 million a day—that's more than two annual National Endowment for the Arts budgets daily, seven days a week. The unexamined idea that we can't afford to invest adequately in cities is embedded in conventional thinking, but the truth is not so much our lacking resources as our addiction to spending them on punishment.

Even when we do invest, punishment often shapes our choices in hidden or unacknowledged ways: we would rather forbid than enable. The public debate over graffiti art offers an interesting illustration. Graffiti art—not tagging buildings and signs with one's initials, but using spray cans, stickers and other arts media to create complex works in public spaces—can be disturbing because it intervenes in the environment, disrupting expectations and often introducing unsettling imagery. I've taken part in quite a few forums and debates on the subject. The typical argument offered to oppose such works turns on two elements, private

---

1. www.costofwar.com.

property and public consent. "They don't ask for permission from the people who own the wall!" opponents of graffiti art say. (Sometimes this is true, although many experienced graffiti artists make permission a point of pride and integrity; often its lack is merely assumed by people who can't imagine otherwise.) They also say, "Now I have to look at this, and nobody asked me if I wanted it there!"

Both assertions depend on not noticing the commercialization of public space, or at least on not recognizing it as a choice in which most city dwellers have no part. It would be interesting to ask random passersby on a major-city street why we allow businesses to fill public space with large-scale advertisements. My hunch is that most would simply accept it as "the way things are." Jacobs prescribes attracting foot traffic as a way to drive out excessive automobile traffic, a positive alternative to banning automobiles. In much the same way, creating protected public space in cities for free visual expression would reduce the room given over to advertising. It would also address both of the common objections to graffiti art. But because we are so used to thinking only in terms of stopping things we dislike, the punitive approach tends to dominate. As everyone knows (and Jacobs plainly says), it almost always exacerbates whatever problem it attempts to solve.

THE LENS OF NEGATIVE LIBERTY

"Stadtluft macht frei" (city air makes you free), was one of Karl Marx's favorite sayings. The human desire to be seen and known remains forever in dialectical interaction with our equally human wish for anonymity and the freedom it confers. Officially, we are all for conviviality and comity these days—myself included. Yet every community builder I know sometimes shares the longing to lock the door and disappear in front of the television, to sit sometimes in silent hope that an unanswered doorbell will discourage an unwanted visitor. Our biases in favor of certain social goods sometimes blind us to personal goods. In addition to company, almost everyone craves what the philosophers call "negative liberty," the freedom from restraint and compulsion that comes most easily with anonymity.

I work with a great many community artists whose own work is to help animate community life, the opposite of anonymity. When people take part in a community arts project, one benchmark of success is whether civic engagement and collegial enterprise will heighten their disposition to re-enter the social arena. One idea is that collective art making is a powerful means of cultivating full cultural citizenship, an experience of meaningful belonging, participation, and mutual responsibility. Another is that the playful space of creative collaboration presents a lower threshold than other forms of civic participation, forming a gateway to community life. Both are true. But even the friendliest neighbor will recoil from an overdose of earnest encouragement, because it cancels the freedom to be left alone. The trick is finding a balance.

THE LENS OF NO THEORY

We are standing at the coastline between worlds. I like to call the old world Datastan, because it has embraced "hard" data—weights, measurements, any form of quantification—almost to the exclusion of other forms of value, with the absurd result that many of the things we care most about are not part of social equations because they can't be quantified. In Datastan, we are willing to sacrifice children's well-rounded education, the kind that teaches them to be resilient, improvisational, curious and creative, for one that reduces education to numeric test scores. In Datastan, we are willing to bulldoze long-lived neighborhoods to make way for sports stadiums and freeways. In Datastan, we confidently propound theories about human communities, and then try editing those communities to fit the theories. The critique of Datastan has been gathering force since the mid-twentieth century. I am moved by the way Isaiah Berlin expressed it in his wonderful essay, *The Sense of Reality*, grounded in the truth that what may be known about human beings is very little compared to what must remain fluid and mysterious:

> To claim to be able to construct generalizations where at best we can only indulge the art of exquisite portrait-painting, to claim the possibility of some infallible scientific key where each unique entity demands a

lifetime of minute, devoted observation, sympathy, insight, is one of the most grotesque claims ever made by human beings. (Berlin 1996, 20-21)

It appears Jacobs was immune to the madness of theory. To tip Datastan into oblivion, the rest of us may need inoculation. Happily, to get it, all we need do is open our eyes and minds.

REFERENCES

Adams, Don and Arlene Goldbard. 2002. *Community, Culture and Globalization*. New York: Rockefeller Foundation. (Out of print; contents may be downloaded from http://arlenegoldbard.com/books/.)

Berlin, Isaiah. 1996. *The Sense of Reality*. New York: Farrar, Straus and Giroux.

Goodman, Paul. 1962. *Utopian Essays and Practical Proposals*. New York: Vintage Books.

Jacobs, Jane. 1961. *The Death and Life of Great American Cities*. Modern Library Edition. New York: Random House.

Pew Center on the States. 2009. *One in 31: The Long Reach of American Corrections*. Washington, DC: The Pew Charitable Trusts.

THE LOGIC OF SMALL PIECES:

A STORY IN THREE BALLETS

Mindy Thompson Fullilove

J ANE JACOBS WROTE *The Death and Life of Great American Cities* (1961) to protest the policy of urban renewal that was dismantling American cities by scooping out huge sections of the nineteenth-century grid in order to install parking lots, megablocks of Corbusian towers-in-the-park, monolithic public housing, and campuses. To help the U.S. understand the harm it was doing, Jacobs lifted the curtain to reveal the mysterious mechanisms that make cities work. She helped us appreciate the city as a highly functional form of human social organization, one capable of contributing in large and small ways to the nation's pursuit of happiness. To understand the seminal contribution she made from the perspective of my discipline, social psychiatry, I begin with the work of Alexander Leighton, whose careful examination of the internment of Japanese people during World War II is one of the pillars of my field.

BALLET ONE: WHOSE STREET?

The Japanese attack on Pearl Harbor, December 7, 1941, triggered a wave of anti-Japanese sentiment in the United States. Shortly thereafter, on February 19, 1942, President Franklin Roosevelt issued an executive order for the internment of Japanese people. Within months, people who had immigrated from Japan (known as Issei) and their children born in the U.S. (Nisei) were forcibly displaced to internment camps away from the West Coast.

Leighton (1945) studied one of those places, the Poston camp, located in the Arizona desert. People arrived having lost their homes and their livelihoods, carrying the few possessions they could pack. They were assigned to cramped barracks, and gradually given work. For their part, the internees struggled to balance disorientation, despair and resentment with hope and re-engagement. The administrators, albeit limited by their own racism and insensitivity, as well as that of the society that had endorsed the racist policy of exclusion, worked diligently to meet the goals of keeping everyone alive and active. The rules of social engagement were contested in the highly fractured social system of the camp. At issue were fundamental questions of power.

The resulting tension came to head over an incident in which several members of the community beat a man who had betrayed his fellow evacuees. Two men were arrested for the assault, and a protest ensued. The leaders of the internees demanded that they be given authority to manage the investigation of the attack and the prosecution of wrongdoing. The administration had no interest in sharing power. Leighton recorded a dramatic showdown between the two sides:

> The Assistant Director [of the camp] said that law and order must be maintained and he entreated the [internees'] Council to have faith in the Administration and to think of their own future. The Vice-Chairman of the Council, a very Americanized Nisei acting in the absence of the Chairman, carried by the intense waves of feeling of those around him, said, "These men [the prisoners] are not even charged. They have not been held legally. Now, if that is granted to us, I think things will run smoothly. If they are guilty, it is up to the people to determine that they are guilty." There was widespread clapping at this, and then he added, regretfully, "If you cannot trust us, then we have nothing more to do. We feel you should give us self-government."
>
> The Assistant Director stood firm. The Council resigned in a body. The Issei advisers followed after a short speech by their Chairman.

All trooped out of the hall and went down to join the demonstrators before the jail. Later, the Block Managers resigned en masse and soon the Administration received word that on the next day there would be a general strike of all evacuee help in Unit I. (Leighton 1945, 170)

Similar confrontations in other internment camps deteriorated into rioting. The situation at Poston was resolved peacefully and positively, in no small measure because Alexander Leighton found a way to help the administrators appreciate the general strike as signaling the emergence of effective community leadership. Rather than stonewalling that emerging leadership, Leighton helped the administration engage with the new leaders in finding solutions to the conflict. The administration's intransigence was converted into willingness to negotiate, and the whole system of the camp was able to evolve into larger and more stable social units.

Leighton emphasized, "Communities undergoing social disorganization also show new organization; break down and repair take place simultaneously." He elaborated on this idea, elucidating the principle that "where stress is severe and social disorganization is extensive, the breakdown-and-repair process is likely to take a violent form consisting in groups of people, each coalesced around a different system of belief, struggling with each other until one group dominates or until an equilibrium is achieved among several dominant groups" (1945, 322). We learn from Dr. Leighton that violence understood as a message can be managed to promote healing of the social fractures.

BALLET TWO: OUR TOWN

Jane Jacobs' description of the sidewalk ballet on Hudson Street is not usually read as a story of power. The bucolic scene is mesmerizing in its kindness:

The stretch of Hudson Street where I live is each day the scene of an intricate sidewalk ballet. I make my own entrance into it a little after eight when I put out the garbage can, surely a prosaic occupation, but I enjoy my part, my little clang, as the droves of junior high school students walk by the center of the stage dropping candy wrappers. (How do they eat so much candy so early in the morning?)

While I sweep up the wrappers I watch the other rituals of morning: Mr. Halpert unlocking the laundry's handcart from it mooring to a cellar door, Joe Cornacchia's son-in-law stacking out the empty crates from the delicatessen, the barber bringing out his sidewalk folding chair, Mr. Goldstein arranging the coils of wire which proclaim the hardware store is open, the wife of the tenement's superintendent depositing her chunky three-year-old with a toy mandolin on the stoop, the vantage point from which he is learning the English his mother cannot speak... It is time for me to hurry to work too, and I exchange my ritual farewell with Mr. Lofaro, the short, thick-bodied, white-aproned fruit man who stands outside his doorway a little way up the street, his arms folded, his feet planted, looking solid as earth itself. We nod; we each glance quickly up and down the street, then look back to each other and smile. We have done this many a morning for more than ten years, and we both know what it means: All is well. (Jacobs 1961, 50-51)

But the point of this metaphor is to use the highly valued "ballet" to elevate and protect everything that is prosaic but necessary in the neighborhood. In my own work, I have heard versions of the sidewalk ballet from all corners of our nation, and people were quite clear that it enabled them to survive (Fullilove 2004). Mr. Charles Meadows, who lived in Northeast—an African American neighborhood in Roanoke, Virginia—told me:

In Northeast, there was no poverty because everybody helped one another. When we could afford two pounds of beans, our wives would cook them up and everybody would have a bowl. If our next-door neighbor didn't have a job, we would help them out. We were independently self-supporting as a neighborhood. We enjoyed it, because we knew we had someone to rely on. The section was so unified at one time, you could start at the Norfolk and Western station and call the names of everybody on every street. We didn't need telephones.

You'd just walk out and call somebody's name, or spread the word. "Hello, Brother John, hello, Sister So-and-so," hollering on both sides of the street. (Fullilove 2004, 82)

Though Hudson Street was preserved, Northeast was lost, bulldozed in 1964. Mr. Meadow's all-inclusive walk-of-hellos was extinguished. And what Jane Jacobs knew would happen did happen: the precious networks could not be rebuilt, because the people were stripped of assets and dispersed. What had been a large and well-functioning social system, capable of nurturing people through good times and bad, was shattered into small pieces. At that time, a new logic came into play.

Within a few years of Jane Jacobs' writing, urban renewal had become one of the causes of the civil insurrections—the riots—that rocked American cities in the 1960s. President Lyndon Johnson appointed a commission, which became known as the Kerner Commission, to help the nation understand the causes of the uproar. The Kerner Commission was quite clear that urban renewal, which had displaced people, undermined their faith in democracy, and diminished the stock of low-cost housing, had been a major contributor to the difficulties people faced in trying to live their lives.

Dr. Rodrick Wallace, a physicist turned ecologist, has conducted numerous studies of fracturing of urban communities. He emphasizes:

It is not the case that small pieces are the same as larger ones, except smaller. There are massive shifts in behavior that represent the response to fewer resources as well as to the implicit societal rejection that accompanies having the government destroy one's neighborhood. New behaviors are required to affirm "I am a person of worth in a community of worth" in the face of such societal betrayal. I am convinced that what are called "risk behaviors" represent a new mode [of] communication generated by shattered social networks.[1]

Wallace, as Leighton before him, emphasizes violence as a form of communication. There is some evidence that our society heard what

---

1. Personal communication. See also Wallace and Wallace (1998).

the rioters were saying, for President Lyndon B. Johnson instituted a number of anti-poverty programs to address the concerns noted in the Kerner Commission's report.

BALLET THREE:
A DANCE FOR SMALL PIECES

Yet there is even more evidence that, if our society heard, it didn't care: policies of displacement continued to be enacted by local, state, and federal governments. One such program was the planned shrinkage, or extreme disinvestment, which was instituted in New York City in the mid-1970s. At the heart of the policy was the closing of fire stations in densely settled urban neighborhoods. Those neighborhoods proceeded to burn down. The loss of housing, which reached as high as 80 percent of the units in some areas of the Bronx, caused massive social disruption. That, in turn, was followed by epidemics of violence, drug addiction, infant mortality, maternal mortality, school failure, family collapse, and AIDS. The burnt-out South Bronx became, in the popular consciousness and as depicted in books like Tom Wolfe's *Bonfire of the Vanities*, the horror off the highway, the wrong exit that turned one's middle class life upside down. The middle class got the message, and stopped going to those places.

Intrepid newspaper writers made voyages of rediscovery, but few stayed long enough to get the sidewalk ballet. One who did was journalist Greg Donaldson, who spent a year between 1991 and 1992 following life in Brownsville-East New York after it had been devastated by planned shrinkage. Greg Donaldson's book, *The Ville: Cops and Kids in Urban America* (1993), is a minute-by-minute description of the rules patterning exchange on the streets of a neighborhood deeply injured by catastrophic urban policies. In the following segment, Donaldson reports what Lonnie, one of the cops he followed, had to say:

> "Say you're walking down this street with your woman," Lonnie goes on, "and some guy around your building says, 'Hey, I want your lady to suck my dick,' and you just grin." Lonnie displays a lame smile. "Then the guys get together and they start talking. You know, 'Hey

I told that guy's woman to suck my dick and he didn't do nothin'.' Then they start getting this idea that they should rob you." Lonnie acts out the robbery with the victim raising his hand in a feeble gesture of protest. Then he assumes the role of the tough guy. "'Put your hand down. I told you not to move your fuckin' hand.' The next thing you know, they have your old lady up on the roof and they really *are* makin' her suck their dicks.

"It's the same if some guy robs your mother on the way home from [the] subway. You get the name and the description... You have to decide what to do. If you decide to take him out, you have to do it right, because if you fuck up, he'll kill you. You come up to him real fast with your head down and your hands in your pockets. Or you get your crew. That's why you need a crew. That's how you act when you live around here, and that is why so many brothers are in jail." (Donaldson 1993, 209-210)

Though this vignette is vulgar and violent—so nasty we are tempted to throw it away in disgust—it is urgent to study this with the same care we have applied to the more pleasant happenings on Hudson Street. In both instances, it is the neighborly eye that governs what is happening on the street. In the aftermath of social disruption, the problem is not candy wrappers, but primitive accumulation.[2] People are starting over by employing violence to expropriate what belongs to others. To maintain one's turf, friends and relations, and possessions, one must be prepared to outdo the violence threatened by others.

The critical insight Donaldson offers is that this is not random violence: it is as highly choreographed as Jacobs' interactions on Hudson. It is, however, a ballet in the language of small pieces: people communicate via aggressive actions, and safety lies in meeting force with force.

---

2. "Primitive accumulation" is often limited to the accumulation of capital in the early days of capitalism. However, the use of violence to accumulate capital through gang and gang-like violence in impoverished communities is a recurring theme in American history. As the capital is often used to enter business—i.e., the Mafia investing in Las Vagas casinos—the parallels are of more than theoretical interest.

"You need a crew," Lonnie says. Being able to organize a small group is essential to survive. But the existence of that survival strategy signals that larger and calmer social units have been destroyed, in this case by urban policies with lethal outcomes, if not intent.

I learned about Brownsville and East New York as part of a study of lethal shootings in schools I conducted for the National Academy of Sciences. Several deadly shootings had taken place at Roosevelt High School in East New York during the time Donaldson was there, 1991–1992. Our retrospective study, conducted in 2001, collected interviews with community leaders and residents, people who had been students at the school, the young men who had committed the murders, police officers, clergy, politicians, educators, lawyers, and others who had been present at the events. They had vivid recollections of that time, and the extent to which society had fallen apart (see Fullilove et al. 2003).

Perhaps most striking was the testimony of the young men who had taken guns to school. They were trying to stand up to the forces described by Lonnie: they felt that if they had not demonstrated their ability to use force, they would have opened themselves up to complete destruction. They were not able to reach out to teachers or parents: adults had a hard time understanding the brave new world in which their children were living. Mayor David Dinkins spoke for that generation when he told the youth to say no to violence. The youth emphatically told us that that was not an option in the world in which they lived.

THE STORY OF THE BALLET

Much of art appreciation lies in the interactive process between the viewer and the artist. It is easy to say "I don't like it" about a piece of art, but that is not the way to a deep appreciation. In using "ballet" to describe the prosaic acts of putting out the garbage and nodding to the fruit seller, Jane Jacobs challenged us to open our senses and our understanding. She was well aware that the scene she was describing was imperiled by urban renewal precisely because it was devalued by power brokers interested in other uses for the land. Her reframing "putting out the garbage" as "sidewalk ballet" created a weapon for protecting neighborhoods. Our task is to understand, as Leighton did, the logic of dances that are less nice. The great use of Jacobs' framework is in approaching scenes where the ballet is alien and alienating. It was easy for planners to condemn Hudson Street, but it was even easier for them to destroy the minority neighborhood of Northeast, and easiest to write off Brownsville/East New York as a disaster zone, needing to be "cleaned out." This is a wrong-headed strategy, because it loses sight of the human relationships that are in place and must be the foundation for betterment. Brownsville/East New York, at its moment of deepest distress, did not need further upheaval, but rather more investment and more respect, just as the Japanese interned in the Poston Relocation Center needed to be heard by the camp administration.

U.S. society has enacted a series of policies—including the internment of Japanese Americans, urban renewal, and planned shrinkage—that have dislocated people and destroyed their social and economic resources. The appreciation for the sidewalk ballet may appear to be a slender thread for hanging our hopes for more humane treatment of our fellow citizens and their social worlds. Yet the sidewalk ballet, a modest living dance, has the power to help us appreciate and treasure urban environments. The tasks before us are expanding our seeing so that we learn to cherish an even wider array of places, and make sure that our governments enact policies that build on these collective treasures, rather than destroy them.

REFERENCES

Donaldson, Greg. 1993. *The Ville: Cops and Kids in Urban America*. New York: Houghton Mifflin.

Fullilove, Mindy T., Gina Arias, Moises Nunez, Ericka Phillips, Peter McFarlane, Rodrick Wallace, and Robert E. Fullilove. 2003. "What Did Ian Tell God? School Violence in East New York." In *Deadly Lessons: Understanding Lethal School Violence*, edited by Mark H. Moore, Carol V. Petrie, Anthony A. Braga, and Brenda L. McLaughlin. Washington, DC: The National Academies Press.

Fullilove, Mindy T. 2004. *Root Shock: How Tearing Up City Neighborhoods Hurts America and What We Can Do About It.* New York: Ballantine Books.

Jacobs, Jane. 1961. *The Death and Life of Great American Cities.* Modern Library Edition. New York: Random House, 1993.

Leighton, Alexander. 1945. *The Governing of Men.* Princeton: Princeton University Press.

Wallace, Deborah and Rodrick Wallace. 1998. *A Plague on Your Houses: How New York Was Burned Down and National Public Health Crumbled.* London: Verso.

"OF THINGS SEEN AND UNSEEN"

Alexie M. Torres-Fleming

JANE JACOBS AND I are unlikely friends. She was a white, middle class journalist. I am a Puerto Rican mother and youth minister with no college degree. Truthfully, I knew little of her until recently, yet as I become familiar with her story, I recognize her as a presence whose ideas and spirit have been with me throughout the past fifteen years of my life. I have never seen her, yet I am deeply familiar with her essence. She lives in my gut conviction that my community is made up of more than streets, buildings, and businesses. It is a brilliant, sacred, living and breathing space whose people are its richest and most powerful resource. I see all of this so clearly now, but it was not always the case for me.

I was born and raised in the Bronx River Public Housing Projects in New York City. I have lived my entire life in the South Bronx, the poorest congressional district in the United States. I am the child of parents who emigrated from Puerto Rico in the 1950s. My mother worked as a seamstress in a clothing factory. My father was homeless until he got a job as a dishwasher and sandwich man at a Manhattan deli. He met Mom at a church dance and married her three months later. Mom eventually stopped working, got her GED and gave up a college scholarship to stay at home with her four children. It grew more and more challenging to sustain our growing family, so Daddy eventually got a job as a maintenance man in our public housing project. As a child, I watched him work in our thirteen-story building, picking up garbage and mopping the floors. He also had the unpleasant responsibility of washing things like urine off the elevator walls and stairwells. He did this while always singing. From him I learned dignity, joy, and contentment.

My mother has always been an active church volunteer. Thirty years ago she founded our church gift and thrift shop where 100 percent of the proceeds go to support the parish and our community. Everyone knew Mom, and neighbors came to her with their needs and the needs of others. In order to respond to them, she became an expert organizer and developed informal networks of support that were not present in the community. She did this while always praying. From her I learned faith, service, and love of others.

My parents were very protective, so my siblings and I were not allowed to play outside. Instead, Mom and Dad would place a chair in the door and watch us as we lay blankets on the hallway floor, talking for hours, doing homework, "sock skating," dancing, and putting on performances. In the absence of any youth or community facilities, that hallway became our place for tutoring, arts, sports, and education. It was there that I learned that community is where you make it.

Later, as I entered my teen years, my local church youth group became an important and extended community space as well. I had a profound formation experience where I felt deeply accepted. I was also discouraged from making church a place to "hide" as I awaited a better world in the next life. I was, rather, taught that faith was not about just making it into heaven someday when so many were already living in hell right now.

Indeed that hell was breaking loose all around me. It was the late 1970s in the South Bronx, the time of "urban renewal," "planned shrinkage," "white flight," disinvestment, and the ultimate "burning of the Bronx." This occurred after police and fire stations where shut down and property owners set their own buildings on fire to collect the insurance money and escape the neighborhood. I remember being perched on the kitchen washing machine, feet up on the radiator, as Mommy cooked. From my ninth floor window I watched my community go up in flames. I can still hear the sound of fire engines interrupting our conversations, smell the fire mingling with Mom's cooking, and taste the smoke in my throat.

It was at that time that I began to have a new and rather distorted view of my home and myself. My beloved community became a place to be feared. At school, church, and on television, I heard it referred to as the "ghetto," a "slum" from which nothing good would come. Fear replaced love, and people stopped gathering in all of the familiar places. I felt powerless and believed that things like this, over which we had no control, "happened to people like us." I heard my neighbors congratulate each other for "making it out," and I too began to believe that the measure of my success would be how far I could escape from my community. That desire was supported by the world around me, and despite all I had learned, "taking care of number one" became my mantra.

I left the South Bronx after high school in pursuit of this "better" place. I got a good job in Manhattan, had several nice apartments, traveled, made money and bought nice things. Against the checklist of what girls like me could become, I had survived the worst and "made it." But in the end, I was profoundly alone and empty. Having bought the American dream hook, line, and sinker, I found that I had everything to live with, but little to live for. I lived with both shame at the powerlessness of my family and community and a deep longing to reconnect with them.

During this time, I was encouraged by friends back home to give back to my community, and so I began to do volunteer work at my old Bronx parish. The church had begun organizing prayer marches in response to the crack epidemic that had devastated the South Bronx after the fires. Crack houses emerged all around the neighborhood, and children and families were lost in addiction and violence. I began attending parish meetings and volunteered to help plan the prayer marches. Despite being gone for so long, I was lovingly welcomed back by all of those I had secretly rejected and looked down upon. The gatherings were inspiring, and the company of those who knew and loved me regardless of how "successful" I had become was comforting.

On a Sunday afternoon in November 1992, about three hundred of us walked, sang and prayed our way to seven known crack houses in the community. It was a simple yet moving action, after which we all went home. Two weeks later, I awoke to the news that drug dealers had torched my church in retaliation. Having run from the fires not a decade before, my first thoughts were, "What did you get yourself into?" and "You should NOT have come back." Fortunately, they were immediately followed by my higher angels that said, "Don't just sit there!" "Go home! This is the moment you have been waiting for." I got on the train and came back home.

The church sanctuary was burnt; windows and statues were broken, including a beautiful statue of the Blessed Mother that people knelt around as they wept. I was equally devastated until another voice came up inside of me and said, "Why are you crying about this building? God does not live here. Every day, what is truly sacred is desecrated down the block from here. When will you cry about that?"

There were press and television crews everywhere. You don't burn a church in America and not get national attention. There was an article in a newspaper the next day, along with a picture of the parishioners crying over the statue. I said, "That cannot be the last image of who we are as a community—us crying over a broken statue." So when the press asked, "What are you going to do now?" I told them, "We are going to march again." The announcement was made, the flyer went out and the death threats began. There were threats against the pastor's life, and warnings that if we marched again, the crowd would be shot into. True to form, the pastor put on a bulletproof vest and we continued to plan.

It was a beautiful autumn day when we marched again. I had spent the night weeping out of fear that no one would show up, but what I saw on that day as I walked down the street changed my life. Over 1,200 members of my community were waiting to march. Young people; single moms pushing baby strollers; immigrant men and women; the elderly; people I recognized from street corners; and the people I had been taught in my "new" world were the most "powerless" were all around me. My father was also present. The man with a third-grade education who had washed urine off elevator walls taught me a great lesson that day. That voice inside spoke up again and said, "This, Alexie, is what real power is, all God's children moving together from the margins to the center, lifting their own voices, struggling for their dignity and their community."

A few months later I quit my job, and along with a few young people founded Youth Ministries for Peace and Justice. I was twenty-eight years old. Ten years after my departure and more than two decades after urban renewal began, my community still desperately needed to be rebuilt. Young people poured into the church basement that became our new youth center, but as quickly as they came in, we had them go outside. We took long walks, and asked them to write about what they saw and what they felt. It took a long time for them (and for me, I admit) to get to a place where we could see past hopelessness. We worked together to overcome the usual "things can't change" and "we just need to get out of here" thinking. They looked to me for answers, but truthfully I had none. We continued to work to take problems apart and understand what made things bad and how to tackle them step-by-step. And it was in these simple meetings that my healing began. Soon we came to discover that what we had far exceeded what we did not have. The most wonderful resource we came upon during these conversations was the beauty and energy of our youth members. Soon after that, with our hearts open and ready to truly see the potential in our community, we came upon the Bronx River. All of those years after being born in the Bronx River Housing Projects and living in a neighborhood called Bronx River, many of us realized for the first time that our neighborhood was named after this 8-mile body of water that ran right through the heart of our community. Of course it was industrialized, inaccessible and polluted, but it was also ours.

We began to imagine how residents, whose only source of water for recreation was the local fire hydrant, might enjoy the river. Admittedly, this was hard to fathom. Then one day a neighbor suggested we drive and follow the river north on the Bronx River Parkway. There, no more than ten minutes away, new visions were opened up when young people saw what the river looked like with its greenways, benches, and wildlife. We learned that day that the river runs through some of the wealthiest congressional districts in Westchester County as well as ours, the poorest in the nation. Young people began to break free from simple answers to the question, "Why is it so different in our community than up here?" Answers that they had internalized, such as "Poor people just don't care as much. They are dirty and not smart enough," or "If we could only get out of here and move up there" seemed less powerful. We slowly began to explore notions of personal responsibility along with ideas such as environmental justice, inequity, classism, racism, and injustice.

In response, the R.I.V.E.R. team (Reaching and Including youth Voices for Environmental Rights) was born, and Project R.O.W. (Reclaiming Our Waterfront) was launched. Our plans were ambitious: restoration of the river both physically and in the minds and hearts of the community who had written it off; development of a greenway along its banks where no one thought it was possible; restoration of an abandoned and contaminated waterfront park; and the cleanup and redevelopment of an abandoned concrete plant into a new waterfront park. Along the way we also became founding members of a coalition to decommission an underutilized highway that blocked access to most of our waterfront.

Our first task was to get the community out and excited about the river. We received a small grant for some canoes and began regularly carrying them to the river. Imagine the sight of youth walking through our "concrete jungle" with 75-pound canoes on their head. We had a Pied Piper effect and drew crowds along the waterfront that many never knew existed. We gave canoe rides, and people would stand along the bridges, stare and laugh as we maneuvered through the 40-plus cars, 10,000 abandoned tires, and other debris that had been dumped into the river and along the waterfront.

Drawing from my childhood "hallway" community-building experiences, we held picnics, cleanups, dances, poetry readings, theater, and the like. We also held canoe "christenings," prayers, blessings and rituals that inspired and reminded us that this was holy water and its revival would give us more than a place to enjoy—it would change *us* in ways *unseen*.

As people became more familiar with the river, we began to conduct planning events that we called "community visioning sessions." We knew that all the canoeing, arts and prayer in the world were not enough to tackle all of our challenges. There were city, state, and federal agencies to confront, and it was not enough to come with a list of complaints. We needed a vision that drew upon an expertise that had been ignored in urban renewal efforts to date—namely, community expertise.

We had to be creative and we had to inspire. People were tired and suspicious of talking heads and empty promises. They were already too weighed down by the struggles of day-to-day work and of raising families in the community. They did not need lectures, people who looked down on them, or provided them with empty promises. They did not need another meeting to attend. So we gathered on our front stoops, in our backyards, in the church sanctuary, and in building lobbies. We knocked on doors, had coffee, and visited church groups, tenant associations, school board meetings, and parent associations: anywhere people gathered and we could get them excited. Not everyone spoke English, so we translated. Not everyone communicated best with the written word, so we gave them tape recorders, video cameras, crayons, clay, instruments, popsicle sticks, glue, and anything else we could get our hands on. We worked to the sounds of music and drumming, and the results were very little "newsprint." Our ideas were expressed in Popsicle river houses, CDs, theater projects, children's books, videos, photo journals, poetry, murals, comic books, as well as reports and maps provided by wonderful partners and technical assistance providers. Along the way we learned that this "process" was as important as anything we could ever "produce." We had gained a sense of united community that gave us the strength to overcome our next hurdle—"the experts."

As we began to navigate the policies, systems, and agencies that were responsible for decisions that were hurting our community, we had to overcome three hurdles presented to us by the experts: language, missionary mentality, and the big fish.

The language barriers we confronted went beyond anything we could tackle with translating equipment. The "experts" create entire new languages with acronyms and jargon. We had to overcome embarrassment and many rolling eyes as we committed ourselves to asking that every acronym be spelled out and every word we did not understand be defined. We hung on until we understood and learned the power of demystifying the language of the experts. We learned that language can be used to keep people out, and that our questions could be threatening to those who stake their entire educations and careers on knowing what others do not. It is a subtle form of power that is not easily surrendered to people that are, at best, perceived as incapable of understanding, and at worst as not deserving—after all, we were the very "problem" they were trying to solve.

Along the way, it was also easy to be taken in by "the missionaries." By this I mean those well-intentioned "experts" that are knowledgeable or skilled or well resourced or famous that would come in and tell us not to worry. They would fix, design, buy and take care of our waterfront and our problems for us. On the hardest days they were a major threat to our developing community and sense of power, but in the end we realized that a Hero or Savior could never replace our emerging trust in our own wisdom and power.

Finally, we had to tackle the Big Fish: the large statewide or national environmental groups to whom we were often referred. We were told they should be our spokespeople and the conduit for our grants. They were the voices the foundations and government agencies trusted and wanted to hear from. But like many of the other "experts," they were not from our community, nor did they have the intimate knowledge of it that we knew was critical in the decision-making process. The Big Fish would agree to token representation by one or two of us "leaders" on their committees or advisory groups, and would be more than willing to speak for us when it meant access to a grant for work that community residents had been leading all along.

These three challenges presented by outside "experts" became so frustrating that we began to regularly carry to meetings a sign that declared, WE LIVE HERE, WE'RE EXPERTS TOO.

In over fifteen years of struggle we have often been amazed at the visions that were buried within our community and at what we have been able to manifest. Today, with the leadership of our Bronx River residents and many other organizations, partners, and technical assistance providers, thousands of people have canoed up and down the Bronx River. Salt marshes have been restored, wildlife has returned, and approximately twenty-five acres of new parkland and greenways will open soon. The contamination at our local park has been completely remediated with one million dollars of restitution awarded to the Parks Department, and an abandoned cement plant has just opened up as a new waterfront park.

There is indeed a lot to *see*, and through it all I have tried to be faithful to all that I learned in that hallway in the projects, at my mom's church store, in my parish youth group, and from witnessing my father at work. But if I am lucky enough to get to leave a legacy to my community, I hope that it will be measured less by what is visible and more by what you don't see—an abundance of pride, hope, voice, confidence, love, trust, respect, dignity, and unity. These are the most treasured rewards—the ones I pass on to my own children, even as I continue to develop them within myself.

Not all work today is sacred. Community planning and development has the power to both crush and elevate the human spirit. Jane believed deeply in the power of observation, in what we see. And while I agree with her, I have also found that this work is as much about what we don't see. Communities are not just streets and buildings: they are the sacred spaces made up of living, breathing people whose hopes and dreams are wrapped up in those same streets and buildings. Planning can elevate or diminish that reality. I have experienced both effects in my life. The most profound and inspiring moments have been about what I don't see with my eyes.

THE FINE ARTS OF SEEING:

PROFESSIONS, PLACES, ART, AND URBAN DESIGN

Rob Cowan

"WHEN WE DEAL with cities we are dealing with life at its most complex and intense," wrote Jane Jacobs. She hit the nail on the head, which is why I used that as an epigraph at the start of *The Dictionary of Urbanism* (Cowan 2005). Coming to terms with complexity and intensity is the key to understanding a city. What each of us sees and understands depends on our own experience: where we come from, personally and professionally. We learn the fine arts of seeing through professions, places, art, and urban design.

PROFESSIONS

Denise Scott Brown, an architect, planner and urban designer, understands that very well. "Put a group of urban designers, architects and planners in a sightseeing bus and watch them as the cameras click," she urges us. "Where do the architects click? At buildings or clusters of buildings, or at objects—bridges, sculptures, pylons. The urban designers click where things come together—buildings against bridges, pylons beside small houses. The planners are too busy talking to each other to look out of the window" (Scott Brown 2002, 51).

The architect and educationalist William Lethaby wrote: "Bad plays need not be seen, books need not be read, but nothing but blindness or the numbing of our faculty of observation can protect us from buildings in the street." And how numb our faculty of observation sometimes is!

Built environment professionals too often see the world through a prism that their education and practice have created, and too rarely leave their offices to look at the places they are designing and planning. Mystified non-professionals too often defer to them. That is why I invented Placecheck, a first step in looking at a place and thinking about how to change it for the better.

"Invented" is a grand word for something so simple. People carry out a Placecheck by going to a place and looking. They ask: what do I like about this place? What do I dislike? What needs to be improved? They may go on to ask some of the more detailed questions in the Placecheck user's guide.[1] Some of those questions are about the physical form of the place. They are the sort of questions that urban designers ask, but why should people not ask them for themselves? Other questions are about what needs to be done to make change happen: about who has the necessary interest, budget, responsibility, expertise, or mandate. The Placecheck method, which is now widely used in the UK, is a simple way of promoting collaborative action. The secret of its success is that the people who live and work in a place are likely to know already what needs to be done. All they need is to be prompted to look, to question, and to start the process.

We need the professionals as well, of course. But where does urban design fit into the landscape of professions? Where does urban design begin, and where do architecture, planning, and other related disciplines end? The answer is: they don't. Urban design is not a profession occupying a niche between the others. It is a way of working.

Yes, there are professional urban designers: specialists in the art of placemaking who choose "urban designer" as their professional label. They deserve more recognition than they generally receive. But many of them are also architects, building conservationists, engineers, landscape architects, planners, or surveyors. One of the defining characteristics of urban design is that it is a process involving a range of disciplines.

Urban design is a way of managing the complexity of places and of creating frameworks for change. It is a way of approaching architecture,

---

1. www.placecheck.info.

though not the type of architecture that is "done" once the project has been photographed for the professional journals. It involves planning, but not the sort that considers the process complete when the plan has been approved. It is concerned with highway engineering, but the type that responds to the particular possibilities of the place, rather than being enslaved to regulations and conventional practice.

A couple of years ago the Urban Design Group in the UK asked its members: which person, living or dead, do you most admire for his or her impact on thinking or action on the built environment? In second place came the urban designer Kevin Lynch (1918-84), whose methods of analyzing and graphically notating urban form are the most commonly used by urban designers today.

The winner—by a mile—was Jane Jacobs. She was not an urban designer in any conventional sense, so why are so many urban designers so passionate about what she stood for? The answer is surely that her insights into what make cities tick, made nearly half a century ago, ring as true now as anything anyone else has written since. Jane Jacobs' writings give us the sense that although it may not be easy to get to grips with places as complex and unpredictable as Birkenhead, Chester, or Liverpool, there is no more exciting task.

Not fitting neatly into any professional category myself, I tend to fill in the "occupation" box in official forms by writing "urbanist," if only to confuse the bureaucrats. Where do I come from? If not from a distinct profession, perhaps from a place, or a series of places. My own experience, and the way it informs the way I see, begins with three cities, located within fifteen miles of each other in the northwest of England: Birkenhead, Liverpool, and Chester.

PLACES

Birkenhead, where I was born, is not a city in the British sense, not having a cathedral and never having been awarded a city charter (though its derogatory nickname is, for reasons that remain obscure, "the one-eyed city"). But at one time, Birkenhead seemed destined to become a city, and a fine one. There were once plans, later abandoned, to build a cathedral.

The town's origins date from the 1820s, when William Laird built a shipyard and commissioned the Edinburgh architect James Gillespie Graham to plan a new town at the site of what had been no more than a village. Edward Hubbard has called the resulting rectangular street plan "one of the most ambitious instances of nineteenth-century planning anywhere in Britain." Birkenhead Park, designed by Joseph Paxton in 1843, was built as the world's first park provided at public expense, and its design influenced that of New York's Central Park. The intention seems to have been, Hubbard notes, for the entire town to consist of stone-faced classical buildings of high architectural quality. But, although the streets were laid out, the high quality envisaged in the original plan was never achieved. Birkenhead has ever since been Liverpool's poor neighbor.

Liverpool, across the River Mersey from Birkenhead, needs no introduction. No city is the subject of more stereotypes. Liverpudlians (or "scousers," as they are called colloquially after a stew that used to be eaten by sailors) are said to be sentimental, roguish, light-fingered, self-mythologizing, militant, grudge-bearing, self-pitying, humorous, and inward-looking. The last of those clichés is certainly inapt, as the urbanist Tim Mars notes. "Liverpool is not inward-looking," he told me recently. "But you could call it semi-detached. Liverpool looks not to England but outward—to Wales, Ireland, Africa, America. Liverpool is the least English of all English cities, with the fewest native-born people living in it. It is the capital of north Wales [even though it is not actually in Wales] and once had thirty-five Welsh-language chapels. It is also, courtesy of the potato famine, the capital of the Irish diaspora. It has the largest Chinese population outside London and the oldest Chinatown in Europe. It is full of the descendants of Chinese, Lascar and Somali sailors." It was through Liverpool that most Irish immigrants came to America. "Liverpool was a multicultural city before the term was invented," Mars told me. "The Mersey sound, Merseybeat and The Beatles happened in Liverpool precisely because of this rich cultural mix and early contact with American popular music through the records brought in from the U.S. by visiting or returning sailors. The nearest comparison is not with other British ports—Bristol or Newcastle, Glasgow or Belfast—but

with Marseilles, that least French, most semi-detached, most multicultural of French cities."

Liverpool, U.S. poet Allen Ginsberg famously said when he arrived
there in 1965, was "at the present moment, the centre of consciousness of
the human universe." Liverpudlians like to imagine that in some strange
way it still is, even though Ginsberg may have thought that Liverpool
deserved the accolade mainly because he himself was there at the time (he
made a similar claim for Milwaukee when he was there). To me, Liverpool has always been the epitome of a great city, combining exceptional
architecture (it has more buildings on the official list for protection on
the grounds of special architectural or historic interest than any other
city outside London), vital culture (often of an unofficial kind), and a
distinctive sense of humour.

Chester, where my parents live, is the third city of my trio. Fourteen
miles from Birkenhead and fifteen from Liverpool, it is a more sedate
place than either. Now the county town of Cheshire, it was founded as
a fort by the Romans. Its main streets—Watergate Street, Bridge Street,
Eastgate Street, and Northgate Street—follow the course of the Roman
streets laid out nearly two thousand years ago. The city walls are the best
preserved in Britain. Today Chester is the very image of a medieval city,
with a medieval cathedral and medieval-looking, half-timbered buildings
(many of them erected in the nineteenth century).

Towns and cities tend to have distinctive variations of familiar urban
forms. But Chester has something unique, in Britain at least, that sets
the curious urbanist looking for clues as to what extraordinary conditions
shaped it. Chester's most striking and mysterious features are the Rows.
These form a network of two-tiered shopping streets of medieval origin,
with an upper pedestrian street running above the ground-floor shops.
A variety of explanations have been given for this form. The historian
Oliver Bott (2001) suggests that the lay of the land was an important
factor. By the thirteenth century, when Chester's first Rows were built,
the main streets were still at around the same level as they had been in
Roman times. The ground level of much of the land behind the buildings, though, had risen due to rubble and rubbish accumulating during

the Dark Ages. The lowest floor of a new building needed to be only a few steps down from the street, Bott explains, if the next floor was to be level with the backyard. This meant that instead of having deep cellars, as in other medieval cities, Chester merchants had their storage at street level, with their shops or offices above.

Richard Morriss, another historian, records the theory that when the Saxons settled in Chester in the seventh century, the ruins of the Roman barracks and other buildings were converted into store rooms, and new shops and houses were built above them, connected by a raised walkway that became the Rows. Alternatively, Morriss suggests, owners were ordered to make their ground floors fireproof following a fire in 1278, which they did by building stone structures at ground level. It has also been suggested that the idea of the Rows came from builders from Constantinople (which had buildings in this form) who were based in Chester while constructing the chain of Welsh castles for Edward I after 1277.

ART

Places, professions… what else opens our eyes? Good art changes how we see the world, and in some cases how people in future generations will see it. Our eyes are opened to forms, textures, patterns, relation-ships, and meanings we might not have noticed otherwise. For me, the experience has rarely been as direct as it was when many years ago I saw an exhibition in London of the work of Boyle family (they call them-selves that, without the definite article). This is a family of artists: Joan, Mark (who died in 2005), their son Sebastian, and daughter Georgia. Since the 1960s they have been making what they call "earthpieces"—three-dimensional facsimiles of the earth's surface made from glass fiber and resin. The subjects, including small areas of street or pavement surface, indistinguishable from the real thing, are sometimes chosen at random by throwing a dart at a map.

You might ask what is the point of hanging on a gallery wall some-thing that looks indistinguishable (except for the fact that it is hanging on a wall) from a small, random piece of the earth's surface. In creating works of art, artists are saying that for them those artworks are significant, meaningful, or beautiful. Boyle family's work helped to open my eyes to the wonderful richness, variety, and uniqueness of every square foot of urban space; to how the most seemingly insignificant bit of crumbling asphalt bears the marks of the person who laid it, the vehicles that have passed over it, the people who have littered it, and the storms that have weathered it.

That is not the most profound of reactions to a work of art, but then this is not the greatest art. I am grateful for it though. The seemingly random edges of a Boyle family artwork serve to emphasise how each patch of the earth's surface is connected to the next, and so on, in an infinite series. For me at least, that fascination with the ordinary makes every place, however neglected, rundown, or unloved, a beautiful expression of some aspect of (to recall Jane Jacobs' phrase again) "life at its most complex and intense."

OBSERVE TO UNDERSTAND

Before action comes observation. No one was a more disciplined and attentive observer than the French writer Georges Perec (1938-82), perhaps best known for his three-hundred-page novel *La Disparition*, which contains not a single letter *e*. Perec was the son of Polish Jews who had migrated to France in the 1920s. His father had been killed early in World War II and his mother had died in Auschwitz. Perec had more reason than most writers to use his art in a desperate search for meaning and identity. He obsessively recorded everyday life in Paris, not always for publication, because he thought it important to notice and question "the habitual."

"But that's just it, we're habituated to it," he wrote in a 1973 essay:

> We don't question it, it doesn't question us, it doesn't seem to pose a problem, we live it without thinking, as if it carried within it neither questions nor answers, as if it weren't the bearer of any information.

This is no longer even even conditioning, it's anaesthesia. We sleep through our lives in a dreamless sleep. But where is our life? Where is our body? Where is our space? (Perec 1973, 210)

In another essay, Perec explained that he valued, in close observation of the everyday world,

the sense of the world's concreteness, irreducible, immediate, tangible, of something clear and closer to us: of the world, no longer as a journey having constantly to be remade, not as a race without end, a challenge having constantly to be met, not as the one pretext of a despairing acquisitiveness, not as the illusion of a conquest, but as the rediscovery of a meaning, the perceiving that the earth is a form of writing, a *geography* of which we had forgotten that we ourselves are the authors. (Perec 1974, 78)

In other words, we observe in order to understand. Only when we understand can we hope to shape the world around us for the better.

The Scottish pioneer planner, sociologist, and biologist Patrick Geddes wrote in 1905: "A city is more than a place in space, it is a drama in time." That insight was forgotten for a few decades as professions—architects, town planners, highway engineers and several others—emerged to compete for the dominant role in remaking cities, and their members failed to see the narrowness of their particular perspectives.

What was so refreshing about Jane Jacobs' writings sixty years later was that she saw the world not through a narrow professional prism, but through the eyes of a journalist and activist. In today's professionalized world, we need all the inspiration we can get—from the new generation of enlightened professionals, from the places we love, from the artists who delight us, and from the passion of the urban design movement—to help us learn the fine arts of seeing.

REFERENCES

Bott, Oliver. 2001. "Medieval Boom Town." In *2000 Years of Building: Chester's architectural legacy*, edited by Stephen Langtree and Alan Comyns. Chester: Chester Civic Trust.

Cowan, Robert. 2005. *The Dictionary of Urbanism*. Tisbury: Streetwise Press.

Jacobs, Jane. 1961. *The Death and Life of Great American Cities*. New York: Random House.

Morriss, Richard. 1993. *The Buildings of Chester*. Stroud: Alan Sutton.

Perec, George. 1973. "Approaches to What?" In *Species of Spaces and Other Pieces*. London: Penguin, 1999.

——. 1974. "Species of Spaces." In *Species of Spaces and Other Pieces*. London: Penguin, 1999.

Scott Brown, Denise. 2002. Panel discussion. In *Urban Design: Practices, Pedagogies, Premises*, edited by Andrea Kahn. Proceedings of the National Conference organized at Columbia University, New York, 5-6 April.

SECTION 3

Cities, Villages, Streets

CITIES AND THE
WEALTH OF PLACES

Daniel Kemmis

I ONLY MET JANE JACOBS once, but it was enough to give me a story to tell my children. In 1993, the Dallas Institute of Humanities and Culture invited me to participate in one of their annual "What Makes a City?" conferences. Just finishing my first term as Mayor of Missoula, Montana, I was excited at the prospect of spending three days in conversation with some of Dallas' civic, business, and elected leaders, and with a handful of the country's leading observers of cities. Above all, I looked forward to meeting two writers whose work had long influenced my own thoughts about cities: Christopher Alexander and Jane Jacobs.

I learned that a unique feature of this speaking engagement was to be a day-long walking tour by all the speakers to visit some of downtown Dallas' key locations. That morning our hostess, Gail Thomas (then the Director of the Dallas Institute), gathered our little group in the Institute's parlor and told us that, before we set off for our tour, she had a story to tell us. Gail and her husband, Bob, had hosted Jane Jacobs at their home the night before, where, over a glass of wine, Gail had asked her guest how it was that she could see so many more interesting and significant features in a city than most people would ever see. As Gail recounted it, Jane said, "Well, I have a secret. Whenever I visit a new city, I take a companion with me."

"A companion," Gail said. "Anybody in particular?"

"Yes," Jane responded, "I ask Benjamin Franklin to walk with me. You see, everything is new to him, but he's so curious and so intelligent, and so he always asks questions that I have to think pretty hard about before I try to answer him. That helps me see deeper into the city than I would otherwise have done."

Watching Jane Jacobs stand there while Gail told the story, I was struck by a certain similarity that she bore to Franklin. Squat and a tad frumpy, with her granny glasses perched on her nose, her eyes twinkling mischievously, she made me wonder if she was telling the whole truth. Did she take Franklin on those walks? Or was she in fact Benjamin Franklin, impatient to find out what was going to happen next, and so returning in the inimitable personhood of Jane Jacobs?

With that experience in mind, I decided to borrow Jacobs' technique as I set about trying to describe what I see emerging in the coming decades. Knowing all too well my own acutely limited ability to foresee anything, I decided to recruit as my imaginary helper that unparalleled observer of cities, Jane Jacobs herself. I decided to walk with her around my small city, and to invite her to ask me questions, or offer observations as we walked, and so to help me see what I might otherwise have missed.

I live in a townhouse condominium situated at the eastern edge of downtown Missoula, on the banks of the Clark Fork River. Since I always turn to the river to see how the city is doing, we started our walk there—with a little small talk.

JJ: How long have you lived in Missoula?

DK: Thirty-six years now, and counting.

JJ: What are the biggest changes you've seen in that time?

DK: Well, just being here on this trail beside the river brings home how entirely different the city's relationship to the river is now than it was back then. This little park was the only riverside park, and there were no riverfront trails. Now there are miles of trails on both sides of the river, and at least a dozen parks.

JJ: How did all that happen? Did the city come into a lot of extra money?

DK: Why do I suspect that you don't really think that was it? No, the whole thing started with a couple of hard blows to the local economy, and particularly to the downtown. First was the development of a regional shopping mall on the edge of town. Downtown retail collapsed overnight, and no one was sure the downtown would survive at all. Then the Milwaukee Railroad declared bankruptcy—the first in a series of industrial setbacks, followed by the closure of several local sawmills.

JJ: All right, I want to hear how that contributed to the development of these riverfront trails and parks. But as you tell that story, I'd like you to think about what it might suggest about this current economic collapse, and how Missoula or any other city is likely to emerge from this crisis.[1]

DK: All right, then, we'll try to look ahead while we are looking back at how another set of economic challenges helped produce these trails and parks. Here's my quick version of what happened. When the new mall caused the downtown to implode, several of Missoula's civic and political leaders moved fast to create tax increment legislation to enable Montana cities to respond more effectively to this kind of challenge. I was serving in the legislature at that time, and this whole idea was new to me, but I helped sponsor the legislation, and then watched what the folks in Missoula made of it. As you know, tax increment financing doesn't increase anyone's taxes, and therefore doesn't raise any more money than would have been raised otherwise. But it plows some of the revenue back into the "blighted area," in this case the downtown, in the hope of increasing the entire community's tax base over time.

JJ: Let me guess: these trails and parks were created with tax increment financing?

DK: Yes, in part they were. There was quite a debate within the redevelopment agency board at that time about whether that was a good idea or not. The argument against it was that the goal was to increase the tax base, and therefore these scarce resources should be invested in tax-generating properties like stores and office buildings. Trails and parks don't pay taxes, so how can you justify this kind of investment?

JJ: But it's clear at a glance that the downtown did in fact revive and is now thriving, and I assume that's in part because the reclaimed

---

1. This imaginary stroll with Jane Jacobs occurred in 2009, over a year into the deepest economic crisis in America in 70-plus years. At the time, no one yet knew where the bottom of the decline might be, let alone what the recovery would look like.

riverfront made it a more attractive place to shop, to do business, and even to live. So do you see a lesson here for how to think about another round of economic challenges?

DK: I'd start by recognizing that what the city's leaders came to, in the course of their debate, was a simple recognition of the value of the river. It's that basic idea of value, and the role that value plays in an economy, that seems like it might shine some light on the future.

JJ: How is it that the river is valuable?

DK: I'm not sure I know, or that I can say for sure. But I want to test the idea that this river in the heart of town is valuable in the way that gold is valuable, and that it might play a role similar to the one that gold has sometimes played in providing a foundation for the economy. I've never entirely understood what makes gold so valuable that people would be willing to stake their fortunes on it, but clearly something about it almost irresistibly draws people to it. And something draws people to a river, too. Look at all the people out here on this trail, walking, running, riding bicycles, and pushing baby strollers. They love being here by the river, and it turned out that giving people a chance to come to the river and spend time together here was a very smart way to bring economic activity back to the downtown.

JJ: Would you say the downtown has prospered, then?

DK: Yes, it has prospered, both in the narrow sense of generating lots of that tax revenue the old debate centered on, and in the broader sense of making Missoula a more attractive place to live and work.

JJ: You sound like you don't want to stop there. Do you suspect that there may be more to prosperity than this?

DK: Well, you asked if the downtown had prospered, and it's clear to me that it has indeed. Earlier you said that it seemed to be thriving, which captures more of what I see. There's something about the activity on this trail that almost compels you to think about prospering in a more complex, more full-bodied way than the purely economic meaning we so often attach to the word. All this fresh-air exercise has to have made Missoula marginally healthier. You've seen strangers smile and greet us, and when you multiply that hundreds of times a day, you have to conclude that the city is also stronger socially because of these trails and parks. So the prospering that was engendered by these investments isn't only a narrow economic prospering, but a much broader, much more complex kind of prospering.

JJ: Can you tie that back to what you were trying to understand about the river being valuable, like gold? And then can you carry it forward to how economies might emerge from this current crisis more sound than they were before?

DK: Well, if the soundness of economies is reflected in the prosperity they produce, then I might argue that the only really trustworthy prosperity is this kind of multidimensional, full-bodied thriving.

JJ: Are you suggesting, then, that places like Missoula might emerge from this crisis more prosperous in that broader sense?

DK: Maybe I am, and perhaps it goes back to our earlier discussion about value, and about what is most reliably valuable. Maybe there's an analogy to an individual who emerges from a life-threatening crisis clearer about what really matters in his or her life. It reminds me of the old saw about economists knowing the price of everything and the value of nothing. That's grossly unfair to economists, many of whom think pretty deeply about values, but it might help remind us that a sound economy has to rest on a sound foundation, which can only be something of intrinsic value. Isn't that why the gold standard was so fiercely defended for so long—because of the conviction that a sound economy had to have something intrinsically valuable at its base? Gold finally came to be seen as too narrow a base for an increasingly complex global economy.

JJ: What replaced it?

DK: As far as I can tell, there was no one thing, which was probably healthy. To a certain extent, the dollar itself eventually seemed to become the new global gold standard. During the period of American hegemony, that made sense, since no matter where you lived in the world, you could absolutely count on America taking care of its own interests, and in the process keeping the dollar strong. Eventually, oil also moved into a foundational role in the global economy. Petroleum-driven machines had assumed such a commanding role in human society that the one thing they all depended on—oil—became perhaps not intrinsically, but reliably valuable. It was no accident that it came to be called "black gold." As the reliable value of both American currency and oil became well established, we started hearing about "petrodollars." But then the global economic crisis, which many people blamed on bad business practices in America, combined with this country's deepening indebtedness, especially to China, cast a shadow of doubt on the reliability of the dollar. Meanwhile, predictions about "peak oil" appeared just as the global concern over climate change began driving home the realization that the world couldn't continue to depend that much on petroleum, even if it were available.

JJ: Let's return to our main theme now: the hypothesis that good cities are themselves an enduring source of value. In those terms, while our century-long love affair with automobiles may have provided a temporary, petroleum-based alternative to gold as a value foundation for the world economy, it did so at the expense of that older and, I would argue, more durable base. So let's examine whether cities, which have suffered for so long under the reign of the automobile, might emerge from this crisis as a recognized source of value in their own right.

DK: I certainly learned both from you and from my own experience to think of good cities as being intrinsically valuable. Like gold, they've stood the test of time as few things have, across the millennia of human history. You taught me to see that good cities generate prosperity, and my experience here taught me that they also generate the kind of multi-faceted thriving, or prospering, that we were talking about earlier.

JJ: All right, you hardly have to persuade me of that. But I want you to take a closer, harder look at what we both see as this inherently valuable phenomenon of the good city. Tell me about this farmers' market, down by the bridge. How did it come about?

DK: This is actually Missoula's second farmers' market. The original one is still thriving, and my Saturday morning visits there with my wife are a ritual part of our week all summer. This newer market emerged in part because the old market had become so popular that it was getting congested, but also in part because of a particular effort to help ranchers further up the Clark Fork Valley. The Clark Fork Coalition, a very resourceful environmental group based here in Missoula, has spent decades advocating the cleanup of toxic mill tailings near the headwaters, and then working on the removal of a dam just a few miles upstream from here. More recently, the Coalition became concerned about the threatened subdivision of ranches in the upper Clark Fork Valley, and about the effects that development could have on water quality. They started working with the ranchers up there, to see if there was anything that could be done to slow down the subdividing. Most of the ranchers didn't want to sell their land, but economic pressures made it almost inevitable. This market was initially conceived as a way to help them sell more of their beef or lambs, at a better price. As you can see, the market is very popular, and with more and more people wanting to eat locally produced food, its popularity is only growing.

JJ: So, let's go back to the analogy with gold. If this farmers' market is in some sense like a golden ingot, tell me how it operates within a regional, continental, or global economy.

DK: Among other things, it generates exactly the kind of import replacement that you wrote about in *Cities and the Wealth of Nations*, with all the economy-building implications that you described there. But because the market makes life better in Missoula, it also attracts to our community, and helps to retain people who value this sort of thing.

JJ: All right, good, we're back to that core idea of something (whether it's gold or a riverside market) being intrinsically valuable, and somehow infusing that value into the larger economy. Can you see how that could contribute to a stronger global economy, as it emerges from this crisis?

DK: I don't see it with any clarity, but it seems important that my neighbors do value the market, and that their valuing is manifested and warranted in several ways. First, of course, they part with a fair amount of money here—sometimes more than they would have spent for the same head of lettuce or leg of lamb at the supermarket. But they value the freshness, the purity, and the local provenance of the food enough to pay a little more for it.

JJ: How else does their valuation manifest itself?

DK: By the (valuable) time they spend here, and by building this time into their weekly routine. Behind all of that lies the fact that most of the people trading at this market are also, every day, trading a certain amount of the higher income they could earn elsewhere for the value of living in this place. They warrant the value of mountains, rivers, and wildlife in that way, but also the value of community.

JJ: So how does that valuing translate itself into or manifest itself in any larger economic system?

DK: In part it manifests itself through what I think of as "nicheman-ship": the resourceful entrepreneurship of people who, because they want to be here, are forever discovering new ways of making themselves valuable to their neighbors or to people further afield. The farmers and ranchers do this too, by producing more of what their city neighbors want to eat. Again, this is import replacement at work, both in the basic sense of substituting locally produced goods or services for those that had previously been imported and, often, in developing new enterprises that then reach out beyond the city and beyond the region.

JJ: For example?

DK: Well, for example, we've now made our way to this converted school building that became the home of Missoula Children's Theater. The theater was started by an artistic entrepreneur who found a way to make a living in Missoula by producing plays that used dozens of chil-dren as actors, and therefore brought in hundreds of parents, aunts, and uncles as paying spectators. But he and his crew got so good at what they did that neighboring towns started asking them to give their kids a chance to act. Now you see this whole parking lot filled with those little red pickups? Next week, those pickups will spread out all across Montana and the neighboring states, each one taking a couple of coaches and a few props out to dozens of communities, enhancing their quality of life while strengthening Missoula's economy. And we could multiply that story with others about conservation organizations, bicyclists, all kinds of activities that started out finding a niche where they could improve life for people here, and then turned it into an enterprise of value to other communities.

JJ: I'm delighted to see a place like Missoula benefiting from some of the dynamics I described a quarter century ago. But now the world economy seems to be worse off than ever. Do you see anything hopeful at that scale?

DK: What I've learned from my regional work this last dozen years is how powerful an economic driver livability has become. There was no way to watch the economic transformation of the Rocky Mountain West across those years without reaching that conclusion. A region whose economy had for decades been based on resource extraction and agriculture found, over a score of years, that the new driver of its economy was the attractiveness of its communities.

JJ: Is this current economic crisis going to change that?

DK: Well, this is what I see. Just focusing now on how this crisis has affected Missoula... some people have lost their jobs or businesses; some have moved away in the normal operation of labor markets. Those most strongly connected to the place are doing their best to hang on, and many of them will become more entrepreneurial, looking even harder for valuable niches. In that way, the fabric of the community will become tighter, richer. So here is my hypothesis: the more people come to value various features of a good community, the less they are inclined to seek satisfaction from costlier or more remote sources. We've already seen that many Missoulians, as well as people in hundreds of other communities, have been willing to trade income for amenities. I would argue that they've actually become more prosperous (even if not more affluent) as a result. What if this economic crisis led millions of people, in communities around the world, to take more satisfaction from what their communities offer them (and from what they offer their communities) than from buying more things they may not exactly need?

JJ: It sounds like you're foreseeing an economy based more on being than on buying.

DK: And not only being, but well-being... which is another way of naming the thriving or prospering that we spoke about earlier. What could have a greater or more intrinsic value than that? If we emerged from this or any economic crisis with a deeper appreciation for the sustaining value of being well together, who knows what might come of it?

JJ: Unless I'm mistaken, you've led us back to your home.

DK: I just followed you. Would you care for a cup of tea?

QUEEN STREET

Elizabeth Macdonald & Allan Jacobs*

WITH NO SMALL measure of joy and good feelings, we take a great street where we find it, and Queen Street, in Toronto, is one. Looking, looking again, and, quite often, measuring all the things and people on a street: this is how we learn about it. Jane Jacobs did that, in her own inimitable ways.

Queen Street is not grand or highly designed, like so many of the wonderful Paris boulevards, nor is it lined with fine buildings or rows of old arching trees, nor did its creators—like those of Princes Street in Edinburgh, or Regent Street in London, or Nevsky Prospekt in St. Petersburg—have a great street in mind when they created it. Queen Street is not a public way about which one might say after a day's outing, "Wow, I was on a great street today." But Queen Street is a great street in its own fashion, a work-a-day street for everyone that also gives positive, memorable structure to the city of Toronto—more than other major streets and certainly more so than the Gardiner Expressway (the elevated freeway that separates most of the city from the Lake Ontario waterfront), which sanity will some day remove.

---

*Macdonald and Jacobs walked and rode on the 501-Queen streetcar many times during between 1999 and 2000. Later, Jacobs visited the street again on the occasion of a symposium to discuss Jane Jacobs' last book, *Dark Age Ahead*. This article was written jointly by Macdonald and Jacobs, each writing, criticizing, and rewriting the other's work.

Queen Street is much too long to be compared to Hudson Street in Greenwich Village where Jane Jacobs once lived and which, at least in part, inspired *The Death and Life of Great American Cities*, but many of its sections contain qualities not unlike those of Hudson Street. Now, as we write this, it seems odd that in our many discussions with Jane about streets and cities, we never spoke about Queen Street. Perhaps this is because she was so taken with making a better Toronto, undoing the damage done by the Gardiner Expressway, and preventing new urban indignities, that she did not concentrate as much on what was already fine and probably safe from redevelopment.

Starting east, at Neville Park in the Beaches neighborhood, Queen Street runs in a straight line west, through downtown, to Roncesvalles— a distance of some eight and one-half miles. In 1800 it was the northern boundary of the city, and later became a lineal spine of the so-called streetcar suburbs that developed into the early 1900s. Draw a simple, explanatory map of Toronto and you will surely draw Queen Street, probably just after Yonge Street, the city's main north-south artery, and certainly before King Street, Bloor Street, St. Clair Street, Eglinton, and the north-south running "concession grid" streets—Dufferin, Spadina, University, or Coxwell. Likely, just before or after drawing Queen Street, you draw the shoreline of Lake Ontario, roughly parallel and not far away to the south.

Beyond giving basic structure to Toronto, Queen Street is most memorable for its streetcar line, the venerable 501-Queen that runs the entire street day and night, and for the small-scale buildings and stores standing on either side.

To begin our imaginary walk, visualize a not very wide street right-of-way, 66 feet across from building to building, with streetcars down the center, and lined with residentially scaled buildings. The road travels across one neighborhood after another, passing through the heart of downtown, then again through small-scale neighborhoods. There was a time when many U.S. cities had streets like this, but they changed irrevocably when they surrendered their streetcars in favor of buses and freeways. (It is ironic that many of those older cars, from Baltimore, Cincinnati, Philadelphia, Boston, and even Milan and Rome, now run on Market Street in San Francisco and along the city's shoreline, to the delight of locals and tourists alike.) Queen Street seems to our eyes a classic example of an unself-conscious nineteenth-century streetcar route that is still intact and still works.

The Beaches neighborhood, though perhaps more upscale than many of the other neighborhoods traversed by Queen Street, is a good place to analyze more closely the street's typical uses and physical details. Movement, particularly auto movement, is slow in the Beaches just as everywhere else along Queen Street. Since the two streetcar tracks take up some 20 feet of the 44 to 46 feet curb-to-curb width, and since as often as not there is curbside auto parking, autos must follow the street-cars, with no way of passing. Streetcar stops are frequent, so vehicular movement is slow-paced. Sidewalks vary slightly in width, but generally are about 10 feet. There are street trees here, as in other neighborhoods, but they are not a major presence (though we would miss some old and large trees if they were gone). The wooden telephone and electric poles, often hung with heavy transformer boxes and strung with heavy wires, are as much a presence as the trees.

So, the public realm of Queen Street, the long, eight-plus mile space between the properties that bound it, is, except for its relatively narrow width and the streetcar line, not particularly noteworthy. Rather, it is the small, human scale of the buildings along the street and the highly varied commercial activities associated with them that make the street special, in the Beaches as elsewhere.

Between Neville Street and Woodbine Avenue, the start and end of the Beaches—a distance that contains about one mile of block front-age (not including street widths)—there are some 237 buildings (120 on one side and 117 on the other). That would mean 45 feet wide for the average building, if it weren't for street frontages taken by a school, a library, several parks, a fire station, and several churches. Actually, the typical building is about 32 feet wide. Most are modest two- and three-story buildings. Many were once single- or two-family houses to which stores were added up to the street. There are also newer two-story utilitarian brick and wood frame structures with apartments above stores, and a few apartment buildings with small setbacks from the street right-of-way. In recent years, several three- and four-floor buildings have been added. There are some 282 stores in this stretch, typically with 16-foot frontages in the older buildings, and a bit larger in the newer ones; so along most blocks there are entrances every 16 feet or less. The basic nature of the street has been set: small for the Beaches and for most of the rest of the street as well. The churches, the school and library, the fire station, and even the delightful Kew Gardens park may stand out by being larger than their surroundings, but even these premises are of a domestic scale.

Stores and services do not exist without people to frequent them. Queen Street is the local shopping area for the many neighborhoods it passes through. Moreover, its many shops—made readily accessible by the streetcar—attract visitors from elsewhere in the city. In the Beaches, on a cold, sunny Saturday afternoon in November, we counted between eight and twelve people passing per minute per meter of width, depending on the configuration and accessibility of the sidewalk area. (Many merchants have displays along their storefronts, restricting somewhat the walkable space, but no one seems to mind.) These amounts compare favorably with pedestrian volumes found on active main streets in many major cities in North America and Europe. There were fewer people on the south side of the street, which casual observations suggest is usually the case. Sunshine probably has something to do with this pattern. Because of the modest building heights, sun reaches the north walks of the public realm even on wintry days, making them more comfortable.[1] Perhaps the south side of the street is more comfortable in Toronto's hot summer, but then the trees on the north may help to shade as well.

Together with more pedestrians, there are many more stores on the north side of Queen Street in the Beaches than on the south—176 to 106 when we counted—a pattern that persists, with a few exceptions, for the entire length of the street. The range of goods and services is impressive: restaurants, coffee shops and bars, food stores, home furnishings, drug stores, flower stores, banks, dentists and doctors, chiroprac-

1. This observation reconfirms a key finding of *Great Streets*: the necessity of physical comfort when it's cold. See Allan B. Jacobs, *Great Streets*. Boston: MIT Press 1995.

tors, travel agencies, real estate offices, a movie theater, hair salons, and on and on. It's all there: places to eat and drink, clothing, food, home furnishing stores, laundries, and hair salons head the list. Invariably, the store windows shine: someone cleans them store by store. Elsewhere, in the other neighborhoods through which Queen Street passes, the stores and services are of much the same type, though they might cater to a lower-income group or to a particular ethnicity. There are exceptions, of course, in specialty areas and near downtown, but by and large the uses are similar.

Along Queen Street, there are many things that constantly engage the eyes. Each of the small structures, even when connected to the next, creates at least one and often three or four vertical lines to catch the eye, if only for a split second. Each store is different than the next and there are few blank walls; moreover, the storefronts' transparency gives knowledge of what lies beyond the façade that defines the street. There are many doorways, two to three for a typical building, and people coming in and out of them, to say nothing of the people of all ages walking along the sidewalks. And let's not forget the big, red 501-Queen streetcars, letting off and picking up passengers every two or so blocks, and the cars inching along behind. Even on a winter's evening, walking along in the slush, a light snow falling, eyes generally downward, one is aware of being in an active and welcoming street.

After the Beaches neighborhood, at Woodbine Avenue, there is a brief pause in the north side commercial activity. West of Woodbine, on the south side, long and relatively narrow new residential streets replace what was once a race track. Three-story apartment blocks face Queen Street, with ground floor stores not much wider than those in the Beaches, only newer. What was once the eastern edge of the race track has become a large off-track betting establishment and movie complex. The north side of the street is lined with small houses, many set back from the sidewalk. Moving west, a housing development with six-story buildings sitting on lawns suggests publicly sponsored housing for moderate income people, the kind that was built in the 1960s or1970s. Beyond, the stores continue.

Streetcar barns at Connaught Avenue are another break in the generally two-story shop and apartment buildings that line the street. Across from the streetcar barns to the north, a well maintained house and the grounds of an old estate remind us of what once was. Moving on, there are short runs of relatively new street-facing town houses and also several relatively new, larger buildings for retirement or senior care living. In the Leslieville neighborhood there is another development of recent townhouses. Occasional community centers and public open spaces break the continuous shopping and housing pattern. Noticeably, corner sitting areas oriented to Queen Street have been built in proximity to parks.

The breaks are but moments in the overall continuous commercial streetscape moving westward toward the Don River. In Broadview, the stores, the people on the street and those leaving or entering the streetcar, the maintenance of the buildings, the existence or absence of grilles over windows, and even the quality of window curtains and blinds suggest the different economic status of the abutting areas. In some blocks there are fewer restaurants and clothing stores, and more vacancies, second-hand stores, business services, and automotive uses than in the previous stretch. People on the street and getting on and off the streetcars are perhaps not as well dressed, and they may be older. But then, seemingly out of the blue there is a particularly inviting coffee shop or restaurant, or a new hi-tech furniture store, or an elegant-looking shortbread establishment that makes you wonder why it's there. Change is happening: upward, downward? Both types of change are accommodated by the small-scale built fabric, which is perhaps the central reason that Queen Street is so interesting: it seems to be a place where for a long time many different people, in different circumstances, have been able to get an economic foothold, perhaps for just a short while before moving on, or perhaps for longer.

Crossing over the Don River, before reaching Jarvis Street and the downtown area, there is a long stretch that has a somewhat gritty and slightly more industrial feel. Some larger buildings appear; more businesses, services, and some automotive uses. More people appear to have minimal incomes, but there is also some new housing, so this area, too, is not static.

Shortly after Parliament Avenue, to the north, there is a large low-income housing development with tall buildings scattered over a landscaped site, the Ross Park Redevelopment area. It stands in stark contrast to the fine-grained cityscape we've been passing through and that can be found on the south side of the street—clearly a public intervention not unlike so many we know in the U.S. To our eyes it is a sad sight. Nonetheless, perhaps the fact of being located on Queen Street, with its many passing people on streetcars, in cars, and on foot, offers residents a prospect of entrepreneurial activity that would not be found elsewhere. On one of our visits, on a sunny day, a few local women were set up on the Queen Street sidewalk offering homemade goods for sale.

The intersection of Queen Street with Yonge Street, we suspect, is Toronto's 100 percent corner, the much desired location that is likely to attract the most people and to command the highest rents from adjacent owners. The Bay department store, a major entrance to the Eaton Centre Mall, and a subway stop below, must give it boasting privileges. Few other intersections are more congested with streetcars, buses, and auto traffic, or as busy with people.

A block or so further along, the old Richardsonesque City Hall and the new modernist one, set back behind a large plaza and fountain (that becomes a skating rink in winter), mark the city center. Even here, though, the largeness soon gives way to a much smaller scale as we approach Spadina Street, reasonably considered the end of downtown.

At Spadina Street we have covered a bit more than half the distance to Roncesvalles. By streetcar in mid-morning, the whole trip will take about forty-five minutes. There are more neighborhoods ahead with different characters and concentrations of uses—textile, button-, zipper-, and clothes-making establishments west of Spadina; antique stores further on, toward Roncesvalles—but by and large the scale of the street remains the same, all the way to the end.

Having seen and experienced the whole street and looked at maps, a notable physical characteristic pops out: most intersecting roads do not line up across the street. In the Beaches, intersecting streets average every 320 feet on the south side and every 260 feet on the north. Only the major north-south streets line up and go through. The minor intersecting streets create T-intersections with Queen Street, suggesting that areas to the north and south were developed at different times, by different developers. This is an important quality. The intersecting streets, usually narrow, often with one-way traffic, focus on Queen Street; people normally have to turn onto it. Along with the street's other qualities, this feature helps it be a connecting spine rather than a divider.

The major crossing streets divide Queen Street and its bordering geography into sub-areas. Likely, some of these areas have seen better or worse days, though it is doubtful that many, if any, were centers of extreme well-to-do-ness. Indeed, traveling the street, the current economic state of its uses and users seems less important than its overall structure and fabric: the street with its streetcars, slow-moving automobiles, and pedestrians; the scale of development, overwhelmingly small and tight, with many owners and many tenants who have stakes in it; and the simple adaptability to change.

Imagine the many people who have ridden the streetcars along Queen Street, who have shopped, worked and lived along it, whose lives have been, in part, structured by its constancy and its activity. Queen Street is a modest, simple, and yet great street. To us, it fits in just fine with what Jane was so concerned with: not grandness, but the everyday goodness of people and urban life.

THE INTERCONNECTEDNESS
OF THINGS

Ken Greenberg

T HE "TWIG ON THE RIVER" theory holds that a twig that falls in the current at the headwaters can alter the river by the time it reaches the river mouth. In those terms, Jane Jacobs was not a twig but a tree trunk. What she offered was a web of interconnected ideas that continues to provide confidence, credibility, inspiration, and guidance for my generation and subsequent ones.

Jane Jacobs passed away in Toronto on April 25, 2006, just one week shy of her ninetieth birthday. For the previous four decades she had lived in Toronto, where she had moved with her family in 1968. While New Yorkers remember her best as a historic figure from the epic struggles of the 1960s, for us Torontonians she became a mentor and a remarkably accessible presence during a crucial period in the evolution of our city. Toronto was hanging on a cliff when she arrived, braced for the full program of anti-city urban renewal measures. Major demolitions were planned for such local treasures as Old City Hall, Union Station, and St. Lawrence Market, along with downtown neighborhoods such as the area south of the high-rise St. Jamestown renewal project. Toronto's streetcars were slated for removal and more urban expressways were on deck—not just the infamous Spadina Expressway, but also those intended for Crosstown and Scarborough to form a complete network.

On November 1, 1969, Jacobs told Toronto's *Globe and Mail*:

As a relatively recent transplant from New York, I am frequently asked
whether I find Toronto sufficiently exciting. I find it almost too exciting. The suspense is scary. Here is the most hopeful and healthy city
in North America, still unmangled, still with options. Few of us profit
from the mistakes of others, and perhaps Toronto will prove to share
this disability. If so, I am grateful at least to have enjoyed this great
city before its destruction.

With Jane's presence and inspiration, Toronto became for me the fertile ground where the streams began to merge. I developed a heightened
awareness of the larger political and social city-shaping forces and of how
city neighborhoods actually work. With its downtown and near neighborhoods still relatively undamaged, it felt like Toronto had the chance to
demonstrate that the real city could evolve and respond to new pressures
and needs without recourse to radical surgery. I took up the challenge of
proving this in my final year at the University of Toronto, and did my
thesis project, titled "Infilling the Toronto Block System", on an existing
downtown neighborhood near the university, proposing an alternative to
the aggressive "blockbusting" and urban renewal model that was being
actively pursued by the local development industry. I was clearly inspired
by Jane and was able to meet with her personally to discuss viable solutions. Later, when I began my work at the City and founded a new Urban
Design Group, she continued to make herself available for periodic conversations and to give advice and reaction to the initiatives we proposed.

She gave us the confidence to unapologetically allow cities to be
cities. Her unique and powerful presence deeply influenced her adopted
city, and continues to do so in ways that confound easy definition. She
never held office in Toronto, nor occupied any official position. The press
sometimes called her a city planner, but that was not her aim. She was
very sparing in her public appearances: "I am busy on my next book,"
was her standard response. She refused to be deified or reified: she never
wanted to be a guru and strenuously resisted the temptation to freeze her
thinking into cult or dogma. She turned down many honorary degrees
and awards, and resolutely rejected being "franchised."

For four decades Jane Jacobs has been for many Torontonians a remarkable person in our midst and also an accessible friend and neighbor, often spotted on her porch on Albany Avenue or in her kitchen making jam and cookies to offer as gifts on holidays. She played a unique role as a catalyst, a keen observer, and a gadfly—irreverent, unafraid, and with an uncanny ability to skewer fuzzy thinking and get to the heart of things.

Though lacking a formal education in city planning or journalism, Jacobs came equipped with remarkable powers of observation and a deep curiosity about how things work. These qualities, combined with a passion for advocacy and a profound indignation, impelled her to write in 1961 *The Death and Life of Great American Cities*, a brilliant response to Robert Moses' plans to eviscerate Lower Manhattan and, more generally, an objection to the widespread devastation wrought by bad postwar urban renewal. Along with other independent thinkers like William H. Whyte and Herbert Gans, she was urgently calling attention to a prevailing wisdom that was dangerously off-track.

Jacobs' motivation was always to unmask unhelpful dogma, to debunk myths, and to show that there are other modes of thought. Her arguments in *Death and Life* were built from the ground up through in-depth observations of everyday places—streets, blocks, parks, and buildings. Her appreciation for complex "self-organizing" survival mechanisms was coupled with frustration with the kind of institutional wrongheadedness—bureaucratic, political, and pseudo-scientific—that impedes the creative process of human adaptation.

Jane's preferred stance in public was as a counterpuncher. She preferred to debate, to react rather than to lecture. Socratic dialogue was her *modus operandi*—a dialectical process of probing and testing. She was famous for debunking nonsense and relentlessly asking hard questions. She was hardly the sweet little old lady; she could be intimidating and tough. She had an insatiable curiosity and generosity of spirit, with an unrelentingly challenging gaze when things didn't make sense and a twinkle in her eye when they did. She always forced us to think harder and look from other angles, and yet showed a willingness to reconsider, never deeming her thinking infallible.

Remarkably, Jacobs' ideas almost immediately resonated in Toronto. Armed with her closely observed truths and empirical evidence, city advocates were able to challenge a still potent set of antiurban values and a pervasive imagery whose twin origins and credentials can be traced back to the great twentieth-century antiurban visions by Frank Lloyd Wright (Broadacre City) and Le Corbusier (Radiant City). In contrast to these models, Jacobs demonstrated that there were sophisticated processes at work in existing cities. She applied the concepts of organized complexity, self-organization, and diversity to elucidate what was wrongly perceived as chaos.

Jane Jacobs was the scientist and we were the engineers finding new ways to test and apply her concepts. Gradually and almost imperceptibly, through a process of infiltration and testing, her ideas have come close to being conventional wisdom both in Toronto and in many other places.

As time progressed, Jane's work evolved into a unified theory, with urbanism as the continuum demonstrating the interconnectedness of things. With each iteration, her tapestry of concepts became stronger and denser, expanding the exhilarating potential of her ideas into an entire system of thought. She dislodged the underpinnings of wrong-headed models for cities—*simplicity* (mechanical toys) and *disorganized complexity* (chaos) in favor of an appreciation of *organized complexity*. This was a new way of seeing the city as a perpetually unfinished and intensely interactive web of relationships. People readily perceived the parallels with the ecosystem model, and the latter itself became better understood—the productivity of heterogeneous wetlands resembling that of dense, mixed neighborhoods.

Jane's line of argument brought intellectual credibility—*not* nostalgia, but hardheaded and practical answers—to our challenge to antiurban values. She took us from a preoccupation with analysis and mechanical models to synthesis,. This was a whole new way of embracing indeterminacy, accepting that cities are perpetually unfinished and open-ended. She put the false dichotomies of public/private spheres in a new perspective, confronting those who wanted to exaggerate the role of either. We still need both the strong and reliable guardian framework and the nimble entrepreneurial innovation she brought to the field. Advocating for both, she was politically unclassifiable on any conventional political spectrum, straddling the arguments of the New Left, "small *c*" conservatism, and Red Toryism.

But it was one thing to articulate these ideas and another to make real change in the modus operandi of a city; these ideas, after all, challenged enshrined practices (legal, administrative, and financial) and decades of indoctrination and habit. It was not enough to pay lip service and continue the same old practices; and this is where the responsibility shifted to us. Jane offered no panacea, no formula to go about making changes. Her gift was not a specific solution but a way of thinking that focused on the interplay of things and not some reassuring, cozy image. While some detractors have tried to pigeonhole her this way, there is no "Jane Jacobs world" and no recipe for one. In the end, she gave us all the material for a life's work. We have only begun to mine the full richness of her thinking—the power of organized complexity, its endless permutations and possibilities.

Almost immediately on arrival in Toronto, Jane played a leading role in the Stop Spadina movement that ultimately halted the continuation of the entire network of proposed inner-city expressways, and got involved in similar efforts to prevent further demolitions of viable downtown neighborhoods for high-rise urban renewal.

In a very real sense, Jane was the confidence-building muse behind Toronto's 1970's Reform Council and the theorist who inspired the city's groundbreaking Central Area Plan, countering the spread of downtown commercial areas into adjoining neighborhoods. Once again, she suggested what needed to happen but never exactly how. Another great testament to Jacobs' teachings in which I participated with her was the Kings initiative, a radical experiment carried out under Mayor Barbara Hall, allowing four hundred acres in former industrial districts flanking downtown to develop organically, eschewing traditional land-use controls in favor of a self-defining mix of uses.

On the private side, a number of highly influential and socially committed entrepreneurs, including Margie Zeidler and the whole Zeidler family, have invested in keeping with Jane's teachings and successfully demonstrated how the city's resilient building stock could be recycled for an extraordinary range of new and innovative uses.

By the 1970s and 1980s these initiatives began to accumulate, and started to visibly reflect a new set of priorities. New medium-density, mid-rise infill developments had emerged, and mixed use was occurring in areas where no one had lived for decades. Affordable housing started to appear on scattered sites. Industrial lofts and converted office buildings then led the way, as downtown itself became more of a neighborhood. And then, there was the condo boom—unfortunately, more about quantity than quality. But still, with a mix of successes and partial successes, Toronto was producing one of the most vibrant lived-in city centers on the continent.

"Toronto the Dull" had begun to be "Toronto the More Interesting" as neighborhood streets came to life. Gradually, the city relearned how to make urban buildings and spaces, framing its streets with pedestrian-friendly building edges and active uses, and occasionally producing excellent contemporary buildings in an idiom particular to Toronto. The city became denser without destroying its neighborhoods. Jane had admonished us to not be afraid of "density" (an abstraction), but to see how it could be introduced while strengthening the grain and structure of the city.

In 1997 Toronto hosted a remarkable event at the Music Hall on Danforth Avenue and the Royal Alex Theatre, "Ideas That Matter," to celebrate Jane's presence among us. A wide spectrum of distinguished thinkers attended, reflecting the breadth of Jane's extraordinary category-defying life's work in areas including urbanism, environment, and economics. The evenings were the highlight; this was the magical moment when Jane sat down on stage for a one-on-one conversation with a well-known journalist to discuss in her unique way the day's events.

Now things have evolved, and while some of the old battles have been won, cities including Toronto are struggling with a whole new series of challenges—lack of resources and inability to provide services, political powerlessness, environmental degradation, demographic shifts, development pressures within the city, and seemingly unstoppable sprawl without. Perhaps not surprisingly, some critics (even somewhat sympathetic ones) have seen these new realities as signaling a limit to the usefulness or applicability of the Jacobs' approach, as if her thinking were limited to the neighborhood scale and the time and place that spawned her seminal works.

Prolific to the end, Jane Jacobs was ever alert to these new challenges and opportunities. Her broad reading of history, economics, environment, and culture had made her finely attuned to the ascending and receding patterns of fragility and durability. She constantly reminded us matter-of-factly that things do go wrong, that there are historical dead ends, and that countries, whole civilizations, and even cities can and do atrophy and decline.

In fact Jane's focus in later years had stretched from the neighborhood to the nation, as she developed a complex relationship with national, provincial, and municipal leaders at the highest levels in Canada, even if they often found many of her partial prescriptions indigestible. What she forcefully advocated was no more and no less than a reframing of our national politics, reflecting the grudging recognition that we are undeniably an urban country whose future hinges on the success of our cities. Jacobs repeatedly called for new sources of funding for cities (including a portion of the gas tax) and for giving cities greater autonomy—initiatives that are being advanced even if turning ideas into reality is proving challenging in the face of inertia and competing political dynamics.

In a similar vein, Jacobs had begun to advance an intriguing prediction about how seemingly relentless sprawl may ultimately be resolved. Suburbia has always seemed to be the phenomenon most impervious to Jacobs' influence. Even as downtowns appeared to be newly popular with a growing cohort of the population, and notwithstanding sometimes heroic "new urbanist" efforts beyond the city core, the advancing wave of low-density suburbs has pushed on unabated.

The suburban paradigm has proven to be the hardest nut to crack, and in her last work, *Dark Age Ahead* (2004), Jane has offered a fascinating new theory rooted in a longer historical trajectory. Along with slum clearance and rent control, one of the most significant housing remedies to emerge from the Depression and World War II was the availability of long-term low interest rates. This development—associated with a number of other factors, including the Interstate Highway program, redlining (making some urban neighborhoods ineligible for loans), and the fact that by 1945 only as little as three percent of the population was needed for agriculture—created an irresistible pressure for sprawl.

Sprawl is still powerful and hard to resist, but what if it were less wasteful and the land more intensively used? In other words, what if there was another evolution in urban thinking and the current first-tier suburbs could become like early species in natural plant succession—an interim, phase-in succession leading to denser and more sustainable patterns in the future?

Suburban roads have the potential to be transformed into multipurpose urban streets, the arterials converted into boulevards shared with transit and cycle lanes. In fact, the groundwork is already laid for all this, and pioneering examples exist in many cities. The major impediment is an extraordinary tangle of intractable rules. Jacobs predicted that with an economic and demographic force majeure, these obstacles would be swept away to allow ingenuity and necessity to operate.

There would need to be real pressure to make this revolution both feasible and necessary. Such a transformation would need to be deeply rooted in the raw power of a demographic force or an economic imperative like the rising cost of energy or, as she presciently hypothesized in 2004, an economic crisis. Like the natural processes of urban "unslumming," diversification, and "import replacement" that she had previously examined, she was laying the groundwork so that when the time came, the ideas would be in place. This was a classic Jane Jacobs kind of argument. Could it be wrong? Might something else happen? Of course. But by knowing that it might happen—and now to a significant extent this crisis has happened—we are better prepared to effect changes with more grace and less harm.

Jane Jacobs' fervent support of diversity has undoubtedly had some influence on the collective embrace in Toronto of the incredible mix of people that has become our most distinguishing characteristic and perhaps greatest strength. Her emphasis on active, vital public space as the frame that binds us and the social infrastructure (health, education, public schools), and on the city as the hatchery of new jobs, has been influential as Toronto moved from defence to offence in the past decades—from saving and preserving to creating new kinds of urban places, from strategic infill sites in the city's core to the projects to regenerate large obsolescent sites on the waterfront and promote a more sustainable growth on the emerging fringes of the city region.

Toronto, by taking many of the paths identified by Jane Jacobs, has become an extremely valuable research lab on urbanism, demonstrating her conviction that cities are the places where problems are solved.

JANE JACOBS:

THE TORONTO EXPERIENCE

David Crombie

IN 1976, THE city of Toronto's "reform council," first elected in 1972, adopted its Central Area Plan to guide Toronto's future. Following a two-year moratorium on new building, the plan, controversial for its day, introduced a number of policies and zoning requirements to strongly encourage residential development downtown. It also argued that neighborhoods should be dense and mixed-use, and should not be demolished in the name of "urban renewal"; that heritage buildings should be protected from demolition; and that transit should trump the private automobile.

Thirty years later, a councillor of that era and later mayor of the city, John Sewell, pronounced his verdict on the impact of the plan. "That plan has been so successful," he said, "that its principles are now, generally speaking, taken for granted. Extraordinary amounts of new housing have been built downtown, much stronger neighborhoods have emerged, there has been fair to middling protection of heritage buildings, and no new roads into the downtown have been built."

Visiting Toronto for the Conference on Pedestrianism in the fall of 2007, Los Angeles urban planner and founder of the Latin Urban Forum, James Rojas, was moved to explain his newfound affection for the city. "I fell in love with what I call its urban messiness," he said. "The city contains the usual suspects on the menu of elements of contemporary good urban form: mixed use, bike paths, transit, street trees, etc. However, there's a sort of less-than-manicured quality to the whole thing and, coupled with a large diversity of people, the city ends up feeling gloriously messy in a functional and walkable way." In his walks, he noted in particular "the small blocks, negotiable streets, fruit stands, varied architecture, distinct neighborhoods, the mix of new and old buildings that are allowed to show their age." Stepping onto Toronto's streetcars was like "simultaneously stepping back in time and into the future," as they increased substantially "the social interaction of myriad different kinds of residents of all backgrounds sharing public space in a palpable way."

The influence of Jane Jacobs on this contemporary portrait of Toronto and the 1976 plan which cradled its dynamism is undeniable to all who know her early works. When she moved to her adopted city in 1968, Toronto's urban reform movement was already well underway. Its various strands of specific causes, interests, and concerns were being brought together through a growing understanding of the power and importance of neighborhoods in the quest for a better quality of urban life.

Her impact was immediate and transforming. She made it clear that the ideas that mattered were the ones which we understood intimately, drawn from our own observations and experiences. She thereby conferred legitimacy on the perspectives and solutions being forged from activities and events in a growing number of neighborhoods where residents sensed both risk and possibility. She understood our distrust of top-down blueprints and our need to determine patterns, principles, programs, and policies from the bottom-up. She exuded faith that human beings could discover the roots of their own problems and act upon them in a constructive way. She understood that livable cities evolve spontaneously, and her distaste for prescriptive planning played to our desire to imagine, innovate, and create.

In the early years of this new century, Jane Jacobs' Toronto is still undergoing significant change. Our celebrated history of extensive immigration and settlement is continuing to transform the city's demographic makeup. The "green revolution" is intensifying and requiring our attention as never before; our natural environment, no longer peripheral in our thoughts, is central to our lives. Moreover, like other urban centers in North America and indeed around the world, the economic basis of Jane's adopted city is experiencing a dramatic shift necessitating new perspectives in creating opportunities. These extraordinary changes in our community, ecology, and economy demand in turn the regeneration of Toronto's public realm and a refocusing of our political life, allowing us to test the continued relevance of the values and the ideas that matter in the Jacobsian city formed half a century ago.

All cities, of course, are different. They all bear their own civic ethos —a civic culture rooted in the needs of its people, their dreams, challenges, experiences of place and founding moments, which are carried forward in habits of mind and heart and ways of doing things. History matters and is always at work, whether we're paying attention or not.

Toronto has always been a gathering place. Even in aboriginal times, Toronto, with its natural network of rivers, lakes, and valleys linking the St. Lawrence to the Mississippi and the west, was at the crossroads of human settlement, trade, conflict, and ceremony. Toronto's first European contact began with Louis XIV and the French Empire and lasted for some 150 years, until the city became part of the British Empire in 1763 at the Treaty of Paris. When European Toronto was founded in the little Town of York in 1793, it began life not as a commercial enterprise, nor as an invading force, nor as a refuge for religious freedom: it came into being as a military outpost of Empire. Its earliest civic code, therefore, was engendered in the colonial administrator's obligation to ensure "peace, order and good government" through an inclusive application of the common law, an emphasis on the virtue of civic order, and an understanding of the primary role of government in shaping the civic culture of the new community. "Peace, order and good government," which would become the "*cri de coeur*" of modern Canada's constitution, provided a context for Toronto's civic life, linking it to its regional frontier and the imperial powers beyond.

As colonials, Torontonians grew accustomed to the idea of belonging to a global sort of citizenship that included the many nations, languages, cultures, races, and religions that owed allegiance to the British Crown. As Canadians, we worked to fuse the remains of the French and British empires in North America. We learned that assimilation of our people was impossible and segregation unacceptable. So we evolved an understanding that cohabitation and coexistence were the only stable, practical and peaceful approaches to both nation and city building. Our constitutional heritage, supported by our practical history and experience, insisted that language, culture, and community were local and place-related and were not inconsistent with significant allegiances beyond our border. We therefore had to erect a political house of many mansions to make substantial room for multiple loyalties and maximum acceptance of individual and community differences.

It is within this context that Toronto has experienced the resettlement of millions of newcomers, welcoming people from all corners of the globe, be they part of a tide of war-torn refugees or individuals looking for a better life and new opportunity. These continuing waves of immigrants have created a city of such human diversity that it is now described as the most multicultural city in the world. Certainly, the demographic base in the past sixty years has transformed the face of Toronto. A 2007 document of the Toronto District School Board identifies a full 71 percent of senior elementary and secondary students as having both parents foreign-born (Manning 2007, 17). Clearly, the Toronto where Jane Jacobs developed her thoughts on urban diversity and in which Marshall McLuhan invented the very notion of "global village" is, as Pico Iyer describes, "a post-modern Commonwealth, a vase that is put together out of broken pieces" (Iyer 2000, 125).

Over the years, we have learned much about newcomers, how they behave, and what they need as they pursue their dreams. Immigrants, for the most part, are neither fighting a rearguard action to preserve old ways nor living in a holding tank, awaiting assimilation. Rather they are participating in a dynamic process, bringing their hopes and keeping what they cherish, while changing, adjusting, and contributing to the new according to their own circumstances, in their own time.

In neighboroods where race, ethnicity, and immigrant experience are determining characteristics, questions and answers of personal identity will be refracted through the light of particular kinships and cultures. Distinctive settlement occurs in response to real human need: the warmth of familiarity through language, cultural habits, work possibilities, and affordable housing. These communities create dependable islands of human touch that offer some coherence and predictability and a web of helpful relationships in an alien and perhaps even hostile world. It is from these "base camps" that newcomers can reach out into contested terrain to pursue their dreams and "negotiate their ethnicity" (Harney 1985, 13).

Neighborhoods have always been especially important to Torontonians. We have understood them not only as physical places of important reference, but as psychic spaces in which human personalities are formed and expressed. They are places where identities are learned and where the rudiments of survival are gleaned and practiced. The city neighborhood is where we learn early and continuing responses to such eternal questions as who am I, where do I belong, and how do I behave.

While the development and diversity of community in Toronto has changed consistently over time, our understanding of the importance of our natural environment has transformed dramatically in the last half century. For too long, in pursuit of our needs and pleasures, our throwaway society has too often poisoned the air, polluted the water, and contaminated the soil with neither care nor curiosity about the long-term damage to both the environment and the chances and choices of future generations. Unswimmable, undrinkable, unfishable water, unusable soil, and unhealthy air became the legacies of our environmental carelessness.

From the landmark work of Jane Jacobs, Rachel Carson, Ian McHarg, William H. Whyte and others in the 1960s and the likes of Anne Spirn and Michael Hough in the 1980s, to the Brundtland Report of 1987 and the Melbourne Principles of 2002, we have moved from insight and advocacy to implementation, from thought to action, as the need for "sustainability" was taking hold in the new century. Globally and locally, the issues of air, land and water have come to dominate the urban agenda around the world.

We are relearning some valuable ecological truths: human beings are part of nature and not separate from it; since everything is connected to everything else, we are responsible for the consequences of our actions—to ourselves, to other people, to other generations, and to other species. The idea, therefore, that we can move in, use up, throw away, and move on is not only morally indefensible but ultimately economically destructive. Our community and ecological and economic well-being are not mutually exclusive, but rather mutually interdependent.

The importance of economic well-being to the future of the city has always been front and center. People come to Toronto in pursuit of better prospects for themselves and their families, and success in that effort is what enables them to set down roots. As Toronto moved from being a colonial outpost to an agricultural economy and then an industrial power in the twentieth century, it demonstrated its willingness to reinvent itself in order to keep what it could of a declining economy and do what was required to participate in the emerging new order. The economic history of the city illustrates that Torontonians have always adapted to constantly shifting economic opportunities and appreciated the power of individual initiative and private endeavor to create wealth for both private use and community benefit. That is why at crucial times of change throughout the nineteenth and twentieth centuries, Toronto found itself able to rise to challenge—to repair, regenerate and reinvent its public realm to serve the needs of a new era.

Moreover, throughout its history Toronto has taken a rather robust view of what should be included within the sphere of public interest and concern. Here the list is long, including everything from education, healthcare, justice, social services, environmental stewardship, public safety and security, to public transportation, libraries and public places, as well as a number of community facilities of private concern which are regulated in the public interest. All of these are seen as our connecting tissues, which widen the circle of accessibility and opportunity, link our individual private worlds, and help fuse our generations to one another. The public realm is the glue that holds the city together and the bedrock upon which it builds its prosperity, its communities and its social peace. Toronto cleaves to the notion that it will be successful because it is civic, not civic because it is successful.

By the end of the twentieth century, however, an increasingly globalized economy, new technologies, new trade partners, and new political attitudes had significantly altered Toronto's economic and social context, and exposed serious deficiencies in a public realm weakened by neglect and too many years of too little investment. Moreover, that indifference was reinforced by the imported political view that "government is part of the problem and not part of the solution"... Indeed, policies of privatization, deregulation, downsizing and downloading began to impoverish the quality of Toronto's public realm.

In the first decade of the new century, though, the process of renewal is again underway. It is made more urgent by the deepening economic crisis, now assuming global proportions. A new balance is being struck between the state and the marketplace. In response, governments are reordering their priorities, policies, and programs; corporations and businesses are redirecting their strategies and resources; and communities and individuals are constantly reevaluating their needs, expectations, and behaviors.

In this regard Jane Jacobs' admonition to always keep abreast of important historical changes is clearly recognizable in the city's Agenda for Prosperity, adopted in 2007. This strategy for economic growth in partnership with provincial and federal governments recognizes Toronto's historic participation in a global economy. It stipulates the need for investment in research and training in creative industries and green infrastructure. It calls for tax relief for small businesses and a program of building public transit and community facilities. Furthermore, it highlights the necessity of refocusing social services and welfare programs to emphasize counseling and job training.

Toronto, however, is more than a city: it is an immense region. Indeed, by the end of the twentieth century, Toronto had become the center of a constantly expanding multi-connected area of some five million people. The region includes within its purview cities, towns, villages, farms, forests, wetlands, lakes, and river valleys. It has become a city-region of continental, even global, significance, connecting people to the places where they live, work, and play, through a complex network of roads, highways, rail, airports, public transit, and now all manner of new communication technologies, from telephones to emails and Blackberries.

Responding to this historic expansion, the Province of Ontario, which has constitutional responsibility for municipalities, has initiated a number of reforms over the years. This has been done in order to ensure a more equitable access to services, a more coherent regulatory framework, and some sense of local accountability.

In 1953 Metropolitan Toronto was established as a regional government imposed by the Province on the City of Toronto and its then twelve "suburban" municipalities, all of whom opposed the new arrangement. This established a two-tier system of local government looking after the affairs of 1.5 million people, half of whom lived in the old city. Each municipality sent members to the new metro government on a roughly representation by population basis. Over the ensuing forty years, this system became more and more centralized as more responsibilities were passed over to Metro. When the appointment of representatives to council gave way to democratic vote by residents, the result was two directly elected local governments.

In 1995, following a review and fierce public debate, the Province amalgamated the government of Metropolitan Toronto with its now six constituent municipalities into one large City of Toronto. The newly created city of over 2.5 million has now been in existence for over a decade, and while some residual angst remains, it has mostly faded away, and its acceptance is no longer under any serious challenge.

However, the amalgamation discussion did raise the fundamental question of what new regional governance should replace Metro and what powers it should be able to exercise. An impressive array of studies, commissions, task forces, forums, editorial comments, and community meetings informed the discourse. Jane Jacobs and many of her supporters took an active and indeed leadership role in the debate. They had strongly opposed amalgamation as being too big for "local" democracy and too small for "regional" government, and in any case felt it would not achieve the cost savings envisaged by the Province. They championed instead a more autonomous, self-governing city-region government for the greater Toronto area, with significantly stronger legislative and fiscal powers. Ideas for achieving that goal included such dramatic notions as reorganizing the Canadian constitution, seceding from the Province, and establishing a city-state.

After more than a decade of public engagement, this strategy has yielded some useful but, given its aspirations, only very modest achievements. The recent amendments to the City of Toronto Act have brought some much needed administrative clarity in Toronto's relationship with the Province. Toronto can now move forward without permission on a number of matters, so long as a provincial interest has not been declared. The City has obtained the right to levy certain new taxes, though it did not gain the direct access to portions of sales or income taxes it had sought. It should be noted that there are indications that these "special powers" are now on schedule to be granted to other Ontario municipalities.

The idea that the governance of the new region of the Greater Toronto Area should be continued by a new expanded version of the old Metro government with increased autonomy has also been rejected. Instead, the Province itself has promoted vigorously and adeptly its own claim to be the effective "regional government" for Toronto. In the past five years, it has established a growth plan, "Places to Grow," for what it calls the Greater Golden Horseshoe—an area much larger than the old GTA, home to about seven million people. Moreover, it has developed a green plan for almost the same area, though not with congruent boundaries. All municipalities must pay heed to these documents in their own planning deliberations. Finally, the Province has created Metrolinx, a new transportation authority for the region.

Why has the strategy to establish a more autonomous, self-governing regional government, inspired by Jane Jacobs and her followers, not met expectations? First of all, its radical reform proposals seem to go against the grain of historic Canadian constitutional experience. Canadians intuitively understand that the price of their many diversities is a constant need to search for unity. That is why reforms reflecting complexity and accommodation are more highly valued than those promoting clarity and separation. Effective reform, therefore, is usually found through imaginative employment of existing constitutional provisions and institutional arrangements, rather than "root and branch" change approaches. Secondly, there are many who worry about the basic assumption that because cities and their regions expand, we should automatically increase municipal powers. In the building of its public realm, Toronto and its region need more, not less, provincial and federal involvement and support. We should not diminish the historic obligations and participation of these levels of government in our well-being in the name of expanded municipal autonomy. Finally, proponents of an autonomous city regional government faced a central dilemma in their approach. Andrew Sancton put it best:

> Making central-city municipalities—and perhaps also their surrounding suburbs—more autonomous does nothing except reify existing boundaries that are invariably seen as arbitrary, outdated, discriminatory, and irrelevant. However, focusing on the economic and social reality of a city means focusing on the city-region as a whole, and determining its territorial extent for the purposes of self-government is not a practical proposition. (Sancton 2008, 4)

The answer to the dilemma, he concludes, is to recognize that the Province itself already has the constitutional responsibility to act as a regional government and is well equipped legislatively, financially, and politically to do the job.

For forty years, the continuing influence of Jane Jacobs on Toronto has been nothing short of extraordinary. As always, her spirit continues to animate the central city of Toronto. What is remarkable is that she is also now having a renaissance in former suburbs that are trying to "urbanize." As they develop mixed land uses and expand public transit, they understand Jane's exhortation to "plan for vitality," and her voice is now being heard and heeded in places undreamt of when she began her journey. For Jane Jacobs, the mother's milk of urban life comes from people passionately and publicly engaged in ideas derived from their own observation, experience, and the willingness to act on them. For her, delivered orthodoxy was the enemy of ideas, so when she came to Toronto, she was not looking for disciples but seeking dialogue. And for us, that has made all the difference.

REFERENCES

Harney, Robert F., ed. 1985. *Gathering Place: Peoples and Neighbourhoods of Toronto, 1834-1945.* Toronto: Multicultural History Society of Ontario.

Iyer, Pico. 2000. *The Global Soul.* New York: Vintage Books.

Manning, Susan, ed. 2007. *2006 Student Census, Grades 7-12: System Overview.* Toronto: Toronto District School Board.

Sancton, Andrew. 2008. *The Limits of Boundaries: Why City-Regions Cannot be Self-Governing.* Montreal & Kingston: McGill-Queen's University Press.

THE VILLAGE INSIDE

Matias Echanove & Rahul Srivastava

INTRODUCTION

ONE OF GANDHI'S many obsessions was the idea of the self-sufficient village—one that would service most of its inhabitants' needs and act as an independent republic of its own. The idealization of the small-scale, self-sustaining and communitarian village was a characteristic reaction to the global emergence of large-scale, bustling industrial cities and trading centers that had changed the way the world organized itself from the nineteenth century onwards. The city had become a larger-than-life figure perceived to be simultaneously mechanistic and out of control, environmentally destructive and socially alienating, while the village was posited as a human-scale alternative in tune with Indian traditions, morality, and spirituality.

As brilliantly argued by political psychologist Ashis Nandy, the archetype of a Gandhian village could not have emerged anywhere else than in the unsettled mind of an urbanite. Gandhi, a city boy by all accounts, produced most of his village visions during his stay in South Africa, and later from his colonial Bombay home. This image, according to Nandy, was as much the product of Gandhi's late explorations of rural India as the fruit of a deep introspection, which slowly brought to surface the ideal vision of a village in him—as in every Indian.

Gandhi's village, however, cannot be reduced to romantic folklore or agrarian utopia. It was based on the principles of industriousness and autonomy, and located the artisan—symbolized by the famous cloth spinning wheel—at the center of its organization. It represented free-dom from top-down political control and economic dependency. Local management of natural resources, including food production, and an insistence on self-made homes, were hallmarks of the Gandhian village. Gandhi believed that any construction had to be built with material solicited from an area of approximately five miles radius around the site (Henderson 2002, 94).

Ivan Illich and other radical critics of the construction industry echoed this in the 1970s. Illich argued that building regulations and the real estate industry took away the ability of people to build their own homes (Illich 1973). Under the guise of defending collective and general interest, construction law has in effect proscribed self-made houses and habitats. Moreover, public spending has been invested into the edification of new towns and housing complexes instead of helping people to build and maintain their own abodes. These new industrial homes, built according to preset norms, are unaffordable to the poor, resulting in the vicious housing crisis that all modern cities are experi-encing today—a crisis manufactured to serve the interest of an industry that far from providing housing to the needy, produces more misery and homelessness. Gandhi responded to the same industrial-urban logic at work in colonial India.

However, as compelling and influential as Gandhi's defense of the Indian village may have been, it was not enough to contain the massive and continuous rural exodus that the country has been experiencing ever since independence. For many, the transition from the village to the city was, and continues to be, experienced as a liberation from social hier-archies and servitude. Indeed, a major voice opposing Gandhi was that of Dr. Ambedkar, a social reformer, ideologue, and revered Dalit leader (from the ex-untouchable community), famous for being the architect of the Indian constitution. While Gandhi was exhorting Indians to go back to the villages, Dr. Ambedkar was urging Dalits to move to the cities, where they could liberate themselves from a backward milieu character-ized by caste-based exploitation, poverty, and illiteracy. One could argue that both Gandhi and Ambedkar's visions were ultimately fulfilled and perverted in India's shadow cities.

Gandhi's idealization of the village was surely problematic to start with. He saw it as an objective reality that could be conceptually posited as a counterpoint to the city. This oppositional logic was typical of Gandhi's time—marked by extreme political ideologies—and it remains one of the most widespread misconceptions about urbanization today. The era of industrial urbanization has typically been represented as a shifting point, when the split between cities and villages became wider and irreversible. This polarization was however more notional than real. Gandhi's emphasis on the village as the locus of economic activity and social progress was a response to Western faith in industrialization and urbanization; but this response became susceptible to other kinds of dogmas and ideologies.

After independence, the Indian government adopted a Gandhian line and largely ignored urban development. Development strategies focused instead on rural areas, where real India was said to reside. Incentives and support were given to cottage and small-scale industries in rural areas. Yet the movement of citizens from the countryside to the city continued. For several decades, this movement did not really worry the government, given that total numbers of people in rural India remained high. The government therefore persisted with its rural bias.

Meanwhile, a version of the village was actually being recreated inside India's sprawling cities. Rural-urban migrants were resurrecting old community ties and arts and crafts in a new form (Nandy 1998, 6). In quest for livelihood, water, and freedom from feudal ties, rural migrants came in millions to the cities and brought with them their skills, talents, and evolving traditions. Hamlets, villages, and settlements mushroomed in and around cities, providing ever cheaper labor, goods, and services to urban residents. These settlements were never seen as legitimate since they were not planned and could not be property audited. Integrating into the city on their own terms, the needs of these emerging settlements were largely disregarded, leading to their marginalization.

Their illegitimacy, though, is as much a result of conceptual fallacies as anything else—a fallacy that insists on understanding the world of habitats in terms of watertight compartments and believes that villages and cities belong to different planets. In truth, cities and villages have always been much more integrated and mutually dependent than Gandhi acknowledged. Jane Jacobs' concept of a city-region recognizes that agricultural villages are an essential part of the urban economy they serve (Jacobs 1969, 17). Inversely, the village has always existed within the city's ethos, fabric, and practices.

Gandhi's dream of a dominant countryside was never realized; instead, it was happening, some would say in a nightmarish way, in the dirty, polluted, and promiscuous city. Rural migrants were building thousands of industrious shacks with locally available materials wherever they could find space: marshland, junkyards, along railway tracks, on the pavements. Incrementally developing and consolidating, self-reliant and defiant, slums flourished to the point that they are now said to be home to more than half the population of Mumbai and many other cities.

Unfortunately, the Indian government never saw slums as striving urban villages, bravely self-developing and worthy of support. Quite on the contrary, to this day they are perceived as shameful marks of underdevelopment, irreconcilable with the country's aspiration to become a modern and civilized nation. While slum dwellers are dismissed as squatters, slums are perceived as natural enemies of city planning and good governance. Thus, the only possible official response to slums seems to be repression, through erasure or willful indifference.

For instance, Dharavi in Mumbai, mistakenly known as the largest slum in Asia, has never been properly retrofitted with water pipes, sewage systems, and electrical infrastructure, nor does the municipality treat it as a legitimate part of the city. Instead, its residents and businesses have had their sheltering and livelihoods threatened by "imminent" redevelopment projects for decades.

MILLION DHARAVIS

Planners and politicians have used Dharavi's unplanned, messy, indeed slummy appearance to justify its destruction. Dharavi is typically pictured as a backward locality, an urban parasite preventing Mumbai from becoming a "world-class city." However, as we argued in a recently published response to the movie *Slumdog Millionaire*, reality stands in sharp contrast to the way slums are usually represented:

> Its depiction as a slum does little justice to the reality of Dharavi. Well over a million "eyes on the street," to use Jane Jacobs' phrase, keep Dharavi perhaps safer than most American cities. Yet, its extreme population density doesn't translate into oppressiveness. The crowd is efficiently absorbed by the thousands of tiny streets branching off bustling commercial arteries. In addition, you won't be chased by beggars or see hopeless people loitering—Dharavi is probably the most active and lively part of an incredibly industrious city. People have learned to respond in creative ways to the indifference of the state—including having set up a highly functional recycling industry that serves the whole city. (Echanove and Srivastava 2009)

Even more remarkably, visitors have observed that many aspects of Dharavi are reminiscent of European old towns and villages, with their labyrinthine and narrow streets, low-rise and high-density structures, mixed-use spatial arrangements, small shops on the ground floor and living spaces on the upper floors, workshops and lively street activity where pedestrian traffic dominates any other mode of transportation. This is no coincidence.

Many neighborhoods around the world share a similar history of incremental development. These are the parts of the city which, though never planned or designed, have acquired a strong identity over time, marked by the evolution and mutation of micro economic and cultural practices. These practices of daily life, to paraphrase Michel de Certeau, shape space and produce context. Space becomes the malleable receptacle of local practices. As practices shape the space they inhabit, they increase its use value. Space becomes not only supportive of, but also conducive to certain uses and practices. This process is at work in these neighborhoods with different levels of intensity and various degrees of autonomy from the larger context. The relationship between space and practices produces its own temporality, connecting a familiar past with a not so distant future.

Incrementally developing neighborhoods can also fall into history, memory or nostalgia when the built environment is artificially preserved long after it ceases to fulfill any function. But more often than not, they evolve in creative ways and acquire new meanings over time, just like SoHo, New York, where galleries, high-fashion and luxury retailers, and stylish lofts have replaced artist studios and squats, which themselves had replaced warehouses and factories.

In Dharavi, the spectacle of a neighborhood transforming itself in fast-forward mode captivates the attention of researchers, reporters, and audiences around the world. Dharavi is constantly *in formation* from the day its first inhabitants, who were nomadic fishing tribes, settled perhaps three centuries ago on this auspicious creek at the confluence of the Mithi tributary and the Arabian Sea. In the early twentieth century came Muslim and Tamilian artisans, who set up tanneries to produce leather goods for Bombay's expanding consumer market. As the city grew, migrants came from all over India, bringing with them their arts and trades. They have established themselves, improvised, struggled, made roots, built up, and moved on. Dharavi is today a major trading hub, central to Mumbai's economy, exporting goods all over the country and beyond.

THE GENESIS OF CITIES

Habitats such as Dharavi have been generated in response to basic human needs for sheltering and subsistence. According to Jane Jacobs, the foundational principles of urban development are intimately linked to certain forms of livelihood, such as hunting-gathering, trading, artisanal production and its scaled-up versions. Historically, only a small proportion of the inhabitants of the political kingdom lived in close proximity to each other—what today we would refer to as urbanized settlements. This population was intertwined in an economy that serviced the ruling establishment and acted as a node in larger networks of exchange of goods and services. Anthropologists like Anthony Leeds see these complexes as urban systems that encompassed vast territories of the kingdom dotted with villages, fields, and inhabited forests, all of which were part of the domain. They were connected to each other through taxation and were interdependent for food, security, and other economic needs (Leeds and Sanjek 1994).

All kinds of inhabited space, and in particular agricultural land and forests, were regulated and controlled. The act of ruling included administering population surveys, controlling people's movements, involving them in construction work as cheap labor, and shaping their livelihoods through economic regulation (Scott 1998).

The industrial revolution supposedly brought in a huge disjuncture in contemporary organization of social life, largely represented in terms of a population movement from rural to urban areas. This move reflected a massive crisis of administration in the nineteenth century and saw the evolution of new modes of controlling rural migrants. Modern urban planning emerged as a response to this need, and the ideal of the planned city—to be eventually emulated by everyone—became some kind of a global norm.

This ideal posited itself as a counterpoint to rural life. Urban planning was defined along the functional lines dictated by industrialization and the cultural values of modernization. Hardly a scaled-up version of the mixed-use and improvised village, the master-planned city was strictly zoned and structured around well-defined activities. It left little space for the grey zones between public and private and living and working areas that characterize unplanned habitats.

The artisanal home, a distinctive aspect of village life, was considered problematic. Home-based manufacture and traditional skills came to be considered outmoded as the factory became the legitimate site of production. Trade of goods and services had to be regulated. The presence of a bazaar-based exchange that floated through the economy and formed an intrinsic part of a village's networks had to be controlled. The segregation of markets and places of residence, work, and leisure was presented as the hallmark of contemporary urban life, necessary for the efficient functioning of highly populated cities. Failure to control spatial use was seen as a failure of urbanization and planning.

URBAN-RURAL: THE CONCEPTUAL VOID

The government, international organizations, and the real estate industry seem unable to respond to the hundreds of thousands of improvised settlements in Indian cities in any other way than through clearance and redevelopment. This happens in spite of the fact that the construction of mass housing and factories has never been able to slow down the growth of urban slums. It also disregards the operational logic of many slums where space is used in a much more flexible way, with functions such as living and working constantly overlapping. Even the most enlightened urban plan trying to bring these functions closer together at most succeeds in reorganizing them in ingenious way, but is strictly unable to merge them operationally. From a planning perspective, any ambiguity in the way space is used is perceived as a potential threat.

The unwillingness to recognize self-developing neighborhoods as legitimate alternatives can partly be attributed to a colonial habit of organizing and controlling space, which has evolved into all kinds of planning directives and urban designs. By and large, heroic planning attempts have failed in post-independence Indian cities, which remain desperately—some would say wonderfully—chaotic at all levels. One space that it succeeded in colonizing completely, however, is the space of imagination. The city is perceived as being modern, high-rise, and motorized (think New York, Singapore and Shanghai), or slummy, messy, and backward. There is no conceptual in-between for a city that is incrementally developing, mixed-use, efficient, and convivial.

Kisho Kurokawa, a much-revered Japanese architect and proponent of the Metabolist movement, locates this conceptual void in Western conceptions of urban order. According to him:

> Western culture rests on innumerable binomial oppositions: spirit and flesh; freedom and necessity; good and evil; conservatism and reform; art and science; reason and emotion; mankind and nature; tradition and technology; capitalism and socialism; the individual and the whole...We have sacrificed much... for the sake of this philosophy of dualism. (Kurokawa 1993, 9)

Similarly, when they are understood as opposites, categories such as "city and village," "urban and rural," "modern and primitive," "formal and informal," and "order and chaos" do become mutually exclusive—with dire consequences for cities, especially in the developing world.

Interestingly, the fact that in Japan these categories were never seen as mutually exclusive allowed for a completely different landscape to emerge. According to Kurokawa, in Japanese cities order includes chaos or "noise," as he calls it in reference to Edgar Morin's theory of noise. This is why Japanese cities are so tolerant of those forms of urbanism that Western notions of planning and urban order would call "irrational," "messy," or even "slummy." Tokyo, says Kurokawa,

> is an agglomeration of three hundred cities... At first there seems to be no order, but the energy, freedom, and the multiplicity that comes from the parts are there. The creation of this new hierarchy is a process that makes use of spontaneously occuring forces. For this reason, it is probably most accurate to say that Tokyo today... finds itself set somewhere between true chaos and a new hidden order. (1993, 11)

However, few other Asian cities have been as accepting of the (apparent) paradox of local self-development in urban land.

Typically, as they expanded their spread and transportation network, Japanese cities have absorbed villages, while allowing them to keep developing in a gradual, incremental manner. In the postwar period in Tokyo, planning was for the most part limited to retrofitting localities with basic infrastructure and transport systems. The government encouraged local self-reliance and did its best to help local actors in their effort to rebuild their neighborhoods. This pattern of development has basically been maintained until today. It explains why Tokyo has one of the best infrastructures in the world, as well as a housing stock of great variety.

In most of Tokyo's neighborhoods one can still find wood and hardware stores selling self-help construction material used by local residents to maintain their houses. This is why, until recently, "the majority of neighborhoods were characterized by flimsy wooden constructions, and slum-type housing dominated many areas" (Hein et al. 2003, 26).

Corrugated metal sheets and wood frames are still a fixture in many parts of Tokyo, particularly in neighborhoods traditionally inhabited by merchants and artisans known as *Shitamachi*, "the lower city." These parts of the city have much more in common with the slums of Mumbai than many would like to acknowledge. In fact, their human-scale, low-rise, high-density typology, and the way they have managed to preserve a strong economic and social life, with corner shops, restaurants, bars, public baths, schools, and shrines, tell as much about their history as about the potential of places like Dharavi.

THE TOOL-HOUSE

More than anywhere else these distant realities converged in the space of the artisan's home, which according to Japanese urbanist and writer Magoroh Maruyama unified "the place of work and the familial space, reinforced the solidarity of local residents and maintained close relationships between neighbors" (see Hiroshi 1994, 385). It also brought together employers and employees, who all stayed under the same roof. Maruyama deplores the exodus of business owners and landlords from their place of work in Tokyo to remote residential areas, which made them indifferent to the fate of their old neighborhoods.

The impact of this incision was most strongly felt in the multipurpose house of the artisan, where most of the goods that circulated in the preindustrial economy were produced. We call this flexible live-work arrangement the *tool-house*, because the space of the house itself is used as a productive tool in all kinds of creative ways. A tool-house emerges when every wall, nook, and corner becomes an extension of the tools of the trade of its inhabitant—when the furnace and the cooking hearth exchange roles, and sleeping competes with warehouse space.

The tool-house is still alive and kicking in neighborhoods such as Dharavi, and a million others all over Asia. Many will argue that this is because Dharavi is wrapped in a preindustrial time and space. We believe that Dharavi should instead be seen as some type of contemporary postindustrial landscape. After all, this is where the industrial, unionized mill workers were absorbed after the cotton mills started shutting down after the 1980s. What could be mistaken for an expression of backwardness is actually happening at an accelerating pace in first world cities like London, New York, and Tokyo. What is the artist's loft if not a toolhouse? Live-work arrangements are making a comeback in rich cities just as they are being castigated in developing cities. Indeed, the mixed-use live-and-work artisan's home continues to live many different lives.

The tool-house can be a container in Kabul, serving as a store during the day and a shelter for the night; a mud structure used as a covered working and resting space in an Indian village; a shack in a Mexican town housing a rural migrant family and its activities; an internet-based home-office operating from an Osaka flat; a warehouse converted into a recording studio with guest rooms in Philadelphia; or a luxury condo apartment used as a party space and social venue in Copenhagen. The value of such spaces is maximized by their capacity to fulfill multiple functions with creative arrangements and flexible forms.

USER-GENERATED CITIES

The tool-house is the multishaped, multifunction building block of what we could call "user-generated cities." Such cities or neighborhoods are typically produced in increments rather than by design, in a piecemeal and decentralized fashion. There is no reason this age-old yet constantly updating urban development process could not be recognized and supported by planners and architects. The production of information about localities, the expression of individual and collective aspirations and visions, the decision-making process, and the implementation of urban plans can all be done with the involvement of motivated local residents.

Fifty years after Jane Jacobs' advocacy work in Manhattan, policymakers and planning departments have yet to acknowledge what local knowledge and expertise can contribute to the planning process. Ignoring local actors comes at a high cost, accompanied as it is by strong oppositions, and more often than not results in inadequate urban development. It is only with a paradigm shift in the way we conceive of cities that we can actually tap into local intelligence and its productive capacity. In an age of "information" in which billions of people are exchanging bits and data across platforms and boundaries, we should no longer rely on the master planner's map and the one-way powerpoint presentations that pass off for community involvement.

Participatory workshops involving local actors, creative people, and professionals, along with user-friendly, location-based web tools can be used to harness individual knowledge and collective imaginations, one neighborhood at a time. Grassroots initiatives are not just multiplying all over the world, they are also professionalizing their output like never before, presenting local development strategies that are often much more sophisticated and better informed than what governments are able to produce. Moreover, neighborhood groups are rarely as conservative as they are often portrayed. We repeatedly see resident neighborhood associations articulating their own agendas in proposals that accommodate the interests of the government. Far from fighting for preserving the status quo, most neighborhood groups fight for change they can control.

The concepts of citizen involvement and public participation have found their ways into planning departments in many cities around the world. However, their rhetoric rarely translates into innovative practices at the ground level. This is probably because at the end of the day, real estate interests, and not planning departments, dictate the urban landscape. But even then, it may well happen that developers, tired of having their projects delayed and stalled by defiant neighborhood groups, actually turn to participatory practices—in hopes that dealing with local interests at the conception stage of their projects rather than at the implementation stage may save time and money.

IN CONCLUSION

Urban renewal and redevelopment projects such as those described by Jane Jacobs in the West End of Boston and the West Village in New York City, or those happening today in Shimokitazawa, Tokyo, or Dharavi, Mumbai, all follow a familiar pattern in which the state supports increasingly large and global real estate bids on neighborhoods. After all, real estate acquisition and development remains the best way to cool off hot money.

The most disturbing part of this process is the fact that the government systematically evokes the messy and makeshift appearance of certain strategically located neighborhoods to justify their redevelopment, even when the proposed structural changes work against the needs and interests of local users. The violence of the redevelopment process is often compensated by tokenistic moves that focus on conserving some heritage symbols or involving a few local representatives in emerging political bodies.

In fact, replacing labyrinthine pedestrian streets packed with small vendors and casual buyers with shopping malls and motorways is not as much an urban makeover as an economic takeover. At stake are the human-scale and organic characters of these neighborhoods, as well as their social, cultural, and economic wealth. The first casualty of redevelopment projects are indeed local businesses, social networks, a sense of shared identity, and the ability of neighborhoods to constantly reinvent themselves.

Most of us remember Jane Jacobs' successful opposition to one of the most powerful builders of all times, Robert Moses. She demonstrated that neighborhoods have the capacity to respond to takeover bids by making the stakes higher through political participation, business association, social cohesion, local skills and knowledge, street presence, collective expression, and self-affirmation. Her writing taught us that these are not only forces of resistance, but also developmental impulses that have a long and complex history, from the village to the city and back.

REFERENCES

Echanove, Matias and Rahul Srivastava. 2009. "Taking the Slum Out of 'Slumdog'", Opinion, *New York Times*, February 21.

Hein Carola, Jeffry M. Diefendorf and Ishida Yorifusa (eds). 2003. *Rebuilding Urban Japan After 1945*. New York: Palgrave Macmillan.

Henderson Garcia, Carol. 2002. *Culture and Customs of India*. Westport, CT: Greenwood Press.

Hiroshi, Tanabe. 1994. *Les "territories" à Tokyo*. In *La maîtrise de la ville: Urbanité française, urbanité nippone*, edited by Augustin Berque. Paris: Edition de l'Ecole des Hautes Etudes en Sciences Sociales.

Illich, Ivan. 1973. *Tools for Conviviality*. New York: Harper & Row.

Jacobs, Jane. 1969. *The Economy of Cities*. New York: Random House.

Kurokawa, Kisho. 1993. *New Wave Japanese Architecture*. London: Academy Editions.

Leeds, Anthony and Roger Sanjek. 1994. *Cities, Classes and the Social Order*. Ithaca, NY: Cornell University Press.

Nandy, Ashis. 1998. *The Secret Politics of Our Desires: Innocence, Culpability and Indian Popular Cinema*. Oxford: Oxford University Press.

Scott, James. 1998. *Seeing Like the State*. New Haven, CT: Yale University Press.

SECTION 4

The Organized Complexity
of Planning

THE OBLIGATION TO
LISTEN, LEARN AND TEACH—
PATIENTLY

James Stockard

I NEVER MET JANE JACOBS. But her impact on my work as an urban planner and affordable housing practitioner has been as powerful as if she had been sitting on my shoulder every day. While other professional forces encouraged me to argue, maneuver, and demand, reading her books encouraged me to build a different set of skills for my work. She taught me to concentrate on listening, on learning from what I was hearing, and on teaching when I had something to contribute. Finally, she taught me patience. Let me explain.

My parents had no idea how important Jacobs was when they gave me a copy of *The Death and Life of Great American Cities*. It was a "notable" book and, knowing little about architecture (my college major), they thought it would be a good gift for my nineteenth birthday. Reading it was truly like planting a seed in my brain. Jacobs' ideas grew slowly at first. For three more years, I continued on the path toward a career in architecture, growing gradually more uncomfortable with that idea. By the end of my senior year, I knew I needed to find a different career. For unusual reasons, I found myself at the Union Theological Seminary in New York City. My internship was on the Lower East Side with a pastor who was very engaged with community issues. As I worked with kids from the church, met their parents, and walked around their neighborhood, many of the ideas about cities and descriptions of invigorating urban places I had read in Jane Jacobs' book grew from words on a page into my own experiences. Her thoughts provided a framework for what I was hearing and seeing in the first urban neighborhood of my adult life. It only took six months for the combination of Jane's ideas and my life in New York City to send me off to seek a degree in city planning.

But wait, you say. Jane Jacobs carried no brief for city planners. Mostly, she hated the way they treated the residents of American cities, and the way they cast aside the built environment with no concern for how cities really work. The icon of the city planning profession at the time, Robert Moses, was the target of some of her most pointed criticism. Why would a young person enamored of the ideas of Jane Jacobs start down a career path that was causing the "death" of cities? Shouldn't one train to be a community organizer or a lawyer preparing to sue those planners?

In a word, no. That seed Jane Jacobs planted had many flowers other than the "city planners are dumb and insensitive" blossom. For one thing, it was obvious that Jane loved cities. Living for a year in what was then her city, I had discovered that I loved them also. And I loved the very things she loved—the serendipity, the liveliness, the many levels of connectedness among neighbors, the variety of people and structures, the history, the beauty. If you loved those elements of the city, it seemed to me you could go learn how cities really work and spend your career preserving the best parts of urban life and creating even more of them.

During my time in school, several other forces nurtured the seeds *Death and Life* had planted. Paul Davidoff and the "citizen participation" movement gained traction among young planners. Chester Hartman, whose always provocative and insightful writing you will find elsewhere in this volume, was one of my teachers and sounded to me like the voice of Jane Jacobs in my classrooms. American cities exploded in the summers of my years in graduate school, clearly because of the extent of racism in urban America and the failure of planners and politicians to practice the principles I had come to believe in. Finally, my first professional employer, Justin Gray, who was to become my mentor, claimed the title city planner, but I'm convinced he would have been warmly embraced by Jane Jacobs.

What all these people and ideas taught me was how to contribute to the process of nurturing the best parts of cities. They never talked about a particular physical form or street pattern or housing policy. They talked about, and practiced, the skills of listening, learning, and teaching. They all had a definition of "expertise" that extended far beyond what one could learn in school. Everybody, they taught me, is an expert at something. Often, people are expert at skills or areas of knowledge in which nobody gives degrees. But that expertise is critical to how cities work. Some are experts at whom and what you will encounter as you walk the streets of a particular neighborhood. Some know how to communicate with youth. Others are experts at whom you have to consult in order to get something done. A few know how to gather people together and build consensus. Many are experts at how people in a place will react to change. After reading *Death and Life*, I believed it would be possible to shape a career as the kind of planner who could take advantage of the full range of expertise to help preserve and shape great urban places.

Early in my career, I read a book totally outside my field. In the beginning of *The Active Patient's Guide to Better Medical Care: Strategies for Working Together with Your Doctor*, Stanley Sagov says something to the effect of:

> Every appointment I have with a patient is a meeting of two experts. I am an expert in chemistry and biology and disease. The patient is an expert in how she or he feels. If we don't each bring our full expertise to the meeting, the results will be less than optimal. And if we don't each take the other's expertise seriously, the result will also be poor.

This seems to me to be excellent advice for city planners—perhaps a prescription "Dr." Jacobs might have issued. My experience in working with dozens of community groups across the country is that we walk a thin road with steep slopes on either side when we engage in our professional activities—especially when those activities are centered on people's homes, as mine usually have been. On one side of the road is the dangerous and slippery slope of believing we have all the skills and information necessary to determine what the future of this neighborhood should be. Sitting in our office downtown, we read the census, draw maps, make projections, and draft new policies with deft strokes on our increasingly clever computers. Those plans are doomed from the day we lean toward that side of the road.

On the other hand, there is the equally dangerous precipice of "I'm just a hired pencil here. Whatever the neighbors tell me, I draw it up nicely and present that to the political leaders." These are the planners the NIMBYs hope to find in their cities, codifying their fears about "those people" moving into their neighborhood.

As usual, that feisty, independent voice sitting on my shoulder seemed to be saying, "There's a third path." Some of my teachers were explaining how a planner discusses complex issues and convinces citizens of the better way to do things when they resist change. Ah, there's the problem, I realized. Our job is not to "convince." As I read Jane Jacobs, I thought the first thing I had to do if I hoped to be a planner who would improve the quality of urban life was to become a great listener. Second, I had to learn from what I heard. And third (this took longer), I would have to learn how to teach. This last part is especially difficult and, in my experience, is the concept planners practice least effectively. We often think it means "to lecture." That's the last thing it means. Let me say how Jane Jacobs shaped my practice.

First, listening. It goes with looking, which Jane talked about a lot. You can only listen if you are truly prepared to hear. And you can only hear if you have not made up your mind before the speaker begins. This was hard for me early in my career. I "knew" about the need for affordable housing. I had "discovered" what cul-de-sacs mean for lively streets. I had "researched" the ways redevelopment can bring new life, new jobs, and new economic vitality to cities. I learned to listen when a community of Polish heritage talked about their feelings for the buildings they had called home for two and three generations. The structures were old and in tough shape, but we found a way to save most of them. I learned to listen when a group of public housing residents told me what the pattern of redevelopment of their site should be. It was based on their real experience with major undertakings in their neighborhood, and they proved to be exactly right. Until I really incorporated the wisdom in *Death and Life*, my reaction to opposition to my proposed plans was to chomp at the bit for people to finish so I could lay down my polished justifications for the conclusions that I "knew" were right. And therefore

I did not hear. I may have looked like I was listening, but often I was only refraining from talking.

I have found over many years of working with community groups that the correct response to most statements about their preferences is to ask more questions. Not trick questions, meant to ensnare people into confessing some sinister secret motive for their opposition or advocacy; but real questions, meant to help people further explicate their statement, to explain how they came to their point of view, or to talk about alternatives that might make sense to them. The fact that we planners have been trained (or have significant experience) in some aspects of city building seems to convince us we have all the answers. In truth, the workings of the cities we love are so impossibly complex that we ought to be humbled (not shy or fearful, but humbled) before the task of comprehending what will be good for them and their citizens. I know I need to be looking for every scrap of information and every piece of an idea I can get my hands on in order to grow wiser about how (or whether) to intervene in their natural growth.

It took me a while to learn that good listening requires paying attention to every part of a statement—the actual words chosen, the emotion behind those words, the larger concepts, the reference points. I found that when I did this I could ask better questions, which helped me obtain yet more information. Further, it often lowered the tension around the conversation if a person felt I was really hearing him or her. I don't mean to be naive or idealistic here. Sometimes the expertise is modest. But each little bit helps.

Task two is learning. And learning is critical. Even when planners hear what people say about a highway going through their neighborhood or an entire community being wiped out by urban renewal, many chalk it up to self-interest or small-mindedness. We rarely learn. Learning means tying ideas together, adding what you know about a person to what he or she is saying, combining the history of a neighborhood with the proposals being discussed, thinking of the actual logistics of changes that are happening through natural forces and how those will interact with some planned intervention. When a community group told me that in their neighborhood duplexes on top of flats would never work, I learned the vitally important lesson that every neighborhood is different and has its own qualities built over many generations. When a training exercise failed, I asked the group what went wrong. They helped me learn to develop exercises that work even when they don't go exactly the way I hope they will. Learning has always taken me to a new place. Sometimes the new information further solidifies a position I have held in the past. Other times it persuades me to modify my stance or even abandon it. But it never leaves me in the same place. If it does, I know I have either not listened or not learned.

Not all opponents of a new affordable housing development in their neighborhood are racists. Some are truly fearful about the possible decline in value of the only significant asset they have—an asset they are counting on to sustain them in their old age. Some are nostalgic for the empty lot where they played ball as a kid and feel its development signals the final end to their childhood. Others take seriously the idea of mixed-use neighborhoods and believe this development will overload the area with affordable housing. And some are racists.

For the most part, the people I have worked with in neighborhoods try to tell you what's on their mind. But they (like we) don't always have the right words. Or they feel as though their thoughts aren't clear enough to express them in a public meeting (hence the need for listening in many different venues). Or they are embarrassed about their concerns. So, simply making note of words is not good listening and does not lead to learning. Appropriate responses to the reasons for opposing affordable housing listed above are dramatically different. There are different questions to ask, different paths for the ensuing conversations, and different stages in the decision-making process. I often sense Jane's spirit advising me to take my time and learn, so I can go down the right path and contribute my expertise to the conversation in a constructive manner.

Finally, what do I mean by our third obligation—to teach? I believe we have an obligation to share the knowledge we have gathered from our professional experience. We need not be falsely modest. We have studied and we have researched and we have read. We have experienced a wide range of previous situations, some of which may bear a resemblance to the one before us. Further, if we have practiced good listening and learning skills, we have gleaned some knowledge from our citizen-partners in other contexts. If we do not share that with the current stakeholders in a useful way, we are not holding up our end of the bargain.

I have sometimes found it difficult to discover the most "useful" way to transmit the information I do have. It's never helpful to lecture people about studies or research data or "what happened in the South End neighborhood five years ago." Good teachers think about the information they have to convey, but they think just as hard about the people they want to receive that information. How do those people learn most easily? Who has credibility with them? When should information be transmitted in group, and when are one-on-one meetings best? Do people hear well in a church basement, or should they be out walking a site? Who understands numbers, and who is afraid of them? Who likes to talk things out, and who likes to take home something in writing and mull it over for the next meeting? Who can read drawings, and who understands models better? What process will result in a group "owning" a decision, rather than simply acquiescing to a proposal they will abandon as soon as they hear the first opposition? There are many questions to ask and answer before we can know how to "teach."

This last step has always been critical for my reflection on my own practice. If I truly believe, based on everything I have learned in my career, that this affordable housing development makes sense at that location, then I should be able to ultimately provide enough information to other people in a manner useful to them so they will agree with me. To assume otherwise is to patronize and demonize all the people who participate in the planning of their cities and disagree with me. It is to assume they can't take in information contrary to their previously held opinions. So if I can't provide information that causes a change in positions, then one of two alternatives seems logically true to me. Either I really don't have enough information, and I'm simply parroting conventional wisdom; or I do have enough information, but I haven't yet found an understandable way to present it. I have mistaken my loud voice or my extensive, jargon-laden vocabulary or my self-satisfied logic for good communication. I haven't learned to *teach*. During an important research project, I found the vast majority of my colleagues in the public housing community arrayed against our methodology and recommendations. Many were longtime friends and much-respected peers. But I really believed in what we were saying. I struggled to find new ways to present the information and new contexts in which to discuss the issues. Over time, many have come to agree with our approach. I do not know how much my patience and willingness to try new ways to present ideas had to do with those results, but I'm convinced that the alternative of shouting down the opposition would have only made the situation worse.

Which is a good segue to a fourth lesson I learned from *Death and Life*: patience. This is hard for planners. We must be patient enough to allow the process of discussion and plan-making and learning by all parties to run its natural course. Nothing is so certain to corrupt a planning process as the statement that "we have to make a decision within the next two weeks in order to file our application in time..." But we must also be impatient enough to find ways for decisions to be made and actions taken at some point. There is no strategy as successful at chasing thoughtful citizen participants out of the public arena and leaving it to those who have hidden agendas than to let the process drag on far too long. If we planners take this mantra seriously, it means we need to be well prepared when we start any planning dialogue with a group of stakeholders. That means we need to have done a great deal of listening and learning before we "start." In essence, we need to be always in the midst of that process. And we need to have the discipline to let the discussions, plans, and revisions "cook" for a while. We need to be constantly listening, learning, and teaching. For most of us, the balance between time in the office doing research and time spent talking with all those involved in decisions about the shaping of their city needs to be bent considerably more toward the latter.

So no, I don't think Jane Jacobs disliked all planners or would have banned universities from offering training in the topic. She simply wanted us to love our cities enough to act more like good citizens– contributing our skills and ideas, listening to and learning from those of others, and working together with our fellow citizens to make a better place for all of us.

BUILT FORM AND THE
METAPHOR OF STORYTELLING

Robert Sirman

SOME MONTHS AGO I was introduced to a Toronto professional in the not-for-profit sector who was writing a paper on vocational renewal. Our first exchanges were limited to emails and phone calls, but it didn't take long before we arranged a face-to-face meeting on her next visit to Ottawa.

We began with the usual introductions. Then she turned to me and said: "Before we start, I have one question. 'Sometimes he makes things happen…'"

I almost fell off my chair.

Jane Jacobs first entered my life in the winter of 1968. I was taking a fourth-year course on urban sociology at the University of Toronto, and *The Death and Life of Great American Cities* was prescribed reading. Published in 1961, the book was already a classic. The year 1968 was also when the Jacobs family moved permanently to Toronto.

I remember this as a time of big ideas. At the University of Toronto many of these ideas centered on communications. Marshall McLuhan (still unknown to many) held court in a former coach house dubbed the Centre for Culture and Technology, where he carried on the work of Harold Innis and promoted outrageous wordplay. One of McLuhan's visual puns was carpeting the coach house with Astroturf. A block to the north, Northrop Frye developed the theory of archetypal criticism and promoted the Bible as the wellspring of Western imagination. What McLuhan and Frye had in common was a belief that all cultural manifestations encoded meaning, a through line for later theories about "reading" the city.

A second major trend was a shift in voice from third to first person, from an insistence on describing reality from an outside perspective—usually rationalized as "objective"—to a willingness to entertain experience-based explanations. Academics became more open to phenomenological explanations, analyzing human actions from the perspective of how actors perceive reality. Participant observation and community-based research took the foreground.

This was also a time of broad de-authorization, when the moral authority of "the establishment" was overtly challenged. The civil rights movement challenged the racially grounded social, economic, and political structure of America, while Vietnam War protesters defied its military authority. The women's movement turned gender-based assumptions on their head, and the generation born after World War II tumbled into adulthood under the banner "Don't trust anyone over thirty." Youth culture, drug culture, and the culture of protest became the new norms on campus.

Jane Jacobs was a pungent addition to this intellectual stew. Here was a mother who left her country of birth to protect her teenaged sons from the draft; a wife prepared to challenge the basic tenets of her architect husband's profession; a thinker turned social activist; and a lay journalist destined to transform the teaching of urban studies, planning, architecture, economics, political theory, and more.

That Jacobs fit comfortably into the university scene in 1968 only reinforces how radical her insights were a decade before. Yet Jacobs' vantage point couldn't have been more conservative. She took people at their word and held them accountable for their actions. She had a straightforward need to believe and felt betrayed by the abuse of power.

What was new was how Jacobs applied these values to the design of cities. Jacobs began from her own experience, from her own response to the environment around her. Some spaces were inviting, others distancing; some streets animated, others lifeless; some materials comforting, others oppressive. Just as McLuhan and Frye wrote about how to decode advertising and literature, Jacobs began to write about how to decode cities. She helped us see that roads and buildings and streetscapes encapsulated information, and that this information played an active part in how people defined themselves and the world around them. Cities communicated meaning.

As simple as this—the application of semiotics and phenomenological principles to cities—may seem today, Jacobs drew a conclusion that was anything but simple: if a city's built form impacts all who pass through it, then all who pass through have a vested interest in the decisions that underlie how the city is built. The end users of a new building or road or subdivision are not simply the landlords or primary occupants, but virtually anyone who comes in contact with the space. To Jacobs, design was political.

Jacobs' writings empowered citizens by shifting the analytical point of view from that of the owner to that of the user, from the drafting table to the sidewalk, from the block to the street. The perspective was no longer that of a low-flying airplane looking down, but of someone standing firmly on the ground looking up. The pedestrian ruled.

From her own experience, Jacobs knew that what pedestrians valued was ease of movement, comfort, security, stimulation, entertainment, a sense of well-being, and the company of others. She saw through class stereotypes in recognizing that working-class neighborhoods were safer and livelier than elite residential enclaves. She championed diversity, and the importance of making room for the "other."

All of this came back to me with surprising clarity when, thirty years later, I found myself heading a large capital development project in downtown Toronto. I was working at Canada's National Ballet School at the time, and soon after my arrival I launched an initiative to triple the School's physical plant from 80,000 to 250,000 square feet. The project entailed the reuse of several nineteenth-century heritage buildings tied together by new infill construction. It covered two city blocks and was designed in tandem with a private condominium development of two high-rise towers and a block of townhouses. Fifteen years would pass from the time I issued the first request for proposals to the opening of the final phase of the project.

Even before the capital project, Jacobs was a conscious part of how I approached my work at the School. One of my earliest observations was how fearful the staff were of outsiders. Drugs and prostitution were big issues in the neighborhood, but rather than asserting control of the street, the School seemed to be turning inward. This made no sense to me in the context of how Jacobs described healthy communities, and I did everything I could to turn the School's energies around to assert its presence on the block. This was not without controversy. When I erected signage outside the front door for the first time in the School's thirty-year history, some staff members told me that if any students were molested I would be held personally responsible.

When the corner restaurant applied for permission to open an outdoor patio, a neighbor rushed to get my signature opposing the application. She pointed out that the patio would be in direct line of sight of the School's residence, where upwards of a hundred children between ten and seventeen lived for eleven months a year. Imagine her surprise when I flatly refused, pointing out that the outdoor patio would finally provide the eyes on the street that were so sorely needed to stabilize the block.

It seemed natural, then, to fall back on Jacobs when I framed my thinking about how the School's larger capital project should unfold. I worked with a large team of consultants, including two brilliant architectural firms—Goldsmith, Borgal & Company, who specialized in heritage preservation and did the master plan for the project, and Kuwabara Payne McKenna Blumberg (KPMB) Architects, who designed the new ballet training facilities that branded the project and integrated the site. I was the client, however, and I knew that without a strong set of underlying principles, I would never be able to provide the leadership needed to hold the project together.

One of my first breakthroughs came when I directed the architects to create a design that would not simply contain the organization's program, but advance its mission. Once expressed, this statement provided a framework for an endless number of subsequent decisions. It freed me from worrying about aesthetics (what the final product would look like) and allowed me to focus on outcomes (what it would achieve).

While many instances like this played out, a couple of examples are especially worth citing. Early on, we made a conscious decision to push the tension between heritage buildings and new design. We were building a home for one of the leading ballet training institutions in the world, and in ballet, as in architecture, there is an ongoing dialogue between yesterday and today, between classical traditions and more contemporary concerns. What better way to reflect the currency of this debate than through the physical space itself, making visible how the past and the future can comfortably coexist. We put as much energy into revitalizing the heritage buildings as we did into designing the new, even using the choice of furniture as an opportunity to juxtapose centuries.

I also insisted on design solutions that would allow visitors to decode the values of the organization from the way space was laid out, to learn about the National Ballet School, as it were, by "reading" the buildings. At the center of the new training facility, in a large open space called the town square, we positioned the School cafeteria. It was the first thing one would encounter after passing through the reception area, and its intended message was clear: here is a place where students are nourished. It is a place where visiting parents and siblings can relax and have a snack, and where staff and students can interact informally throughout the day. It is only upon deeper reflection that one realizes how intentionally provocative the placement of food services is within an institutional culture long associated with eating disorders.

All of us on the team went to great pains to ensure that the design served the primary users of the space and not simply the design professionals or the landlord, but in the best Jacobs tradition, we went much further. Knowing that we were designing for children as well as adults, we pushed the notion that built form should be giving—one is tempted to say forgiving—in its relationship to the user. We rejected the notion of "back space" for any part of the facility to be used by students, including those spaces not on public view, and demanded that finishes and materials meet the same standards throughout. When conceiving the exterior of the buildings, we promoted the citizenry as end user, and insisted that all external perspectives be treated as the "front."

The architects came with a vision that prioritized the design of connective tissue rather than primary organs, of spaces linking specialized functions—stairways, corridors, foyers, thresholds—rather than containing them. This was music to my ears, consistent as it was with the priority Jacobs placed on the street, the ultimate in connective tissue.

Glazing can be harsh or it can be invisible; it can push you away or draw you in. The architects chose design strategies to achieve a visual fluidity that pulled the city in and let the program out. The most dramatic example is the series of three stacked studios suspended above a busy commuter street, each two stories tall, that give dancers the illusion that they are soaring over the city, and offer passersby brief glimpses of one of the world's great art forms. But quieter examples also abound, from extended internal vistas to intimate garden views.

I lived with this project for so many years that is hard for me to reconstruct at which point I stumbled upon each particular insight. One of the lead architects, however, had such a singular epiphany tied to Jacobs' legacy that I can't resist recounting it here. When the firm of KPMB joined the project, the master plan was essentially in place. KPMB's challenge was to bring that master plan to life by designing a new training facility that would wrap around an 1856 mansion and connect a number of heritage properties at each end of the site. KPMB, with a strong international reputation for contemporary infill, was ideally suited to the assignment, and they did not disappoint.

KPMB's designs complemented the adjacent condominium development with a counterpoint of strong vertical and horizontal forces that was nothing short of musical. The two developments were seamlessly integrated through form, function, and finishes, and the new designs echoed the scale and sensibility of the heritage buildings with a sensitivity that was anything but ordinary. Yet despite the quality of their work, the architects at KPMB seemed somewhat reserved in their enthusiasm, even omitting the project from a new book they published during the period. Something was missing.

Then one morning, when the construction approached the halfway point, one of the lead KPMB architects called me, highly agitated, to tell me that something important had happened. While touring some visiting architects from Paris, he had driven them by the School on route to another destination. To his great surprise, the visiting architects were enormously excited by what they saw. They could think of no design precedent in Europe, they told him, and pumped him full of questions about where his inspiration had come from.

This peer feedback came as a revelation. Rather than viewing the design simply as infill, he saw the project through his colleagues' eyes—from the perspective of the street. It was as though Jane Jacobs had taken him by the hand and led him from the drawing board to the side-walk. The larger streetscape took shape before his eyes, and he could hardly believe that its bigger significance had eluded him. The thought struck him that this may well turn out to be his signature project.

As subsequent events would attest, his European colleagues were not crazy. In 2007 the American Institute of Architects recognized the project with an Award of Excellence, only the fourth time a Canadian project had been so honored. In 2008 the project was awarded the highest design honor in Canada, a Governor General's Medal in Architecture, and was one of the five recipients of a Global Award for Excellence from the U.S.-based Urban Land Institute (the other four were in Amsterdam, Beijing, Portland, and Tokyo).

Perhaps closest to the spirit of Jacobs, the project was recognized as "Best in Show" in the 2005 Pugly Awards, a people's choice online competition in Toronto to select the best and worst new building of the year. When I left the School to head the Canada Council for the Arts, the architects celebrated the event by giving me a pair of cufflinks in the shape of miniature pugs.

"'Sometimes he makes things happen...'"

"It's a quotation," I replied.

"Yes, but what does it mean?"

One of the new National Ballet School buildings is fronted by a large plane of glass suspended above the ground at a slight angle to the sidewalk. This vertical plane, almost four stories tall, features a design embedded in the glass using an enamel baking process called ceramic frit.

Architects most often use frit glass to cut down on solar transmission, but in this case the application is decidedly artistic. While part of the glass is left blank, most of it is covered by a repeated series of markings, some large, some small, with handwritten script below. The markings look at first glance like musical notes on a five-line staff. Below the staff, the handwritten script reads: "Sometimes he makes things happen, sometimes things happen to him."

The treatment was deliberately designed to provoke questions: Is that music on the windows? What do the words say, and why are they there? The answer to each triggers ever more questions, and a narrative unfolds that ultimately leads to an awareness of what goes on in the buildings behind those windows.

The design is not music at all, but dance notation in the hand of a graduate of the National Ballet School named Peter Ottmann. It records a variation from Act I of *The Nutcracker* choreographed in 1995 by James Kudelka, also a graduate of the National Ballet School. The choreography was created less than a hundred yards away on the stage of the theater named after one of the National Ballet School's founders, Betty Oliphant. It was first set on principal dancer Jeremy Ransom, also a graduate of the National Ballet School, and captures a sequence in which his character entertains children, played on stage by National Ballet School students. The handwritten script below the notation is a verbal direction from the choreographer to the dancer, to the effect that sometimes the character is to appear to be in control of things, and other times not.

The design fulfills many functions: it entertains, it animates, it provokes. It is permanent and ephemeral at the same time. It transforms the street into a performance space, it triggers the active engagement of the viewer, and it invites the outsider in.

Built form as an embodiment of storytelling: pure Jane Jacobs.

"That's an amazing story," my visitor said. "You should write it down." And so I did.

4.3

STEPS TOWARD
A JUST METROPOLIS

Chester Hartman

I THINK OF JANE JACOBS as the consummate advocacy planner—
a concept and term launched in 1965 by lawyer and planner Paul
Davidoff with the publication of his classic "Advocacy and Pluralism in
Planning" in the *Journal of the American Institute of Planners* (subsequently
renamed *The Journal of the American Planning Association*). Paul challenged
the traditional notion and practice of planning, dominated by the physical
dimension and bearing the conceit of "public interest" as the motivation
and thrust of planners' works. He pointed to the significance of the social
and political dimensions of planning, and showed clearly the class bias
of much of the profession's work—notably at the time the impact of the
urban renewal program, which was destroying neighborhoods peopled
by poor and minority residents to the advantage of upper-income housing, high-end offices and retailers, convention centers, dining and entertainment facilities, and other elements of urban life for the largely
white middle and upper classes. From his lawyerly perspective, Davidoff
proposed that, in addition to recognizing and acknowledging the realities of urban planning as then practiced, planners of a more progressive
bent should begin to work for the interests of those communities and
populations being harmed by the work of traditional planners, and should
openly describe themselves as playing an advocacy role.

Advocacy planning has, over the decades, become an accepted (left)
wing of the profession. Influenced by Jane's work—and by my own deep
involvement, as a graduate student, in the National Institute of Mental

Health-funded study of the impact of bulldozer-style urban renewal on the 7,500 residents of Boston's West End, a classic Jacobean neighborhood (also portrayed in Herb Gans' *Urban Villagers*)—I initiated, from San Francisco where I relocated in 1970, The Planners Network. At first this was simply a communications/support vehicle (via a periodic newsletter) for social justice-oriented planners, and has henceforth morphed into a formal organization housed at Cornell University with nationwide membership, regular e-communications, an annual conference, and since 2002 a quarterly magazine, *Progressive Planning*. A related professional organization is Architects/Designers/Planners for Social Responsibility (ADPSR), dominated by the first-named profession, and with presence in several cities as well as a formal role at the American Institute of Architects conferences. Furthermore, the Association of Collegiate Schools of Planning (ACSP) recently recognized a formal sub-entity, Planners of Color Interest Group (POCIG), which supports and mentors minority academics in the planning field, creates an identifiable perspective among academic planners, and also organizes events at the annual conferences of the Association of Collegiate Schools of Planning.

Jane motivated and inspired a great many people, and helped to organize them, but I think of her largely as an individual force, not part or builder of an organization. However, her example and the Davidoff article were a very big deal for many of us, leading us to create organizations. In the Boston area, a small, interestingly heterogeneous group—including an architect, a lawyer, a sociologist, an anthropologist, a planner, a transportation expert, and a psychologist, most with full-time academic positions—decided to formalize some of our individual work as Urban Planning Aid (UPA), a planning "firm" making its services available (free of charge) to community groups threatened by highway, urban renewal, and other public as well as public/private plans. Our aim was to analyze the impact of such plans, critique them and, as necessary, propose alternative plans that would benefit, or at least not harm, those communities. Shortly before that, a similar group in New York—Architects Renewal Committee in Harlem (ARCH), started by the recently deceased architect Max Bond—had led the way, as did the work of Walter Thabit in New York's Lower East Side. UPA worked with black neighborhoods in the Roxbury and South End areas of Boston, fighting off destructive "renewal" plans, critiquing their impact on working-class neighborhoods and local jobs/businesses, and organizing to successfully stop the proposed Inner Belt highway from splitting Cambridge in half (as well as damaging adjacent towns). Jane Jacobs-like, I organized an open letter to state and federal highway officials ("Do We Need the Inner Belt?"), published in *The Boston Globe* and signed by no less than 528 MIT and Harvard professors, including such big names as John Kenneth Galbraith, Derek Bok, Samuel Huntington, Noam Chomsky, Bernard Malamud, Edward Banfield, and Daniel Patrick Moynihan (who personally delivered the petition to Transportation Secretary Alan Boyd in Washington). The use of big names to publicize issues and influence decision-makers was very much in the Jacobs mode, and is replicated in similar current efforts.

Interestingly, Jane did not directly relate much to universities (other than frequent guest lectures), but others and I began to bring the advocacy approach into graduate curricula in the relevant fields and write about it. I also helped produce a formal statement, signed by well-known and respected MIT and Harvard planning faculty and other practicing professionals speaking in the name of the Boston chapter of the American Institute of Planners, to oppose the destruction of a small enclave of homeowners in the Allston section of Boston, right across the Charles River from Cambridge and quite near Harvard's Soldiers Field stadium—all being done to reward one of the mayor's developer friends, who planned a luxury high-rise apartment building in its place. Largely as a result of my work with UPA and these related projects, I was invited to join the City & Regional Planning faculty at Harvard. I accepted the offer, immediately creating a student version of Urban Planning Aid, the Urban Field Service, as an alternative to the traditional "studios." Graduate student teams assisted community groups with a wide range of problems, often having more than just Harvard planning students: MIT planning students, Harvard law, divinity, and public health students. Such "real-world" options, sometimes mandatory, are now formal classes in many, if not most, planning programs. My occasional teaching gigs in recent years—at Columbia and University of North Carolina—involve student projects to assist community groups, *à la* UPA and Urban Field Service. At Columbia, the class I organized worked for the tenants association of a public housing project in Manhattanville, just north of the university. At UNC, we worked with a small, tight-knit black community in Durham (a miniurban village), successfully fighting off the state's plan to convert it into a highway exchange, and in the process developed a plan, later implemented, to strengthen the community. Following the Gulf Coast hurricanes, a number of planning "studios" involved work in New Orleans—Cornell, MIT, Pratt Institute, and Harvard being among the leaders.

One firm prediction is that concerns of social justice and racial fairness will occupy ever more established places in the planning profession—graduate education, professional associations (the American Planning Association has minority planners divisions), conferences, and academic as well as more popular publications. A quite recent development is the Right to the City movement, stressing protection of low-income and minority residents of cities as they face displacement from various market forces and government programs, and loss of essential services. With nodes in eight regions throughout the country, the emphasis is on grassroots organizing, supported by sympathetic academics and, occasionally, by the staff of official planning agencies. Community organizing entities such as ACORN, the Midwest Academy, National Training and Information Center, Industrial Areas Foundation, US Action, PICO, Wellstone Action, and others provide training, funding, and support for work of this type. Not unrelated is the stirrings of a "right to housing" movement—see the volume I co-edited with Rachel Bratt and Michael Stone, *A Right to Housing: Foundation for a New Social Agenda* (Temple University Press, 2006), especially its contributions on the broader economic environment for housing, affordability standards, the housing finance system, organizing, social ownership and financing, rural concerns, the special needs of women and the elderly, racial segregation/discrimination, and the role of the courts. (Regarding race and racism issues—an area Jane paid insufficient attention to, in my view—I urge readers to consult *The Integration Debate: Competing Futures for American Cities* [Routledge, 2010], the set of essays by leading scholars and activists in the field sociologist Gregory Squires and I assembled for a 2008 conference at the John Marshall Law School in Chicago.)

It remains something of a question whether the judicial system will be a progressive force on these issues. The late David Bryson and Florence Roisman put forth an important analysis of this element of our government in their chapter, "The Role of the Courts and a Right to Housing," in the above-mentioned *A Right to Housing* volume. My own experience after moving to San Francisco to join the staff of the National Housing Law Project, then housed at the University of California-Berkeley Law School, is that litigation (something Jane rarely resorted to) can be very effective. The Law Project was co-counsel with San Francisco Neighborhood Legal Assistance Foundation in a West End-like situation, the Yerba Buena Urban Renewal Project in downtown San Francisco, home to some 4,000 mainly elderly white male residents living in single room occupancy hotels. Like the West End—where the aim was to replace the tenements with upscale high-rise housing with a view of the Charles River—the motive was to change the entire South of Market Street area, expanding the city's growing financial/commercial/tourist district. Like the West End, exaggerated, distorted, and damaging characterizations of the residents were propounded (Redevelopment Agency head Justin Herman—the West Coast version of Robert Moses—was quoted as saying, "The land is too valuable to permit poor people to park on it.") The residents had inexpensive housing (rare in the area), in a flat part of the otherwise hilly city, with close access to inexpensive restaurants, secondhand shops, and other support services. The "hotels" themselves were minicommunities housing people who knew and took care of each other. Desk clerks were quasi-social workers, performing all manner of services for the residents. The lobbies were round-the-clock gathering spots. (The Agency, in a move calculated to destroy this sense of community and prompt early move-outs, removed comfortable lobby seats, withheld services, and replaced the desk clerks with unfeeling, unhelpful employees.) Like the West End, there was little to be done to stop the bulldozer: the Moscone Convention Center, luxury hotels, high-rise office buildings, fancy shops, and restaurants now are SOMA—the South of Market "neighborhood." But at least the residents, lots of whom were former union members, formed their own organization (TOOR—Tenants & Owners in Opposition to Redevelopment) and got Legal Service lawyers to mount effective countermoves and litigation. They successfully sued to stop the displacement process as a clear violation of federal law—the first time a court had ever done that—and, guided by an excellent, sensitive federal judge, Stanley Weigel, secured a consent decree that produced four well-designed permanently affordable developments scattered throughout the project area, with a total of 963 units, all developed/managed by TODCO, TOOR's housing arm. (For details, see my book *City for Sale: The Transformation of San Francisco*, University of California Press, 2002.)

A very recent court case I was involved in as an expert witness was heart-warming with regard to what the legal system can provide by way of protecting communities. It involved a large trailer park—Duroville— in Riverside County, California, on Indian reservation land, home for up to 6,000 people, mainly agricultural workers (population figure variable, related to seasonality). Due to poor, irresponsible management, which has produced extremely serious health and safety conditions for the residents, the Bureau of Indian Affairs sought to empty the park through the eviction process, rather than accept the renovation plan of California Rural Legal Assistance. I prepared a report on the likely results of displacing thousands of poor, minority families into an upscale housing market and testified at the trial. Shortly thereafter, the federal judge, Stephen Larson, issued a remarkable opinion, citing the importance of the strong community ties that existed there—the tribe is of Mexican origin, and they speak their own language—despite (perhaps, in response to) the poor physical conditions. Most gratifyingly, he referred to Duroville as a "village," perhaps picking up from my reference to the Gans book/concept in my testimony. An excerpt from this eloquent opinion:

> Duroville… is not a business, it is a village; thousands of our fellow human beings call the Park home. It is not nearly as safe or as healthy as we would want it to be; it is, nonetheless, home for a community of people who are poor, undereducated, disenfranchised, and, in many respects, exploited. The Court must also add that, despite these dis-

advantages, these very same people, based on evidence at trial, are an honest, hard-working, proud, colorful, and family-oriented community of people committed to educating their children and raising them to be productive and successful members of our society... Some are undocumented, some are resident aliens, and some are United States citizens; this complicated combination of immigration statuses places many of the residents of the Park at the crossroads of our Nation's incongruous immigration and agricultural policies that on the one hand portend that undocumented workers lack legal status, while at the same time predicating the economic efficiency of an agricultural industry on their hard work; it appears to the Court that we have, once again, established a rather "peculiar institution" to service our agricultural needs... The evidence at trial clearly established that to accede to the government's... request to promptly close the Park, without identifying where the vast majority of its residents would then live, would create a major humanitarian crisis. For the Court to close the Park under current conditions would create one of the largest forced human migrations in the history of this state. Unlike another forced migration in the state's history—the internment of Japanese citizens during World War II—there is not even a Manzanar for these residents to go... As unsafe and unhealthy as the Park may be... it nonetheless offers a shelter in place for a people who otherwise have nowhere to go.

Although the residents now can feel secure, the details of the CRLA rehabilitation plan still need to be worked out. With a new, Native American director of the Bureau of Indian Affairs (Larry EchoHawk), and a Senior Policy Advisor for Native American Affairs (a member of the Cherokee Nation) at the White House, things are clearly looking up at Duroville.

The new federal bureaucracy of course is an important piece of the immediate future. HUD appointments have been first-rate, as have those of the White House domestic staff—including for the first time a key Urban Affairs advisor and at least one terrific appointment (MIT planner Xavier deSouza Briggs) as Assistant Director for General Government Programs at the Office of Management and Budget.

SUMMING IT UP

So what does all this mean for today and the future? To me, one of the permanent lessons has to do with what it means to be and function as a professional, which has applicability far wider than just urban planning; it relates to doctoring and public health, education, the criminal justice system, the food system, lawyering, the sciences—every profession. Jane Jacobs was a great force in bringing about this more realistic, more helpful understanding and practice. Development and expansion of Planners Network-type organizations is terribly important, as well as the conscious introduction of efforts along these lines into professional education curricula and professional associations.

Another lesson, of course, is appreciation for neighborhoods, networks, social support, and social capital—the kind of work that has seen continuation in important writings such as those by Mindy Fullilove and her concept of "root shock," and which now is seeping into more sophisticated analyses of the costs, as well as the benefits, of idealistically motivated mobility programs such as HOPE VI and HUD's Moving to Opportunity efforts. With greater understanding of and respect for those living in communities across our metropolitan areas—people who are disproportionately poor, minority, and immigrants, and who consequently have less political power—we can begin to live up to our democratic credo. We need a lot more efforts to investigate realities and costs, to create social (and racial) impact statements of the likely results of planned efforts, particularly those involving government funds and powers. And we need more simple, direct *observation*. Possibly Jane Jacobs' greatest contribution in the way of investigative technique was to use her eyes, to be open to seeing everything in the surroundings without prejudgment or screening.

Clearly, the World Wide Web can play an important role in how we collaborate, organize, respond to threats to our neighborhoods and communities, and generally engage people to create better human settlements. In particular, we need to connect all of our systems, avoiding what has been labeled "the silo mentality." Housing, education, wealth creation, health, employment, the criminal justice system, and immigration all have important links to one another. Our professional work, research, activism, graduate training, professional associations, policy proposals, and programmatic work all must begin to make those connections. We will be far more effective in working toward social justice and making progressive change to the extent that we begin intentionally removing those silos.

Not until June 30, 2000, did I actually meet Jane Jacobs. We had lunch at her house in Toronto, arranged by our mutual friend David Gurin, a planner who, like Jane, had emigrated from New York City many years ago. It was of course a lovely and meaningful visit, one which emboldened me to ask her to write the foreword to *Between Eminence & Notoriety: Four Decades of Radical Urban Planning* (Rutgers Center for Urban Policy Research, 2002), the collection of some three dozen of my past articles. She at first politely declined—begging off by saying I really had no need for such a lead piece. But then she changed her mind. As she wrote in that foreword:

> I had just written him, declining… when I happened to receive a phone call from a reporter asking me for a quote on why middle-class people (her code word for whites) were returning to cities when a generation earlier they had fled cities as unfit places to live or bring up children. She was astonished when I told her that hundreds of thousands of middle-class people had been forced against their will to leave cities because their homes and businesses were demolished in the name of slum clearance and urban renewal, or their neighborhoods degraded and ruined by highway clearances. Nor was she aware that poor black ghettos do not locate themselves spontaneously; she knew nothing of financial redlining, social blockbusting, and planned pushing about of minority populations. By the time our conversation ended—she incredulous at my words, I incredulous at her innocence—I had made up my mind to crumple my letter to Chester and write him, instead, Yes, I want to put in my say that your book is needed, especially by people too young to have lived through the kinds of events it chronicles.

So, thank you, unidentified reporter. And thank you, Jane, for The Book, that lovely foreword to mine, and for your life…

ILLUMINATING GERMANY:

OBSERVATIONS ON URBAN PLANNING POLICIES IN THE LIGHT OF JANE JACOBS

Peter Zlonicky

IF WE OBSERVE the changes in planning policies and practice that have occurred in Germany in the last fifty years, we might think that politicians and planners have carefully read Jane Jacobs' *The Death and Life of Great American Cities*. Her observations and reflections on the "peculiar nature of cities" and the "conditions for city diversity" seem to be hidden guidelines for recent policies and practices. Since publication of the first edition of *The Death and Life* in 1961, we have witnessed profound changes in the German cityscape. What were German planning policies and practices at that time? And how is the situation today? What did we learn from Jacobs' book?

Reconstruction of German cities after World War II came to an end around 1963, the same year that the first translation of *The Death and Life of Great American Cities* appeared in Germany. At that time, politicians and planners were concentrating on the development of new towns following the British models. It was a period of hope. Creating new towns meant Germans might have a chance to avoid the typical problems of nineteenth-century cities: traffic congestion, insufficient housing, and social conflicts. After the disaster of Nazi planning ideologies, with their inhuman, big-scale urban politics, planners tried to refer to both the Bauhaus modernism and the International Style of the 1920s and 1930s. An outstanding example of the influence of modernism on planning practices during this era was the 1957 "Interbau" (International Building Exhibition) in Berlin, where German architects in exile like Walter Gropius were invited to create modern architecture in a new urban context, avoiding any memories of the city's past. Le Corbusier, too, was asked to realize another *"Unité d'habitation"*; since the scale and the splendid isolation of Le Corbusier's architecture could not be integrated in the urban context, the *Unité* was realized only at the fringes of the city. A second source of inspiration for planning practice was the revival of International Style, epitomized by the *Congrès International d'Architecture Moderne* (CIAM).

These earlier planning strategies had shared some common elements in their attempt at advancing the idea of the "functional city," overcoming the overcrowded, polluted, anti-social city of the nineteenth century, and reconnecting Germany with the international urban debate. Some basic tenets were:

- Replacing structures from the nineteenth and early twentieth century with modern structures;
- Separating residential and manufacturing area in the city space;
- Separating car traffic and pedestrian movement (the influence of car industry on city development was strong);
- Creating low density structures in new towns.

The "functional city" seemed to offer a solution to every problem traditional cities presented, and to disclose access to all aspects of modern life. However, at the time, some sociologists criticized the results of this "functional" urban development. The first was Edgar Salin, who in 1960 complained that the city of Basel had lost its rich urban life amidst the new urban structures. Alexander Mitscherlich criticized the inhospitable structures of the new cities in a short pamphlet titled "Die Unwirtlichkeit unserer Städte," published in 1965; his well-formulated opinion had a deep impact on public discussion. On a more scientific level, Hans Paul Bahrdt paid homage to some basic elements of traditional cities and to their clear separation and balance of public and private spaces in his pamphlet, "Die moderne Grossßtadt," published in 1961. But despite their articulate critique, these publications failed to affect planning policies.

The first German edition of Jacobs' book represented a break with mainstream planning policies. It stressed the value of public space, social contacts, lively streets, neighborhood relations, and the importance of density and complexity instead of monofunctional uses. The debate Jacobs ignited spread all over Germany, sparking discussions among planners and politicians alike. Even today, her observations and wisdom guide us as we deal with contemporary challenges.

The problems Germany faces today are numerous and even more complex than they were in 1963. The gap between rich and poor is growing, as well as social segregation in neighborhoods, with areas ridden with unemployment and poverty on one hand and privileged districts for the wealthy on the other. Future quality of life in cities depends to a large degree on how well the local governments will succeed in addressing the problems of unemployment and poverty. Urban design and architecture cannot concentrate exclusively on city centers,[1] but should contribute to the improvement of neglected neighborhoods suffering from architectural facelessness. Land and planning policies can provide these neighborhoods with a new identity, while actively working against social segregation.

However, urban planning should not be limited to these aspects. Other urban issues such as energy conservation and education reform can, and should, be part of the urban planning agenda. The challenge to address issues of environmental sustainability and the growing needs of an emerging and more diverse population demands the same sense of observation and response that Jacobs brought to bear on problems of the last century.

For example, the threats of climate change and the increasing scarcity and rising cost of energy resources—the latter fueling the danger of more energy wars—have gradually infiltrated public awareness. Little of this consciousness, however, can yet be noticed in the current planning of cities, traffic, and the built environment. The modernization

---

1. As opposed to the United States, in Europe the "inner city" has traditionally been home to the more affluent population, while lower-income and newer immigrant populations are relegated to the periphery of cities.

and retention of existing buildings to make them more energy-efficient could release vast, and until now unused, energy-saving potential. The conversion of our power industry to a decentralized energy industry with renewable sources is long overdue. These issues generate new criteria in urban design. For instance, clear preference should be given to rail-based public transport systems rather than highways. Similarly, redevelopment of our "brownfields" and the preservation and retrofitting of the existing built environment must take precedence over new development of the pristine and undeveloped green spaces outside the city.

In education, wealthy Germany lags far behind other, smaller European nations. So what does this have to do with urban development? Instead of waiting for the federal and state governments to agree on educational reform, cities should postpone expensive projects and focus instead on building and upgrading day-care centers and all-day schools within cities. We should also provide better training for women and men in educational professions and employ social workers to assist our youth. As cities compete to attract well-educated, young, affluent inhabitants, the important criterion for future generations will be the availability of a good, up-to-date education system, rather than elaborate entertainment centers.

Beginning in 2000, a fundamental shift in public debates on sustainable development and projected demographic changes occurred, propelling the creation of new urban development policies and initiatives. As a result, the German government raised the following questions for discussion and debate:[2]

- What constraints need to be overcome in order to further the development of our cities' potentials? How can the conditions for sustainable urban development be made more effective?

---

2. In Germany, unlike in the United States, "participation" takes place not through the civil society as much as through the political system. Germany has a multiparty parliamentary system wth proportional representation. Diverse and minority opinions are often reflected not through civic organizations, but rather through parlimentary debate and the cobbling together of governing coalitions at all levels of government—local, regional, and federal. For example, in order to get a ruling majority, a city administration might relegate the environmental portfolio to a member of the Green Party.

- What strategies will encourage competitive, strong, and vibrant cities, able to take responsibility for their urban regions and rural areas?
- How can a successful concept of the city be developed to safeguard future innovation, as well as offer social coherence and high-quality living and housing?
- How can a broad alliance of responsible stakeholders be consolidated, and municipal self-administrations strengthened?
- Which new partners can be won for long-term urban development strategies? What are the possible alliances? How can citizens in particular be better informed on urban development policy and motivated to actively participate in it?

In 2007, some recommendations were published in a document titled *Memorandum: Towards a National Urban Development Policy in Germany*. The Memorandum proposed participatory guidelines for creating new urban development and planning policies. Included was a recommendation that

> a campaign should be developed to raise public awareness of urban development options and to engage committed citizens and businesses in the planning process. It was felt that this participatory process should also be extended to partner countries in the European Union to foster regional collaboration. The proposed campaign comprises many projects, initiatives, conferences, publications, exhibitions, and partnerships.

In 2007 this led Germany to propose a common approach to urban development policies for the entire European Union. The ministers of all twenty-seven members of the EU signed a policy paper called the *Leipzig Charter on Sustainable European Cities*. While allowing for a recognition of the different historical, economic, social, and environmental backgrounds of European cities, the ministers of the various member states agreed upon common principles and strategies for urban development policy.

The main components of the Charter come together to create what we in Germany call a *Baukultur*. In the broadest sense of the word, *Baukultur* is the sum of all the cultural, economic, technological, social, and ecological aspects influencing the growth and evolution of cities. To accomplish this, the Charter suggests several ways to advance common goals, including:

- Integrating urban development policies throughout the European Union;
- Ensuring access to high-quality public space;
- Preserving architectural heritage;
- Modernizing infrastructure and increasing energy efficiency;
- Advancing innovation and education within a framework of lifelong learning;
- Integrating community-based, participatory processes among all stakeholders;
- Paying special attention to deprived neighborhoods.

Both the *Leipzig Charter* and the *Memorandum* are based on the "European City" model—the "genetic footprint" or "genius loci"[3] of cities in Europe. But a critical question remains: is the "European City" a viable model for future urban development? What are its characteristics? Are they associated with a specific type of city? Is there even such a thing as the "genetic footprint" of the European city?

In his book *Die Europäische Stadt* (2004), Walter Siebel, a renowned professor of sociology, specializing in regional and urban research at the Carl von Ossietzky University of Oldenburg, lists five main features of the "European City":

- A historically shaped place where civil society was able to evolve;
- A written history of hope and political and economic emancipation;
- A place characterized by particular lifestyles and by the experience of difference, as well as by the separation between public and private sphere;
- A shape and form that evolved over time, also as a result of planning;

---

3. The distinctive atmosphere or pervading spirit of a place.

- The regulatory influence of the welfare state, shaped by the values and the moral principles of urban stakeholders.

The European city is a place of constant transformation of its building stock, public infrastructure, commerce and service facilities, culture, and economic structures. It is in this *constant transformation* that the European city reveals its inner strength. In all its many different shapes and forms, the European city still retains its constituent features and remains distinguishable among the world's urban settlements. Therefore, can the European city provide a model for urban development? What does it do better than other urban models?

Transformation is a perpetual task. Reshaping and rebuilding our cities is the key challenge of the twenty-first century, the "urban age." The adaptive reuse of industrial and military infrastructure buildings has become commonplace: it creates economic opportunities, such as the possibility to start a recycling economy. Additionally, the reuse of old buildings can aid in preserving social milieus. With sustainable development projects such as Hamburg's Hafen City, with its Brownfields to Greenfields initiative, programs like From Backyards to Frontyards in industrial regions, and the re-urbanization of inner cities, current European planning experience is now internationally acclaimed, and reflects Jane Jacobs' ideas.

These transformations have a very positive impact on the job market, employment, and training. "Creative milieus" not only attract young people to the cities, but also trigger economically viable downstream projects or, as Jacobs described them, "spillovers." The practice of creating temporary uses of existing, underutilized areas helps to stabilize existing building stock as well as prepare for new uses in business and municipal activities. These hybrid *social infrastructure* facilities must be given a wider range of uses relevant to the city: an example here is the Community Learning Center initiative, thanks to which underutilized schools are now used several hours a day by a diverse population. It remains to be seen how buildings that shape the city's identity but are bordering on dereliction can be secured and made available for new, long-term uses. There are already promising examples of churches being used as extended public spaces, gaining a new significance as places for social interaction.

The issue of immigration and the growing diversity of the European city adds a new relevance and dimension to the discussion about the social infrastructure and the use of space in cities. While the benefits of immigration to Germany's national interests is evident, at the local level immigration still generates conflict, and without the proper social infrastructure it overburdens local communities. Stakeholders in marginalized neighborhoods must play a major role in addressing this matter, a fact that is not recognized widely enough. Often it is the migrants and their local, ethnic economies that help to keep these endangered neighborhoods alive and, like in the United States and elsewhere, contribute to the revitalization of the city itself.

Adaptability and the ability to regenerate are strong features of European urban districts. Citizens perceive the public spaces that characterize the European city as public property. It remains to be seen just how affordable housing can be upheld as an essential communal asset. Here, experience and insight gained with the Social City program[4] can provide guidelines for securing the quality of the European city and may provide lessons for cities in the United States and elsewhere.

That the regeneration of neighborhoods is a *permanent ongoing process* is now universally accepted in Germany. The European city seems capable of turning the transformation process into a benefit, rather than a loss. Public debates have contributed to making change acceptable and profitable. However, some questions still remain. Where is the Jane Jacobs of today who reminds us of the importance of human values in our cities, who knows how to overcome social and economic polarization, how to create education and hope for young people, how to build green cities, and how to rebuild public space and participation? Who has a vision for the decades to come?

---

4. The Social City program is an effort to catalyze an ongoing development process in a neighborhood based on a comprehensive—social, economic, and physical—approach to revitalization and regeneration. The process focuses on fighting spatial segregation and transforming marginalized and blighted areas into self-sufficient neighborhoods with a positive outlook for the future.

REVIVING CITIES

Jaime Lerner

J ANE JACOBS WROTE *The Death and Life of Great American Cities* in the aftermath of one of the greatest transitions in our history—a rapid and intensive process of urbanization that has now consolidated worldwide. But apart from the maze of disillusioned planning models, failing policies, and crumbling utopias, urbanizing areas were undergoing astounding transformations, which left behind a fantastic array of challenges and possibilities. It is necessary to embrace this legacy. It is in the cities that decisive battles for the quality of life will now be fought, and their outcomes will have a defining effect on the planet's environment and on human relations.

As a human construction, the city is more a structure of change than a model of planning, an instrument of economic policies, or a nucleus of social polarization. The soul of a city—the strength that makes it breathe, exist, and progress—resides in each one of its citizens. Jane Jacobs understood that. Through acute observation, she realized the power that relationships, diversity, cohesion, identity, and density have to shape, for better or for worse, the quality of the urban environment. And all of us who dedicate ourselves to the study and practice of cities should never forget that.

There is a widespread idea that most large cities and metropolises are misshapen agglomerations with little quality of life; chaotic and violent, they are the sites of an ongoing war. However, a more generous approach to our cities would allow us to understand that, instead of being problems, the influences that shape a city can provide opportunities for innovative solutions. We perform at our best when we focus our energies not on the shortcomings of a current situation, but on its possibilities of positive transformation.

Behind every big transformation there is a small transformation. Simple elements that are easily implemented are the seeds of a more complex system in the future. Although we live at a time when events happen at a galloping pace and information travels in a blink, the decisions regarding urban problems are postponed due to a systematic lack of synchrony with the speed of the events. To start at all is to innovate! Imagine the ideal, but do what is possible today. Solutions for twenty or thirty years ahead are pointless, because by then the problems will probably be different. The future will require new ways of thinking. Therefore, we need urban policies that can effect change now. The present belongs to us, and it is our responsibility to open paths. We cannot burden future generations with problems created by our own.

Those responsible for managing a city must keep their eyes on the future and their feet firmly grounded in the present. Those who focus solely on the daily needs of the population will jeopardize the prospects of their city. On the other hand, those who think only about the future, disregarding the daily demands, will lose the essential support of their constituents and will not accomplish anything.

It is necessary, then, not to lose track of the essence of things; to discern within the complex flow of information available today what is fundamental and important to a city's ongoing health; and to distinguish the strategic from the daily demands. A clear understanding of future objectives is the best guide for present action, one that allows us to connect the present with a future idea. As Jane Jacobs already pointed out, is the progress that only promotes an increase in scale without considering improvements in quality, accessibility, and identity truly human?

The increase of demand in growing cities has been routinely met with increases in scale. Urban problems have been described as quantitative: an "excess" of people and a lack of resources. In the case of urban congestion, for instance, this simplistic line of thought suggests that if there were more money, we could address the increasing demands of automobiles by appropriating more areas and building more and bigger overpasses, and everything would be solved.

In fact, a more human city provides its inhabitants with a decent range of housing options and an appropriate infrastructure; good conditions for traffic circulation, through a coherent network of streets and an efficient public transportation system; and ample possibilities of employment, both in terms of accessibility and in terms of wealth generation. A more human city fulfills not only objective needs, but also subjective ones, such as access to information or leisure opportunities. A more humane city doesn't have to be bigger or smaller: it only needs to be a city where people have a place.

For instance, in the late 1960s the downtown area of Curitiba, Brazil, was facing serious congestion problems and the degradation of its old historic buildings. In my first term as mayor, we took a bold initiative: we decided to close one of the busiest downtown streets to traffic and to create the first pedestrian mall in Brazil. The project had to be realized quickly, for there was opposition from retailers, who believed the initiative would push customers away. Indeed, the opposite happened: the response of the population was so enthusiastic that the retailers' representatives asked the city to extend the mall. We created a new identity for the revived Rua XV de Novembro, dubbed "Rua das Flores": we put in place a new set of especially designed urban furniture and planted flower beds—and no matter how many flowers people took home each day, we replanted them, until people understood that those flowers were part of the streetscape and let them be. On the weekends, kids and their parents would take art supplies—brown paper, brushes, and paint—and enjoy themselves together for hours. In time, the shops renewed their façades, and subsequently the historic buildings were renovated as well. The Rua das Flores, with its coffee shops, newsstands, shoe shiners, mimics, and posh and simple shops, regained its place as the beating heart of the city, where people could gather to gossip or debate politics or make art: a true open-air living room for Curitiba.

If the city is the essence of society, the street is the essence of the city. Analyzing the North End streets in Boston, or Hudson Street in

New York, Jacobs highlighted a paramount aspect of good urban life: the street integrates people and urban functions, and is the core of co-existence. The street is where all cities begin, and has to be the path to the future as well. Those who don't understand the street in its plenitude cannot understand the soul of a city. As Jacobs wrote in *Death and Life of Great American Cities*, "Streets and their sidewalks—the main public places of the city—are its most vital organs" (Jacobs 1961, 37).

My strongest hope resides in the speed of transformation. Demographic projections based on the high birthrates of twenty or thirty years ago have not been confirmed, shading a more encouraging light over the next years and decades. Renewable energy sources, less pollutant automobiles, and new means of public transportation and communication are mitigating the chaos that had been predicted for large urban centers. The evolution of technology and its democratization offer new perspectives to cities of all sizes and shapes.

In terms of physical configuration, the cities of the future will not differ significantly from the ones we know now. What will differentiate the good city of the future will be its capacity to reconcile its citizens with nature. Socially just and environmentally sound cities—that is the quest! In dealing with economic and environmental issues, this quest will foster an increasingly positive synergy between cities, regions, and countries. The lack of resources is no longer an excuse not to act. Still, a certain sense of urgency is vital to the transformation of our cities. The idea that action should only be taken after all the answers and the resources have been found is a sure recipe for paralysis. The planning of a city is a process that always allows for corrections; it is supremely arrogant to believe that planning can be done only after every possible variable has been controlled.

Sometimes, when the solution is not in space, it can be in time. To that end, we are designing in Curitiba the "Portable Street." Inspired by the *bouquinistes* of Paris, this piece of urban furniture made of fiberglass or metal can comfortably accomodate street vendors, adding a new element to the urban landscape. It is an "itinerant acupuncture:" it can be set up in areas that need an injection of life at night, for instance, when regular shops are closed. Formal and informal sectors can share the same space at different times for everyone's benefit: the keyword is coexistence.

A city has to be a mixture of functions, income levels, and age groups. The more you mix these elements, the more human, the safer, the healthier the city will be. Every city has a particular design related to its history, which may be hidden under the layers of the natural and built environments. There is a strange archeology that connects in time ancient paths and buildings, meeting points and references—all that has been dear to the city's life—and gives them a new meaning. Once this underlying design is discovered, it can be consolidated through mass transportation and land-use policies and articulated along the streets. This vision will define the pattern of growth of the city.

Biodiversity is a concept that also applies to human beings— intended as "sociodiversity." As in the natural environment, isolated "fragments," however diverse, cannot create the synergy that only comes from interaction. The proliferation of gated communities and of segregated and poorly served neighborhoods, for example, derives from a compartmentalized understanding of the city, to the detriment of all. The integration of functions and the mixture of incomes are beneficial to the whole. Democratic process demands that all strata of the population participate in the making of the city. The integration of diversity and the coexistence of multiplicity are therefore the most crucial goals for those striving to reach a more humane urban environment.

I believe there are three imperative issues that need to be addressed when establishing the priorities of a city's future: *mobility, sustainability, and identity*.

In terms of mobility, the future is on the surface. Entire generations cannot be sacrificed to the wait for a subway line, while a complete network of surface transportation can be set up in less than two years. The key to mobility resides in the combination and integration of all systems: subway, bus, taxi, cars, and bikes. However, these systems cannot compete on the same space. People will select the most convenient combination according to their own needs and travel with a "mobility card." All providers and operators of the different transportation services mode will work in partnership. For instance, in 1974 we started the Integrated Mass Transit System of Curitiba, with a twenty-kilometer axis of dedicated lanes transporting 25,000 passengers per day. The bus companies that operated independently in the city were involved as partners in the decision process. A co-responsibility equation was created, in which the city provided some infrastructure (the dedicated lanes and bus terminals, for example), established itineraries, and set and collected the fare. The companies were responsible for the fleet and its operation (adjusted to new comfort parameters) and were paid back per kilometer traveled. In time, we were able to consolidate a single-fare system that now transports daily over 2.2 million passengers in Curitiba and its metropolitan region along over eighty kilometers of dedicated lanes.

Regarding sustainability, the main idea is to focus on what we know about the problem, instead of what we don't know. And, above all, it is necessary to transfer this knowledge to children, who will then teach their parents. Although the use of basic construction materials such as cement, metal, glass, wood, and plastic in a sustainable manner can help improve the situation, it is in the overall conception of cities that the largest and most significant contribution to a more sustainable society can be made.

Children can be taught how simple, everyday actions are interconnected: for instance, how each one can contribute to a more sustainable environment by reducing the use of the automobile, living closer to work or bringing the work closer to home, saving the maximum and wasting the minimum, and separating the garbage. Sustainability is an equation between what is saved and what is wasted. Therefore, if sustainability = saving/wasting, when wasting is zero, sustainability tends to infinity. Waste is the most abundant source of energy.

A sustainable city cannot afford the luxury of not using districts and streets with good infrastructure and services. Its downtown area cannot remain idle during great portions of the day: it is necessary to fill it up with the functions that are missing. The "24-hour city" and the multiple-use infrastructure are essential to sustainability.

Finally, identity. Identity is a major factor in the quality of life; it represents the synthesis of the relationship between individuals and their urban habitat. Identity, self-esteem, and a feeling of belonging: all of them are closely connected to the points of reference people have in their own city. These are not limited to architectural heritage. Rivers, for instance, are important landmarks. Thus, instead of hiding them from view or burying them in concrete, cities should establish riverbanks as valuable territories. By respecting the natural drainage characteristics, cities can make sure the preserved areas provide necessary relief channels for episodic flooding, and still be used most of the time for recreation in an economically and environmentally appropriate way. Parks can work according to a similar logic, providing territories that people can relate to, and interact with.

Historical districts are also major reference points; however, these areas often suffer a process of devaluation and degradation. Finding ways to keep these districts alive by connecting identity elements, recycling outdated uses, and hosting a mix of functions is vital. Have the "old" coexisting with the "new": before tearing a building down, consider new possibilities of use. "Recycling" is to provide an old building with a new cultural content. As Jacobs wisely wrote in *Death and Life of Great American Cities:*

> The district, and indeed as many of its internal parts as possible, must serve more than one primary function; preferably more than two. These must insure the presence of people who go outdoors on different schedules and are in the place for different purposes, but who are able to use many different facilities in common. (Jacobs 1961, 196)

Once the scenario and priorities are set, we have to make it happen, and to make it happen quickly. For that, it is necessary to thwart a "triple trap": we have to avoid our own bureaucracies, our own political problems, and our own insecurities. Strategic, timely interventions can release new energy and help consolidate it toward the desired goals. This is what I call "urban acupuncture": it revitalizes an "ailing" or "worn out" area and its surroundings through a simple touch in a key point. Just as in the medical procedure, this intervention will trigger positive chain reactions or "spillovers," as Jacobs described them, which will help to heal and enhance the whole system.

Many cities today need urban acupuncture because they have neglected their cultural identities; others because they have neglected their relationship with the natural environment; still others have turned their backs on the wounds left by economic activities. These neglected areas, these "scar marks," are precisely the targets for the acupuncture.

A city is a collective dream. To build this dream is vital. Without it, there will not be the essential involvement of its inhabitants. It is crucial that those responsible for urban policies project an optimistic future scenario, so that the majority of the population will commit to it. To build this dream, this scenario, is a process that acknowledges and welcomes the multiple visions that managers, inhabitants, planners, politicians, businesses, and civil society have of their city. It also demands a sharing of responsibilities by all actors involved. The more generous this vision, the more good practices will multiply and, in a domino effect, will constitute a gain in quality of life and solidarity.

Looking back at what Jane Jacobs wrote almost fifty years ago, it is amazing how relevant to the well-being of our cities her analysis remains and how, after all this time, it is still so hard to implement her ideas. As the ultimate human construct, cities are to be cherished. They are the refuge of solidarity. They can be the safeguards against the inhumane consequences of the globalization process; they can defend us from the challenges the latter poses to our identity.

On the other hand, the fiercest wars are happening in cities, in their marginalized neighborhoods, in the clash between wealthy and deprived ghettos; the heaviest environmental burdens are being generated there, due to our lack of empathy for present and future generations. And this is exactly why it is in our cities that we must progress toward a more peaceful and balanced planet.

REFERENCES

Jacobs, Jane. 1961. *The Death and Life of Great American Cities*. Modern Library Editions. New York: Random House, 1993.

Design for Nature,
Design for People

RECOGNIZING WHAT WORKS:

A CONSCIOUS EMULATION

OF LIFE'S GENIUS

Janine Benyus

J ANE JACOBS WAS a pattern recognizer, a patient heron of a woman who could stare at a stretch of ordinary life that experts had stepped over a hundred times. Cocking her head this way and that, she would watch and wait, tolerating degrees of ambiguity that would drive most observers to stab at early, and false, conclusions. With Jane, insights didn't come in bits and pieces, and they didn't come and go. Once revealed, her patterns held as obvious and as whole as a trout in the morning light.

But Jane's penchant for overarching patterns, for general truths, is not nearly as common in the exploratory arts as one would think. Young scientists, for instance, are deeply schooled in caution and critique, essential vertebrae of the scientific method. Rewards run to those who can disprove their colleagues' theories, and over the years, the average scientist spends far more time finding the exception to the rule than finding the rule itself.

You can imagine theories as birds flying over blinds of hunters stationed at each and every scientific meeting. The hunters shoot rounds of objections to the proposed rule, and whole rafts of shaky theories plummet from the sky. Those nearer the truth fly on, at least until the next conference or journal issue. Those who can see through seductive theories are cheered as heroes, and this encourages most of us to be shooters, not flyers. Debunkers, not Darwins.

But Jane was a flyer as well as a shooter, and in every intellectual culture, that takes courage. She found deep ubiquitous patterns in urbanism, architecture, planning, economics, and was hunting for them in biology as well. That's where our lives intersected. For fifteen years I had been writing books about organisms and the ecosystems that they inhabit, adapt to, and ultimately create. After five books, I was awash in examples of how organisms match and make their places: the sperm whales that change the relative density of their oil to dive deep; the edelweiss that avoids UV light with a network of fiber-optic leaf hairs; the thorny lizards that wrest water from the sand with capillary-embossed bellies; and everywhere, solar-harvesting leaves that can tilt to follow the sun, curl to release the wind's fury, and warn neighboring trees that a hungry caterpillar has landed.

But I also realized that biology's technological feats were best kept secrets outside specialized journals. There was no way for designers, engineers, architects, chemists, and city planners—the people who make our world—to easily and systematically access these wonders. I felt convinced that if they could study life's well-adapted designs, their questions about sustainable manufacturing, agriculture, chemistry, transportation, building, you name it, would be answered.

It made me wonder: Was there anyone consciously emulating life's patterns to solve human challenges?

A potent question can fertilize a book and start its dividing. This one led me to dozens of articles about leaf-inspired solar cells, spider-inspired fiber manufacture, prairie-inspired agriculture, and forest-inspired economies. I started to collect examples of nature's tutelage, first in a file folder, then a file drawer, then a whole cabinet. At that time, nature-inspired innovation was just beneath the surface: rising but yet unnamed. I dubbed the process "biomimicry," and motioned my readers over for a look. Jane, of course, was the very first person to arrive.

Jane called me out of the blue in the fall of 1997 and asked me to speak at a conference called "Ideas that Matter." "I'm giving your books as Christmas presents," she announced. I was dumbstruck to hear the voice of the woman who had taught me, at a distance, to write an honest sentence. As a budding writer, I had dissected her prose the way an admiring cabinetmaker touches the seams of fine joinery. In one of life's sweet turns, I got to thank her publicly during the first, trembling speech of my life.

The imaginary place that I conjured in my talk was a park bench where scientists and inventors sit together, unwrapping sandwiches and helping one another solve knotty problems. A wind turbine engineer looking for a way to increase blade lift would hear how humpback whales reduce turbulence with scalloped flippers. A vaccine manufacturer struggling to retard spoilage would learn how the resurrection plant suspends its processes for months without refrigeration. A cement manufacturer looking for a way to curb CO_2 emissions would learn how coral reefs form ceramics without kilns, absorbing CO_2 as their prime ingredient. The bench was a place of crosspollination, a metaphor for the diversity that Jane celebrated. Great cities, she taught us, are places of mingling that spawn innovation. They are estuaries between salt and fresh water, nurseries of new ideas.

Biomimicry was another ecotone of great promise, and I dreamt of ways to naturalize it in the culture so that biological knowledge could flow unimpeded into human systems' design. I wondered what might happen if the park bench really existed as a network of actual and virtual places where innovators could sidle up to biologists and ask, "How would nature solve this?"

In the meantime, inventors were thinking along the same lines. The phone began to ring the year the book came out, and innovation groups from companies like Interface, Patagonia, Nike, GE, HOK Architects, and Boeing asked whether I could send over some biologists to brainstorm with them, to tell them how life works. They were fascinated by the research in the book, but impatient about results. They wanted to do biomimicry in real time.

My next pivotal call came from Dayna Baumeister, a then doctoral candidate who would become my business partner in the Biomimicry Guild. She had read the book and glimpsed the outlines of a whole new career. "I want to do something that makes a difference," she said. "I don't want to spend my life studying one organism when the biosphere that supports all life is unraveling." I told her about the requests from inventors, and we began to dream of being "biologists at the design table."

Next thing we knew, we were in engineering labs, product design studios, and in city planning and architectural charrettes, talking about the creatures we loved more than anything else in the world. Innovators would ask questions that they had been trying to solve for years, and then listen, on the edge of their seats, as we told them about nature's well-adapted solutions. They were floored by life's deceptively simple designs: the hooks and barbules that zip up a bird's feather, or the bumps on a leaf that cause rainwater to ball up and lift away loose dirt. First there was envy—"Why didn't we think of that?"—and then a deepening regard, a whole new way of viewing and valuing the extraordinary organisms in their midst.

Our most gratifying moments happened outside, when designers met their mentors eye to eye. One of our first trips was to the Galapagos Islands, where wastewater treatment engineers sailed from island to island, snorkeling half the day and hiking the rest. At first they were not sure why their bosses had sent them on such a boondoggle. "We already do biomimicry," they protested, "We use bacteria to clean our wastewater!"

"That's a bioassisted technology," I explained, "using or domesticating an organism to help you produce something. It's as old as breeding cows for milk or using yeast to make bread."

They tried again: "We use orange-peel extract in our cleaning; surely that is biomimicry!" Not quite, I said, "That's bioutilization—harvesting an organism or its product—and that too has been around for millennia."

"What's new in biomimicry is what we're *not* doing. We're not domesticating the producer, nor are we extracting its product from the wild. Instead we're borrowing its idea, its blueprint, its recipe, its ecosystem strategy. Scientists are studying abalone, for instance, because its inner shell is twice as tough as anything we can make. Rather than harvesting or farming the abalone for its inner shell, we're making a kiln-free, layered ceramic ourselves. We're borrowing the abalone's design principle and mimicking its chemistry so that the organism can stay in the wild to teach us another day."

The engineers were still skeptical when we took our first hike on a shell-strewn beach. Flip-flopping over millions of shells, I asked them to give me one challenge that they were trying to solve. "We call it scaling," they said, "the mineral buildup that causes pipes to close up and clog." Their solutions—scouring with harsh toxins, digging up pipes, or using bigger pumps—caused problems of their own.

As a biologist, I'd never learned what the mineral buildup in pipes was composed of, nor had they, as engineers, learned what makes a seashell so tough. I scooped up a handful of shells and told them that this too was calcium carbonate—a curse to pipes, but housing to mollusks. "Shells crystallize out of seawater in a pattern choreographed by the mollusk," I told them. "First, the soft-bodied creature releases a protein scaffold studded with landing sites. Calcium and carbonate ions from the seawater settle on the sites and crystallize into layers. It's self-assembly, with no fire required."

It was a delicious moment, one that happens often in this field, when we realized that human design challenges are not so different from other organisms'. A shell crystallizing out of seawater is a form of scaling, directed by an organism that has perfected the process over millions of years. Finally, one of the engineers voiced the obvious question: "If shells crystallize automatically out of seawater, why don't they keep getting larger? What stops the scaling?" At that, all chatter stopped, and they all leaned in.

"In the same way that a protein starts the crystallization," I said, "the organism releases a stop protein that ends the crystallization by adhering to the growing face of the crystal. And there's a product you can purchase today that mimics this protein; it's called TPA, and it won this year's Presidential Award for Green Chemistry."

Well, that was it. From then on, I had to physically pluck them from their rapt snorkeling, and whistle them in from the islands. On all fours, exploring everything in site, twenty full-grown nature's apprentices were searching for answers: "How does nature aerate? How does nature move water without pumps? How does nature digest cellulose? Seal leaks? Reinforce cylindrical structures? Manage bacteria without creating resistance?"

I watched a quiet engineer named Paul stand motionless before a mangrove as if in deep conversation. He finally called me over and pointed: "This mangrove needs fresh water, but its roots are in saltwater, which means it somehow desalinates using only the sun's energy. No fossil fuels, no pumps. Do you know how we do it? We force water through a membrane at 900 pounds of pressure per square inch, trapping salt on one side. When it clogs, we apply more pressure, more energy."

Then Paul asked the question I've been working to solve ever since: "How is it that I, as a desalination engineer with a five-year degree and twenty-year experience, never once learned how nature strips salt from water?"

Jane believed that there was really only one body of knowledge, and that our pursuit of separate silos was illusionary. She would have loved what we do. Today, biomimicry is a design discipline with thousands of practitioners worldwide. If you google biomimicry or its synonyms, you get 28 million pages. There are centers for biologically inspired design, where engineers learn how nature adheres, distributes fluids, manages tensile stresses, communicates, senses, computes, and more. The worldwide patent database is filling with new innovations that owe a debt to chameleons and octopi and butterflies. Richard Bonser's survey of the worldwide patent database showed that in the twenty years between 1985 and 2005, patents with bio-inspired or biomimetic in their names increased by a factor of 93, against a background rate of 2.7 for all patents.

The flow structures needed to move biological insights into design are beginning to take shape. Tools such as the Biomimicry Institute's AskNature.org are now online, giving innovators a way to search by function through thousands and someday millions of life's best ideas. In addition to organizing the world's biological literature by function, the website is a matchmaker, bringing biologists and engineers together at last. The next generation of biomimics is also on their way. Schoolteachers can download Biomimicry Institute curricula, professionals can take a two-year certificate course, and several universities are offering biomimicry as a minor for designers, engineers, architects, economists, and other world-makers.

The real story is who is now practicing biomimicry and why. In the decades prior to 1990, most biomimicry research was funded by the military and space agencies like NASA. Penguins and dolphins and bats provided models for weapons and rockets and stealth radar. But lately that equation has shifted, with companies and communities using bio-mimicry not to wage warfare or to leave earth's orbit, but to keep everything alive on our first home. The number one question consultees ask is how they can be as sustainable as nature in their products, processes, and even policies.

Some of the answers lie in individual technologies borrowed from the champion adaptors in any environment. In sun-scorched places, architects are mimicking the pleats of a self-shading cactus to reduce a building's cooling needs. In places prone to soil-robbing monsoons, engineers are mimicking the root structures of plants, adding a horizontal dimension to their foundations.

Building skins are becoming more life-like, with dye-based solar cells inspired by photosynthesis, lotus-inspired paints that clean themselves with rainwater, and concrete that "scars" to heal a crack. Roofs can be swooped like a drip trip of a rainforest leaf, while support columns can be feather-light aluminum, reinforced with a porous structure learned from a porcupine quill. Windows can be covered with an antireflective coating that drinks in light, a secret borrowed from the eyes of night-flying moths. Rather than painting a surface, designers are creating transparent thin films that will refract light the way a butterfly's wing does, leading to tunable walls whose layers can be adjusted to create a slightly different color with each season.

The architectural news is filled with examples. A new research center in the Namib Desert is gathering water from fog, using a droplet-scavenging material inspired by the local fog-basking beetle. To recirculate and clean the water, there's a five-kingdom eco-machine that mimics the patterns of a marsh. A midrise in Harare, Zimbabwe, keeps occupants cool without air-conditioning using a natural ventilation system inspired by local termites. London's sexy Swiss Re building mimics the shape of a water-filtering marine sponge to spiral breezes around its sinuous floors.

Even the "bones" of a building can have nature as their mentor. Claus Mattheck has created a software program based on the way trees and bones constantly reform, moving material from where it is superfluous to where it is needed. This stress-sensing software has been used to optimize buildings and bridges, lightweight a car by 40 percent, and even sculpt a "bone chair" that provides strength with the bare minimum of material, leading to an organic and beautifully skeletal frame.

Energy is sipped and waste is unthinkable in the natural world, and increasingly in the bio-inspired one as well. Replacing building fans with nautilus-inspired blades designed by PAXfan can lower energy costs by 35 percent and noise by 75 percent. Interface's carpet tiles, inspired by the random order on a forest floor, are each slightly different, allowing the tiles to be replaced one at a time without the sore-thumb effect that leads to early landfilling.

What would please Jane most about biomimicry in buildings is what is happening at the systems level, as a greater understanding of ecosystem patterns works its way into place-based city design. At the Biomimicry Guild, we begin each project with a "Genius of Place" report that reveals the ecological story of the place and catalogues the functional strategies of native organisms. In Phoenix, the succulents teach us how to make the most of a scant rainfall, while in New Orleans the live oaks teach us how to handle a hurricane with grace. By tapping the embodied wisdom of living well in place, our designs become truly vernacular.

Next, at the level of a large development or city, we're asking nature to set the bar, creating performance metrics based on the emergent properties of ecosystem services. These gifts of a healthy system include building fertile soil, cleansing the water, cooling the air, maintaining genetic diversity, mitigating pest outbreaks, fixing CO_2 in long-term soil storage, and more. Our Ecological Performance Standards challenge a city—buildings, hardscapes, and landscapes—to provide the same level of ecosystem services as the native ecosystem that it replaces. Success is incredibly tangible, in actual metrics derived from the ecological literature: degrees Fahrenheit of summer cooling, tons of CO_2 stored each year, millimeters of soil formed, and gallons of water absorbed and then released in a storm. Guided by these aspirational goals, we're urging developers to create cities that give back—that are actually generous.

What I see in biomimicry is a move from mimicking individual organisms' adaptations to emulating entire systems of solutions. From here, the next step is the study of the mega-patterns embodied in all organisms and ecosystems, and this is the part that Jane would love. As it turns out, life's 30 million species, in all their diversity, share a small but crucial set of common strategies. These ubiquitous, universal patterns read like a code of conduct for living here on earth. You find that all life is locally attuned and adapted, that it is diverse and resilient, that it builds from the bottom up, is nested and modular, leverages interdependence, and relies on information and cooperation. It performs chemistry in water, at ambient temperature and pressure; it runs on sunlight, shops locally, optimizes rather than maximizes, creates with mistakes, and processes in cycles, endlessly reconfiguring a safe subset of the elements in the periodic table.

Patterns like these are incredibly powerful as frameworks for running a circular economy, and for knitting communities into a food web that treats everything as a nutrient, and nothing as waste. These patterns of interliving seem obvious to us now, but they have been whittled and honed for 3.8 billion years by one simple, consistent innovation method: natural selection. Jane appreciated the power of this continual improvement engine. She knew that the fastest way to innovate is with a partner, in a coevolutionary loop of flower and bee, wolf and moose, bacterium and host. For biomimics, nature is our partner, our mentor in answering the question, "How shall we live here?"

Jane Jacobs saw deeply into the hidden complexity of life, and toward the end of her writing career she realized that the grandmother of all systems was the fluttering, blooming, branching world outside our windows. She knew that the fastest way to change is for societies to change what it is they compare themselves to, what is that they admire.

As designers, we can choose to be more like the organisms that we admire. All it requires from us is a quieting of human cleverness, and a heightened sense of appreciation for the living world around us. It helps to develop a nose for general truths, and a respect for what works, even if it comes from a rhinoceros instead of a Rhodes Scholar.

Too often, we overlook the ubiquitous in our search for the glittering gold of rarity. In the natural world, that which is common in a sea of immense diversity and uniqueness, is that which is telling us something. It's easy to emulate great ecosystems, Jane Jacobs would have reminded us. Visit places that are thriving, notice what they have in common, and amplify the patterns that work.

If our species is to come home to this planet at last and for good, we have to do what all organisms have done, which is to take care of the place that will take care of our offspring. In every wild neighborhood on this planet, life creates conditions conducive to life, and that is the pattern that works.

"CODEVELOPMENT"
AS A PRINCIPLE FOR NEXT
GENERATION INFRASTRUCTURE

Hillary Brown

JACOB'S GREAT GENIUS was finding pattern in complexity. Hers were profound insights into how urban density and diversity generate productive human relationships and invigorate local economies. Where others sought to mitigate density and subdue complexity, she celebrated the layering of urban activities as "exuberant diversity" (Jacobs 1961, 150). Jacobs also teased out relevant connections between physical settings and social behaviors. She showed us that a healthy urban tissue (a city's physical and social infrastructure) grows organically from collective knowledge, collaboration, and local vision. Such place-based fabric takes input from a wide range of actors and integrates multiple, complex systems, ultimately taking shape according to natural principles of development.

For one of the most influential urbanists of our time, Jacobs possessed an uncanny grasp of the workings of nature and ecology, which has long inspired me as an architect. It underpinned my own environmental leanings, and it moves me to conjecture here about her observations and "radically new principles for rebuilding cities."[1] To what extent do her ideas about "nature-based" development align with today's privileged term, "sustainability"? And from there, how might such sustainable or ecological principles help us better meet one of the most

---

1. Douglas Martin, "Jane Jacobs, Social Critic Who Redefined and Championed Cities, Is Dead at 89," Obituary, *The New York Times*, April 26, 2006.

vexing challenges for an urbanizing world: upgrading and re-engineering society's civil infrastructure?

The application of Jacobs' gentle doctrines for urban vitality to public works may enable us to more productively reinvest in our bridges, dams, highways, waterworks, powerplants and grids, rail systems and seaports, and other industrial-era constructions; to better manage and mitigate negative effects; and to make constructive contributions to the development of regions, communities, and neighborhoods. Her ecological approach, I argue, befits programs such as the American Recovery & Reinvestment Act, 2009, or other stimulus plans that seek to return America to economic health by redeveloping our nation's infrastructure.

1. CODEVELOPMENT AND SUSTAINABILITY

Jacobs' natural principles of development are spelled out in her *Nature of Economies*. Fascinated by "ecology as the economy of nature" (Jacobs 2000, 110), she argues that human society and its social artifacts and behaviors are in the end bounded by nature, and are not exempt from the universal natural processes of development, growth, decay, and stability. Moreover, development (intended as qualitative growth or change) does not occur in isolation or along a linear path, but is transacted within a diversified matrix, "a web of interdependent co-developments" (2000, 19). Codevelopment, as Jacobs defines it, is the sum of symbiotic relationships among living and non-living things, networked energy and nutrient flows, recycling and waste elimination, etc. Codevelopment, in other words, is an ecological process, a capacity to self-organize and optimize the whole resulting from the interaction of collective parts.

Today, these principles of codevelopment (self-organization, optimization and co-creativity) have begun to resonate deeply within the fields of planning and design. For instance, codevelopment is a foundational principle of the green building movement. Over the last decade and a half, the real estate and construction sector has begun to reject conventional building practices linked to environmental degradation, and to promote those that support planetary health and well-being. Codevelopment principles are exemplified by some leading forces of change such as the U.S. Green Building Council and the Living Building Challenge, each through a creative, self-organized, consensus-built process that incorporates innovative best practices and channels input from thousands of nationwide volunteers representing diverse sectors of the building industry. The design tools developed by these organizations promote the optimization of building performance by capitalizing on what's free, natural, and of minimal impact, and by stressing the interaction and interdependency of diverse elements. Solar orientation and natural ventilation, for example, can reduce or eliminate the need for mechanical systems; daylight can replace electrical energy use, eliminating lighting's waste heat and resulting in smaller cooling systems and operational savings; and similarly, harvested stormwater can irrigate planting (substituting for high-quality potable water) and replenish underground aquifers, while reducing pollution outflows.

Realizing such synergies typically depends upon a codeveloped or cocreative process. To build green, it is necessary that daylighting and curtain-wall experts, horticulturalists, civil and mechanical engineers, and architects undertake a self-consciously collaborative and mission-driven process—what we now call "integrated" design. Using computer modeling, the team can optimize the interactive effects of building massing, orientation, and envelope materials, achieving significant savings.

The mechanics of cooperative, symbiotic development has also become almost axiomatic today for planners working to repair distressed urban areas. The involvement of communities and neighborhoods in the redevelopment process increases self-reliance and the likelihood of local economic growth. Networking all the participants to the planning effort around common agendas may forge productive social networks, which in turn may foster social entrepreneurship and more civic-minded behaviors. The rise of environmental justice coalitions, the emergence of community development corporations, and the community gardens movement, to name just a few, are all examples of how codevelopment can foster shared values, reciprocity, and the restoration of vital intercultural and transgenerational relationships.

Jacobs' ecological instructions for city building also align well with what seems to be a larger emerging social narrative, one that begins to look to nature for example. Through alternative principles and practices, we are starting to question the longstanding anthropocentric agendas of many disciplines. We have begun to acknowledge natural processes not only to avoid costly environmental impacts—"external" price tags that society must pick up—but also, opportunistically, to avail ourselves of nature's free offerings. Significantly, in many natural and social sciences, less instrumental views of nature have begun to prevail as we reassert a social, spiritual, and aesthetic kinship with the biophysical reality of natural systems.

Many other new directions today in design and planning can be said to reflect this ecological and collaborative perspective. No doubt Jacobs herself would subscribe to the sustainable urbanism movement, which envisions low-impact settlements linked to public transportation systems, higher density, and mixed-use neighborhoods scaled for walkability and supported by local infrastructure. The landscape urbanism movement recognizes the ground plane, a composite of both natural and engineered systems, as the formal organizing tissue for contemporary urbanism. Both landscape architects and urban ecologists have led us to appreciate how natural and engineered (read co-developed) vegetation and soil in cities not only perform vital environmental services, but also play a proactive restorative role. Urban trees and plantings clean and cool air, metabolize pollutants, store water, reduce noise, add color, support biodiversity, and store carbon. A popularized theory that crosses many disciplines, the "biophilia hypothesis," argues that humans are psychologically, aesthetically, and spiritually predisposed to take pleasure in and "affiliate" with nature (Kellert and Wilson 1993). This theory links humanity's successful evolution to the ability to read and respond favorably to the multiple visual, tactile, acoustic, and thermal cues nature offers.

Holistic thinking, inclusive codeveloped solutions, and acknowledgment that much of human cognition is grounded in nature: these are the essential attributes of an emergent ecological worldview. It is one that starts to understand how human settlements are products of, and subject to, the nuances of "complexity, diversity and symbiosis" (Naess 1989, 3). It begins to reject many traditional tenets of planning and design—rational simplification, ordered hierarchies, and separation of uses. Finally, it is one that recognizes how re-energizing our symbiotic relationship to nature in an urbanizing world is perhaps one of the most urgent demands and potent opportunities of our time. These perspectives represent true templates for "sustainability," and bring to life Jane Jacobs' teachings on how to decouple environmental degradation from social development while shaping a more vitally rich society.

2. CODEVELOPED PUBLIC INFRASTRUCTURE: MULTIPURPOSE AND NATURE-FRIENDLY

How can these principles be applied to improve the way we currently build infrastructure? For one, they help us see that our current infrastructural typologies are too often the products of fragmented planning, monopolistic behavior, and contradictory regulatory regimes. Piecemeal regional and state land policies, for example, have left the bulk of housing developments of the last half century stranded without access to public transportation. As near monopolies, railroads have traditionally denied right-of-way crossings to coal slurry pipelines—a more efficient means of delivering coal to power plants—since coal transport by train is one of their major revenue sources. Ultimately, such fragmentation leaves us without a federal mechanism to enact valuable trade-offs among transportation infrastructures.

In contrast to our competing or even redundant infrastructural systems, nature cooperates and networks (codevelops) by combining energy exchange, waste handling, and hydrological functions—the very needs served by human infrastructures. Nature creates synergies among living things. Progressive infrastructure projects might similarly, by virtue of a highly cooperative, integrated design process, combine multiple functions within single sites or facilities. These complexes might even incorporate community-based services. This "co-location"[2] of facilities—the placing of multiple entities within a distinct location as a mutually advantageous sharing of infrastructural real estate—is a hallmark of Jacobs' vital

---

2. Co-location is also the term adopted by the information technology industry to describe data centers that house different customer servers designed with shared security resources.

ecological urbanism. Collapsing various uses into shared space reduces redundancy and frees up real estate, answering the need for density on an urbanizing planet; therefore, it should be a guiding principle in the development of next generation infrastructure.

Below, I will share some exemplary projects that embody some or all of these principles—integrated vs. segregated infrastructure, socially and culturally embedded assets, and effective use of natural systems. They can be found worldwide.

The Khaju Bridge over the Zayandeh River in Isfahan, Iran, built by Shah Abbas II in the seventeenth century is a preindustrial public works masterpiece combining each of these attributes. Its central main aisle was originally designed for horse-drawn vehicles, with outer vaulted aisles for pedestrians. The bridge also functions as a dam. The closing of the sluice gates between the arched spans causes the river level to rise, irrigating upstream gardens via a series of channels. A mid-span octagonal pavilion serves as a social (originally, the princely) vantage point. On its downstream side, cascading steps afford public access to the river, where people can socialize, bathe, or wash their laundry. At present on Fridays its lower shady vaults provide cooling comfort as the chambers resonate with the sounds of Isfahanis singing.

Dating from the late-eleventh through the mid-nineteenth century, the community stepwells (*vavs* or *baolis*) in the arid areas of Western India are feats of water engineering steeped in traditional knowledge of weather patterns, geology, and hydrological behavior. Uphill dams capture monsoon rains that through infiltration supply deep water wells. Varying in level seasonally, water is accessed by descending a geometric maize of stairs, or in some cases through staircases cut through shaded chambers that offer summer refuge to people collecting water (see Livingston 2002). Like the Khaju Bridge, the stepwells embody preindustrial man's capacity to erect multipurpose, tectonically elegant structures well-embedded in the social and cultural landscape.

Some noteworthy projects built today have begun to illustrate this essential infrastructural symbiosis. The most straightforward example are multimodal bridges. The Enneus Heerma Bridge, linking the Dutch island of Zeerburg to the urban district of IJburg, carries multiple lanes of vehicular traffic, two tramlines, two bicycle lanes, and pedestrian footpaths. It also "umbilically" connects public utilities between the island and the mainland, by conveying water mains, drainage, and other services (Wurth 2003). In Dubai, the mile-long Sheikh Mohammed bin Rashid al-Makto Bridge will, when completed, transport cars, light rail, and offer amenities for bikers and pedestrians. This winning, composite design calls for the co-location of a metro station, a planned ferry terminal, a public amphitheatre, and a nature center on the artificial island housing the bridge's central support, itself manufactured from the project's dredged material![3]

In the water-scarce developing nation of Namibia, a proposed solar-power station with an integrated greenhouse (the "Greentower") would generate sufficient energy to power the nation's capital city. Large-scale vegetable and grape cultivations would be co-located beneath the plant's thirty-seven square kilometers of glass panels. A central 1.5-kilometer-high shaft is designed to house turbine generators driven by the superheated air. Evaporated water would also be condensed for reuse, and, if eventually sited in reasonable proximity to the Atlantic, seawater would be piped in and desalinated for irrigation (Weidlich 2008). Here a single facility would have the capacity to produce food, water, and energy—all carbon neutrally.

In an unprecedented combined effort of its departments of Parks and Recreation and Environmental Protection, New York City has co-located a major new water filtration treatment plant beneath the Mosholu Golf Course in the Bronx. Above it, nine acres of intensively planted green roof are configured as an additional driving-range. While this covering helps disguise the station underneath, a moat formed by biofiltration trenches encircling the facility below additionally cleanses stormwater for golf course irrigation (Chaban 2009).

These last two examples fully illustrate the aspirations of "codeveloped" infrastructure: they employ natural systems to help solve complex environmental problems, and they serve more than one purpose or function. "Co-located" or jointly used facilities can also produce less

---

3. Conversation with Sudhir Jambelakhar, Principal, FXFowle. May 26, 2009.

construction-related disruption and eliminate duplicate services. In some cases, such as the below-grade treatment plant, this doubling up serves to hide facilities perceived as noxious by society.

In Japan, for example, electrical substations (notoriously noisy and unsightly constructions) are often sited beneath other facilities. One is even sited below ground, near the seventeenth-century remains of Nagoya's famous landmark, Meijo Castle. Substations can be found beneath public parks or sidewalks in London. Zoning restrictions and the public perception of these structures as nuisances, however, largely preclude their mixing with other uses in the U.S. (see Cohen 2008). An exception (grandfathered in by virtue of its destroyed predecessor) is the rebuilt substation serving all of Lower Manhattan. At the base of the new 7 World Trade Center, the latter resides in a concrete bunker wrapped by artful stainless steel panels, rising eleven stories beneath an office tower extending over 1.7 million square feet. Like other infrastructural elements, the substation is an unavoidable fact of life, and this example shows how it can effectively cohabit with other uses.

3. A SYNERGY OF USES FOR THE BENEFIT OF THE COMMUNITY

The ultimate imperative for ecological, co-developed infrastructure is the provision of local or neighborhood benefits. Whereas traditional public works reject shared use for reasons of security and safety, many noteworthy infrastructure projects now intentionally include public social, educational, or cultural functions. Co-locating and safely integrating community-based educational, recreational, or cultural facilities within a complex adds local value and may help reduce or eliminate the local controversies that frequently surround the siting of infrastructure facilities perceived as deleterious. The handsome Waterfront Nature Walk at NYC's upgraded Newtown Creek Sewage Treatment Plant in Brooklyn resulted from a collaboration between the Department of Environmental Protection and local community activist groups. Formerly beset with a history of oil spills and combined sewage overflow events, today's elegant quarter-mile walkway restores and enhances the local public waterfront access. The project was in part accomplished through the assignment of ten million dollars for community environmental benefit projects in the Greenpoint section of Brooklyn, the largest such allocation in state history.[4]

Other examples illustrate the same pattern. In Hiroshima, Japan, the Naka Waste-to-Energy Facility is sited in a public park that produces electricity from the city's 220,000 tons of solid waste, while the c-generated hot water serves a local indoor pool. Its educational "waste museum" showcases the art of solid waste handling and incineration.[5] The towering structural framework of an especially dramatic waterfront facility proposed in the Canary Islands—a solar-powered desalination plant—forms a handsome backdrop for the "Teatro del Agua," an outdoor performance venue for this underserved industrial port.[6] When operational, this facility would produce fresh water from the sea using only solar-powered evaporators and condensers.

The authors of *Infrastructure & Community: How Can We Live with What Sustains Us?* (Singer, Cruz, and Bergman 2007) make the case for a neighborhood-integrated infrastructure as a fundamental means to deliver environmental justice to a community hosting infrastructural facilities.[7] To offset or eliminate disruptive or noxious by-products associated with power-generating or waste-handling services, they mandate practices that integrate bio-remediative (biologically decontaminating) processes into infrastructural facilities. They also recommend new tools such as the "community benefit agreements"—positive economic and environmental features embedded in the development project in exchange for community support. These agreements have helped realize otherwise controversial projects, such as the expansion of Los Angeles International Airport (LAX) (2007, 9). Here, in 2004, a private agreement between a broad

---

4. www.dec.ny.gov/environmentdec/49083.html.
5. www.arch-hiroshima.net/arch-hiroshima/arch/delta_others/naka_e.html.
6. *World Architecture News*, September 5, 2006.
7. This publication contains several case studies of works by the Michael Singer studio. These innovative projects pioneer an environmentally and socially conscious approach to infrastructure design. The report can be downloaded here: www.edf.org/documents/7182_Infrastructure_and_Community.pdf.

coalition of community-based organizations, labor unions, and LAX operators provided compensatory benefits to the affected community valued at $500,000 (Baxamusa 2008). These included noise and air pollution mitigation, local hiring practices, traffic reduction, and long-term studies to evaluate public health impacts. Ultimately, we need innovative development agreements and flexible templates that use integrated design to counter engineering orthodoxies that normally mandate isolating or securing-off many public works. The facilitation of community-embedded infrastructure opens the door for PIMBY ("please in my backyard") to supersede NIMBYism.

4. A FUTURE-ORIENTED VISION

Symptomatic of our general national disinvestment in the public realm, public utility and transportation infrastructures are currently the products of fragmented planning and regulatory regimes. Many short-term planning efforts are vulnerable to the vagaries of political cycles. Coupled with our relatively weak regional planning capacity, we lack the integrated, interagency frameworks and financial instruments for budgeting, constructing, and operating joint or "multiplex" projects. Additionally, design professionals may lack a shared technical language, a familiarity with interdisciplinary collaboration, and an inkling of how to affect policy—all prerequisites for realizing successful innovative projects.

Today's economic stimulus package has so far focused on rolling out "shovel-ready" infrastructural projects. Taken together, they're a drop in the bucket against the $2.2 trillion investment needed over five years to return America's infrastructure to good condition (American Society of Civil Engineers 2009). Even worse, none of the proposed interventions examine the basic infrastructural models—modes of delivering goods, people, or services—required to reduce our carbon footprint and our dependency on foreign oil. Built conventionally today, these assets, with their 75-100 year life span, will chain us long-term to energy- and resource-intensive consumption patterns. For the most part, they are single-purpose. They often occupy vast real estate. Many are noxious facilities, frequently visited upon non-white communities or low-income neighborhoods.

How can we implement more "co-developed" and ecologically savvy infrastructure? The convergence of global economic and environmental crises may actually push us towards bolder models of development, with "yield-more-for-less," synergistic results. A new national strategy demands a unified and compelling vision, and in particular infrastructure-delivery processes that support and reward innovation, cooperation, and coordination among all involved entities. Infrastructures, simply put, are the lifeline of our economy. Jane's voice rings in our ear: "I'm convinced that economic life is ruled by processes and principles we didn't invent and can't transcend, whether we like that or not, and that the more we learn of these processes and the better we respect them, the better our economies will get along" (Jacobs 2000, 32).

Jacobs, who once spoke of "technologies as extensions of our bodies" (2000, 143), would likely support such a next generation of infrastructure, one that is capable of multitasking, i.e. working with, not against natural systems; one that is embedded in community; and one that reduces our carbon emissions. Inevitably, she would take the position that in the long term, our economic and environmental stability is inextricably linked to such holistic and integrated problem-solving and planning.

REFERENCES

American Society of Civil Engineers. 2009. *2009 Report Card for America's Infrastructure*. Washington, DC. www.infrastructurereportcard.org.

Baxamusa, Murtaza H. 2008. "Empowering Communities through Deliberation: The Model of Community Benefits Agreements." *Journal of Planning Education and Research* 27, no. 3: 261-276.

Chaban, Matt. 2009. "Fore! Nation's Largest Green Roof atop Bronx Water Plant Doubles as Driving Range." *The Architects Newspaper*, February 26. www.archpaper.com.

Cohen, Hope. 2008. *The Neighborly Substation: Electricity, Zoning, and Urban Design*. New York: Manhattan Institute for Policy Research.

Jacobs, Jane. 1961. *The Death and Life of Great American Cities*. New York: Vintage Books.

——. 2000. *The Nature of Economies*. New York: Modern Library.

Kellert, Stephen R. and Edward O. Wilson. 1993. *The Biophilia Hypothesis*. Washington, DC: Island Press.

Livingston, Morna. 2002. *Steps to Water: The Ancient Stepwells of India*. New York: Princeton Architectural Press.

Naess, Arne. 1989. *Ecology, Community and Lifestyle: Outline of an Ecosophy*. Cambridge, UK: Cambridge University Press.

Singer, Michael, Ramon J. Cruz and Jason Bregman. 2007. *Infrastructure and Community: How Can We Live with What Sustains Us?* Environmental Defense and Michael Singer Studio.

Weidlich, Brigitte. 2008. "Nation Switches On to Solar Power." *Green Economic Initiative*, November 2. www.greeneconomyinitiative.com

Wurth, George J.J. 2003. "Enneus Herman Bridge, IJburg, The Netherlands." *Structural Engineering International* 13, no. 1.

JANE JACOBS BASICS

Richard Register

ONE DAY ABOUT fifteen years ago, I was reading one of Jane's books. The impulse suddenly hit me: maybe I'd just give her a call. When I dialed the information operator in Toronto—you remember, the actual person who would answer the phone, sound human and give you the number—there was Jane Jacobs' phone number for her home on Albany Street. And she actually answered the phone! Like most people I suppose, I thanked her for her great work. Far from sounding irritated, her tone of voice was more like, "Gee, who's this guy? Maybe he has an interesting thought or two." She sounded friendly and, I liked to think, a little curious.

I went on to say I appreciated her construct about cities building their economies in an import-replacing process, as Venice did in its relationship to Constantinople: trading salt and lumber for glassware, cloth, and other goods, then learning how to make the same products there in Venice. Noticing the role of replacing imports with local production was a powerful economic insight. She wasn't the first to point to this aspect, but she enriched the idea and gave it new emphasis. The relationship of the city to its "hinterland" or resource base was basic and ecologically right: she envisioned cities engaging with their hinterlands in a reciprocally supportive economy; nature delivering resources and services; and people providing support for nature's flourishing. Peter Berg and the others who have refined that idea and called the hinterlands "bioregions" are simply adding detail to the relationship imagined by Jane Jacobs.

But that wasn't the most important part of our conversation. She said the city was the invention that assembled and physically organized a great diversity of resources, producers, tools, and cultural ideas. Complementary specialization could happen there to an extent impossible in diffused geographies. Her notion coincided with urban theorist David Engwicht's when he said, "The city is an invention for maximizing exchange and minimizing trade." It also fits with my slogan: "Access by proximity!"

I added, though, that something was missing in her perspective: the role of the creative individual and creativity in general in launching the whole enterprise. Sure, Venice started making refined products after a number of decades trading salt and lumber with the producers in Constantinople, and in turn Venice played the same role mentoring other cities in Europe. But who invented the glassmaking techniques of Constantinople in the first place? I thought it would have been productive to explore the role of the creative process. She considered it to be incremental, but I still felt that something was missing, maybe a deeper appreciation of the dynamics of creativity. What about the inventors, artists, playwrights, and imaginative craftspeople proud of their work? Their ideas and the sheer creativity behind the products patronized or purchased by the wealthy and exchanged around the world needed more attention, I thought.

When we hung up, I was thinking of the process of incrementally gathering ideas and techniques around some unnamed basic principles. Perhaps, at least I wanted to think, she was left wondering a little more about the creative act itself.

BASICS AND PROPORTIONALITY

What's most special about Jane Jacobs, besides her warmth and clear vision regarding people in their built environments, and besides a capacity for outrage that led her to oppose freeways through Manhattan and flee with her husband and sons to Canada when our fine country wanted to draft them to drop napalm on the villagers of Vietnam? What's most special is something extremely simple, I believe, yet something that almost got lost in the twists of contemporary civilization: the basics. Sounds awfully bland, but it is serious, and the glories of something healthy can grow from there and only from there.

"Basic" is something that is at the root of your building's foundation: all the rest lies upon it. Jane Jacobs emphasized the kind of community that is not the intentional community of friends and think-alikes, but the obligatory community of civility and respect of real differences, justice, rights and duties. Her community is the *celebration* of rich cultural differences cemented together into economic transactions that deliver useful and enlightening goods and services. Her basics rang true to me, and could and should be built upon for the benefit of us all.

Yesterday I returned from a trip to the beginning of the end. After World War II, a great wave of suburban expansion swept out like a tsunami from the kind of city Jane loved, gaining speed and scale, consuming millions of acres of natural landscapes and agricultural fields alike, bridging waters and sloshing up mountain sides... until it ran out of money and gas. Now the wave of development has started to reverse, but not the damage. Few noted that the worst economic crisis since the Great Depression began in suburbia's impossibly overpriced and automobile-dependent far-flung reaches. Fewer still would prescribe the sort of city that Jane had imagined as a major part of the solution. That city, of course I would say, would be an ecocity running on a small fraction of the energy and land required for the car city, powered by solar and wind, linked by foot, bicycle, elevator, and streetcar, and fed by organic agriculture very light on land-hogging meat.

Hearth and Home at Liberty is the name of a would-be development of 558 single-family houses by mega suburban developer Shea Homes. I arrived at this stillborn town near Rio Vista, California, by car. (The far suburbs built for the car are accessible only to the car. Don't try to get there by train or bus—you never will.) There, forty-two blocks of dirt and weeds were surrounded by almost brand new streets, sidewalks, lamp posts, stop signs, fire hydrants, and bundles of flexible plastic utility pipes looking like giant spaghetti extruded from the bare ground. They marked the spots where houses were supposed to go. The cozy "Hearth and Home" site, supposed to deliver "Liberty" at the end of a long forced drive, proves one thing: there is nothing cozy or liberating about it. It may represent the end of a world; but what next?

We need a sense of proportion. That is as basic as designing urban environments in the fine grain and at the human scale—where the "human scale" is exemplified by the cozy neighborhood that can accomodate strangers, shopkeepers, customers, and relatives, as well as friends. Another basic: the car is too overbearing to be a design criteria in any healthy city. The proportions work like this: the car is thirty times as heavy, ten times as fast, and takes up sixty times the volume of a person. That's why you can't design around it. Think basic!

Another example: for all the climate change conferences led by the UN and others, have you ever heard mention of city design or urban form? I haven't. What's the largest creation of our species? Cities. How can it be that typical European cities as prosperous as American sprawling cities consume about a third as much land and energy per person? Proportions and small-scale development don't seem to be part of the formula proposed to solve our environmental problems. I'd maintain that a sense of proportion should be something basic. Certainly better insulation, recycling, and renewable energy systems are good ideas; but add urban reshaping inspired by the European compact model and see just how big energy savings can get.

Finally, for all its countless problems, the city is *important*. It's the key single thing we can substantially redesign that effects practically every aspect of life, economy, and ecological health on this planet. That's basic.

AND NOW...?

More to the point, what to build and how to build it now? I've been working on the idea of the ecocity for more than thirty-five years; others, like Ian McHarg and Paolo Soleri, for forty and forty-five years, respectively. Before the three of us, similar goals could be found in Lewis Mumford's writing from the 1930s through 1960s and in the work of the Garden City planners of one hundred years ago.

The world has not been swift on the uptake. Until now we have been pretty much marginalized and ignored even by our designer and architect friends who focus on one building at a time and don't get paid for whole cities. But the New Urbanists are inching in the ecocity direction with their coordination of modest density and transit nodes. The "smart growth" movement, a more urban version of that approach, takes a couple steps farther toward a true ecocity urbanism. But to get there I think we will need the kind of completeness that life had in the community and which Jane loved so much in the city. The so-called "ecocities" that have been planned and, in a couple cases, built in China and in Abu Dhabi are incomplete. In China everything revolves around the car, which means the pedestrian environment is missing, including the pedestrian-friendly architecture of interlinked buildings. The potential to have the full range of ecocity design features, such as bridges between buildings, rooftop terracing, and multi-story solar greenhouses, has yet to be explored.

Australian architect Paul Downton calls a small but complete part of an ecocity an "ecocity fractal": such a project, as small as two or three blocks, could exemplify the working and the organization of the whole. The functions there would include housing, shopping, jobs, commerce, supply of basics like food and water, and a celebration of nature through open creeks and panoramic plazas. And, of course, it would be an environment for people, not cars. Build such a "fractal," and a sense of the whole could really be experienced and fully grasped.

My worry is that we are closing in on a time when money and cheap energy might get so short in supply that nobody will muster the wherewithal to build the ecocity. Whether the current economic "downturn" drives people to innovation or hardens fears and reaction has yet to be seen. What I do know is that since I started working on ecocity projects, which was almost exactly when I began reading Jane Jacobs' and Paolo Soleri's work, we have burned up about 85 percent of all the oil humanity has burned to date, and likely about 60 percent of all we will ever burn on this planet. We may well have lost the opportunity that was such an exciting notion for me back in the 1960s and 1970s. I certainly hope not.

Now we have a radical and, dare I say, delightful change in leadership in the United States with the Barack Obama administration. But we also have inherited an astounding range of social and environmental problems and a damaged set of international norms and styles of conduct.

The evaporation of U.S. economic foundations may lead us to become aware of nature's economy of resources, or we might head off toward a Jared Diamond-type of collapse—this time taking all people and societies with us.

I'm hoping for the best and will offer another tool to move toward an ecological urban design. That's what I call ecocity mapping: take a map of your city. Find the centers of most vitality. The centers can be made more dense and functionally diverse with time. The architecture can get far more interesting with eco-architectural elements. Bring small manufacturing back into town. Remove buildings as they age and wear out, rather than replace them with new car-dependent infrastructure. Voilà! The city will be changing in the ecocity direction and faster than you'd ever expected.

And to get right up to date, I'm trying to convince Congressman Earl Blumenauer from Portland to adopt legislation that would spread the ecocity mapping scheme throughout the country. Congressman Rusong Wang is already working in that direction in China, where he is a member of the Chinese Peoples Congress. He has recruited me to work on a city that has made its living on coal for the last 50 years—and coal is running out in 2012. This could be a world model for how it is possible to shift from energy consumption to energy conservation by ecocity design.

JANE JACOBS:

ENVIRONMENTAL PRESERVATIONIST

Roberta Brandes Gratz

PRESERVATIONISTS MAKE GOOD environmentalists; environmentalists do not make good preservationists. Preservationists
understand conservation must cover more than buildings; environmentalists often don't see the same connection. Environmental conservation
should include both the natural and built environment, since they are
inextricably linked. Upgrading and recycling functional buildings can
be the highest form of environmental conservation, green building, or
sustainable development.

This is a fundamental lesson of Jane Jacobs and, as an urbanist, this is
also what I see. Everything is connected, interdependent, part of a complex web that is not easy to recognize but is, nevertheless, the hallmark
of urbanism. Nothing is siloed.

Yes, an increase in wind energy would be great; but windmill siting
can devastate natural and built landscapes and underwater aquatic life.
The roads, the power lines, and the infrastructure needed to connect
windmills to the grid can be highly destructive of the natural environment, to say nothing of birds, bats, and fish.

Impacts must be weighed.

Yes, more electric cars and hybrids will help clean the air we breathe,
but it won't do anything to tame traffic, minimize the amount of land
devoted to blacktop, limit sprawl, regenerate pedestrian-oriented places,
or rebuild communities.

LEED (Leadership in Energy and Environmental Design) is the privately created standard by which the design/build industry rates levels of green construction. However, it can be misleading. A gold standard LEED Wal-Mart is still environmentally destructive because of its siting in a greenfield and its car dependency. In fact, a green Wal-Mart is an oxymoron.

New energy-saving green buildings, with all the latest technology bells and whistles, are the current fad of new construction. But the new is valued at the expense of the often still functional old. The value calculation for the new should be measured by a formula that gives appropriate value to what is being lost. It is hypocritical to give a developer LEED points for recycling elements from a demolished, highly reusable historic building without taking points away for demolishing that building in the first place. And it is ludicrous to give comparable points for saving a building and installing a bike rack.

These are the kind of connections made when the web thinking of Jane Jacobs is applied. The kind of observation Jacobs encouraged was to understand how cities actually work—no theories, no ideologies, no fixed assumptions. Observation reveals the inextricable connections. Nothing is one-dimensional. Again, nothing is siloed.

Public discourse sometimes recognizes that embodied energy of standing structures exists. But where is the calculation of its loss? How do you weigh the energy-consuming production of new materials against the energy-saving conservation of old ones? How do you measure the negative environmental consequences of innumerable truck trips for removal of debris? How do you measure the ballooning content of landfills? How do you measure the loss of materials, some of which are no longer available, like wood from old growth forests, the cypress and barge board commonly used in old New Orleans houses, or the horse hair used for insulation in threatened old theaters? How do you measure the need to import from afar the material required for new buildings in contrast to greater reliance on local suppliers? And how do you measure the cultural diminishment when the demolished building is an important historic landmark?

Not all environmentalists make poor preservationists. Some—though not the majority—recognize both the environmental opportunity and the aesthetic appeal of standing old buildings, whether architecturally unique or not. The premier example of this is EcoTrust, whose headquarters is in Portland, Oregon. EcoTrust was founded in 1991 on the principle that good stewardship of the environment goes way beyond cutting our dependency on foreign oil. In fact, EcoTrust was founded to pursue a new type of economic development—conservation-based development—that recognizes the kind of connections Jacobs made between nature, community, and what she called "reliable prosperity."

EcoTrust created new business models inspired by nature itself, integrating social, economic, and conservation principles. It established the first environmental bank and started an ecosystem investment fund. The headquarters building is a veritable gathering place for conservation-minded programs and includes private and nonprofit environmental-based tenants. Jane was an enthusiastic supporter of EcoTrust, a rare case in which she agreed to serve on a board. I had the privilege of touring the building with Jane in 2004, not long after it opened. It could not have pleased her more.

What I observed pleased me as well. I am a passionate historic preservationist, but I recognize that some grand old buildings—certainly not all—can be enhanced in the hands of a skillful contemporary architect, particularly an environmentally committed one.

EcoTrust converted an ordinary 1895 Portland warehouse into a model green building, preserving much of the exterior and interior elements, while inserting innovative energy and water-saving systems, recycling or reclaiming 98 percent of its construction waste, and earning the first LEED gold rating for a restoration. This conversion would probably not have qualified for preservation tax credits based on the Department of Interior standards for historic buildings, but many old buildings don't warrant slavish restorations. Conversely, many historic landmarks should not be subjected to this kind of overhaul, respectful as it may be of their original character. Some landmarks are indeed too important for details to be lost; however, it should certainly be recognized that most standing buildings, whether historic landmarks or not, have a head start in converting to a green structure compared to any newly built ones. Landmark treasures, such as Lincoln's ancestral home or the Empire State Building, can be or have been environmentally upgraded.

A great example is the award-winning restoration of the 1887 Eldridge Street Synagogue, the largest restoration in New York City of a historic landmark that is not affiliated with an institution, government agency, or private development. It is green building at a higher standard than LEED yet acknowledges.

Conservation, localism, and recycling are essential to true green building and sustainable development. In the case of the Eldridge Street Synagogue, the whole city, not just the building, benefited economically, socially and culturally from the restoration in both temporary and permanent ways. The synagogue now functions both as a continuing synagogue and distinctly as the Museum at Eldridge Street.

The localism aspect is, in many ways, the most interesting and least understood benefit of historic preservation. For the synagogue, three high-skill New York City firms—one in DUMBO (Down Under the Manhattan Bridge Overpass), one in Staten Island, and one in Williamsburg, Brooklyn—restored the 66 stained glass windows. A Williamsburg firm with ten to fourteen Brooklyn employees restored the 237 intricately detailed brass fixtures and 75-bulb chandelier. A Manhattan-based firm used forty-five of their mostly Brooklyn-based skilled artisans to conserve and restore the exquisitely detailed interior paint work. A Brooklyn salvage firm provided replacement timbers from demolished buildings. One Long Island City woodworking firm restored the 154 benches, and another restored wood window frames and doors. And that is just the start.

The attic insulation is recycled blue jeans. The bathroom stall partitions are recycled plastic milk jugs, and the sink countertops are made with recycled glass, mostly soda and beer bottles reprocessed at the Brooklyn Navy Yard. Virtually every material element found in the deteriorated building remains, a fundamental goal from the start of this rescue effort in 1986, when water was pouring through the roof, pigeons nested in the ceiling, and dust was so thick on the pews that initials could be left clear as day. Elements that couldn't be restored were replaced in kind with recycled material.

As a rule, 60 to 70 percent of rehabilitation costs go to labor and the rest to materials, many of which can come from nearby salvage. That ratio is reversed for new construction.

When Jane fought the Lower Manhattan Expressway that would have wiped out Little Italy, Chinatown and what is now SoHo, she understood not only the destructive environmental, social, and economic consequences the plan would bring to the city, but also the positive environmental, social, and economic consequences of allowing the existing district to reinvent itself. The positive results both in conservation and historic preservation terms are beyond measure.

This was back in the 1960s, and Jane also made the inextricable link that the health of everything in the built and natural environment starts with transportation. It was the car-comes-first era, a mindset she criticized from the beginning. At the heart of all her advocacy of walkable, vibrant streets was the fundamental need for the critical infrastructure element of a viable transit system. As usual, she was ahead of the times.

The essential truth is that preservation is the first and most fundamental step of green building and good environmental stewardship, even if not recognized as such in the LEED rating system. In the Jane Jacobs lexicon, it was that and more. Preservation is essential to a vibrant, economically viable, stable, and diverse city. The Jacobs' quote "Old ideas can sometimes use new buildings. New ideas must use old buildings" is well-known. But consider what she said leading up to that quote:

> Cities need old buildings so badly it is probably impossible for vigorous streets and districts to grow without them. By old buildings I mean not museum-piece old buildings, not old buildings in an excellent and expensive state of rehabilitation—although these make fine ingredients—but also a good lot of plain, ordinary, low-value old buildings, including some rundown old buildings… If a city has only new buildings, the enterprises that can exist there are automatically limited to those that can support the high costs of new construction.

She then observes the uses that are made of new and old buildings:

Chain stores, chain restaurants and banks go into new construction. But neighborhood bars, foreign restaurants and pawn shops go into older buildings…Well subsidized opera and art museums often go into new buildings. But the unformalized feeders of the arts—studios, galleries, stores for musical instruments and art supplies, backrooms where the low earning power of a seat and a table can absorb uneconomic discussions—these go into old buildings…

As for really new ideas of any kind—no matter how ultimately profitable or otherwise successful some of them might prove to be—there is no leeway for such chancy trial, error and experimentation in the high-overhead economy of new construction. *Old ideas can sometimes use new buildings. New ideas must use old buildings.* (Jacobs 1961, 187–188, italics added)

This doesn't mean she was against new buildings; she just understood way ahead of most people that most kinds of old buildings are flexible and adaptable for new uses. Years ago, when Westbeth was still new, I remember her marveling at the creative conversion of the old Bell Labs into an artists' cooperative combining live/work, exhibition, and communal spaces. She admired Richard Meier's design: "The building spoke to him," she observed.

The place for new buildings, she argued, was alongside, in between, or (where appropriate) in place of old buildings, what she called "infill." She saw new buildings as the latest layer of an organic, evolving city; however, this presupposed that the existing area was not wiped away. "Adaptations, ameliorations, and densifications," that was what a healthy changing urban fabric was comprised of.

Her words here reflect another basic Jacobs' tenet: the essential need for diversity. Diversity in Jacobs' terms, it must be noted, is not the same as "mixed use" in planners' and developers' terms. An all-new development with the so-called mix of uses that includes residential, commercial, and retail falls into the category Jane refers to as "economically too limited—and therefore functionally too limited to be lively, interesting and convenient. Flourishing diversity anywhere in a city means the mingling of high-yield, middling-yield, low-yield and no-yield enterprises" (1961, 188).

Today this is heresy in cities that worship new development in the mistaken belief that it will work as an urban regenerator. True new economic development follows organic regeneration; it does not cause it. Real estate development follows economic development; it does not cause it.

The diversity Jane considered so critical cannot be achieved in newly manufactured communities or districts. She had little patience for highly touted, newly minted so-called "new traditional places," whether billed as transit-oriented, pedestrian-oriented, or mixed-use oriented, especially when such districts were inserted like a patch in city areas where authentic urban fabric still survived nearby. These new inserts too often did not reflect the organized complexity of an organically evolved place.

"There is no use wishing it were a simpler problem or trying to make it a simpler problem," she wrote, "because in real life it is not a simple problem." Instead, what is called for must reflect or help organically encourage the organized complexity she identified as the essence of a city. The kind of infill buildings she valued fit comfortably within existing scale and reflected a variety of types developed by and for a variety of small and large users, enabling a "multiplicity of choices and complexities of cross-use." Thus was possible the genuine diversity that marked an authentic urban place.

Interestingly, Jane writes in *Death and Life* that "zoning for diversity" is, in effect, partially achieved by a landmarks preservation law, even though New York's was a few years away when she wrote it:

> Zoning for diversity must be thought of differently from the usual zoning for conformity, but like all zoning, it is suppressive. One form of zoning for diversity is already familiar in certain city districts: controls against demolition of historically valuable buildings. Already different from their surroundings, these are zoned to stay different from them. (Jacobs 1961, 252-253)

She notes that a slightly advanced development of this concept was proposed by Greenwich Village civic groups for their area and adapted by the city in 1959. Height limits were drastically reduced, making sure that "lower buildings remaining could not be further replaced by excessive duplication of the more valuable high buildings." And, she added, "Again sameness was zoned out—or, in effect, differences zoned in—even though in a most limited fashion and on relatively few streets." The city's landmarks law followed six years later, and Greenwich Village was the second designated historic district.

As I see it, the most important chapter in any of Jane's books is the last one in *Death and Life*, titled "The kind of problem a city is." In it, Jane presents the underpinnings of her web thinking, an understanding of "cities as problems in organized complexity—organisms that are replete with unexamined, but obviously intricately interconnected, and surely understandable, relationships."

She draws here on the work of Dr. Warren Weaver, former vice president of the Rockefeller Foundation. Weaver argued that the history of scientific thought could be understood in three stages. In the first one—from seventeenth to nineteenth century—science dealt with problems of simplicity, in which two variables are directly related to each other in their behavior. During this time, from theories of light, sound, heat, and electricity came the telephone, radio, car, plane, movies, turbines, and other improvements.

The second stage was characterized by the ability to deal with problems of disorganized complexity with billions of variables. This highly mathematically based development led to probability techniques and statistical approaches to understanding problems. Here one could ponder the behavior of atoms and billiard balls, heredity and thermodynamics. In effect, this is modern physics.

However, Dr. Weaver observed that not all problems could be approached in either of these two ways, particularly in the field of life sciences such as biology and medicine. "Much more important than the mere number of variables is the fact that these variables are all interrelated," Jane quotes Weaver. Since the essential feature of these problems is a form of organization, he labeled these problems "organized complexity."

As Jane quotes him: "What makes an evening primrose open when it does? Why does salt water fail to satisfy thirst?" All these questions or problems involve many factors to be studied simultaneously, but they are not problems "to which statistical methods hold the key. They are all problems which involve dealing simultaneously with *a sizable number of factors which are interrelated into an organic whole.*"

The distinction between disorganized and organized complexity is very significant in the Jacobs' canon. Disorganized complexity is the chaotic jumble of things none of which makes sense or relates to any other. Organized complexity may still look like chaos to the less aware observer, but careful scrutiny reveals a logic to the complex mix. The connections among elements add up to a form of organization, the fabric of a place. "Order exists beneath the chaos," Jane said. These connections are lost when an area is "cleaned up," "renewed," cleared and redeveloped, rather than strategically repaired. Social, economic, and physical connections are the assets to be built upon, improved, and added to a process I call "urban husbandry" in my first two books, *The Living City: Thinking Small in a Big Way* (1994) and *Cities Back From the Edge: New Life for Downtown* (1998).

We have Jane to thank for persuasively demonstrating that urban challenges cannot be approached in an effective way unless they are examined through the organized complexity lens—through interrelationships, interdependencies, and organic connections. This goes to the heart of her criticism of the silos of city planning, transportation planning, project development, and housing planning, all of which rest too much on a kind of thinking in which organized complexity is unacknowledged. In the same vein, preservation and environmental conservation are inextricably linked.

Web thinking is the core of what Jacobs is about. Thinking this way does not permit looking at the environment without acknowledging the intricate connections to the built world, nor looking at the physical, social, or economic world without considering the environment.

In her fifth book, *The Nature of Economies*, Jane points to the inextricable connections between the environment and the economy. "If we stop focusing on *things*," she writes, "and shift attention to the processes that generate the things, distinctions between nature and economy blur" (2000, 9). Here again balance, environmental impacts, social values and physical consequences all come into play, as they had done in her earlier, probably most significant work, *The Economy of Cities*.

"Development is an open ended process, which creates complexity and diversity" and "operates as a web of interdependent co-developments" (2000, 17, 19). Thinning the city as urban de-densification planning policies have done for decades and still do, she noted, also thins the earth's resources—a criticism of urban sprawl dating from before the term was popularly invented.

As I see it, the re-densification of cities is the critical issue of the twenty-first century. The advance of sustainable development depends on it. The housing of low and middle-income people depends on it. The strengthening of the national economy from the ground up depends on it. And, of course, the improvement of the natural environment depends on it. But that densification needs to follow Jacobs' principles, not with high-rise barracks for the rich or poor but with "ameliorations and adaptations," along with new additions appropriately fitting in and in scale with what exists.

Each of Jane's books underscores the connectivity of everything and the processes that tie everything together. The *Nature of Economies* is particularly interesting because the title could easily be turned around to *The Economies of Nature*. Economies, she illustrates, like nature, function according to complex processes that cannot be reduced to convenient dogmas, theories, or statistical abstracts. Like cities and nature, observation reveals the essential clues to those processes.

Fundamentally, everything Jane writes is about economy. Not THE ECONOMY, but economy in its broader sense of thrift and value, economy of resources—whether natural or man-made. In her web thinking, everything is connected in a holistic way into the interrelated system that is economy. In this way, Jane provided the bridge between the two concepts of preservation and environmentalism: both are really about economy. The building of each on the other is a logical and natural imperative.

REFERENCES

Gratz, Roberta Brandes. 1994. *The Living City: Thinking Small in a Big Way*. New York: John Wiley & Sons.

——. 1998. *Cities Back From the Edge: New Life for Downtown*. New York: John Wiley & Sons.

Jacobs, Jane. 1961. *The Death and Life of Great American Cities*. New York: Random House.

——. 2000. *The Nature of Economies*. New York: Random House.

5.5

FOR YOU JANE

Jan Gehl

J ANE, I AM somewhat hesitant as to whether it is proper to address this little story to you. However, I feel rather strongly about talking directly to you. Not only were you for decades my faraway and highly valued idol, but later also a trusted friend, with whom I had most valuable and cherished exchanges. So Jane, here is another link in the chain of letters we exchanged over the years.

It was a great day, November 13, 2008, when New York City Commissioner of Transport Janette Sadik-Khan launched the Department of Transportation report on "World Class Streets: Remaking New York City's Public Realm."[1] Everybody and his uncle was present, and the atmosphere was jubilant. Finally, after all these years, a plan to remake the New York streets had been designed that showed concern for people instead of automobiles. Or rather, it was a plan to achieve a better balance between pedestrians, public life, bicycling, and motoring throughout New York.

It took quite a while to get to this day from the troubled days in 1961 when your fight for a better New York was argued and carefully documented in your book *The Death and Life of Great American Cities*. Forty-nine years to be precise, but now the day has finally come. After all these years, the city has finally been blessed with a visionary leader-

---

1. The report can be downloaded here: www.nyc.gov/html/dot/downloads/pdf/WCS_Gehl_08_print.pdf .

ship that not only wants to seriously address the climate challenge and environmental issues by making New York a much more sustainable city: it also fully realizes that a good city can be created if its people are welcomed heartily and invited to walk and enjoy their city in its public spaces. Please walk, please bicycle. Those are the new invitations that were seldom heard previously.

Of all places, this groundbreaking meeting was staged in the AIA Center for Architecture on La Guardia Place in Greenwich Village. While the crowd was rejoicing listening to the details of the new Great Streets Plan, I sat quietly, contemplating the fact that this lovely building, which is now a perfect community house for the American Institute of Architects, would not have been there today, had it not been for your impressive work to rally the Village against Robert Moses, his fellow traffic planners, and their far-flung ambitions to carry through a vision of a Lower Manhattan Expressway. This expressway would have meant getting rid of Greenwich Village and Soho, and replacing these hopelessly derelict and old-fashioned city districts with some really up to standard high-rise family residences, standing far apart in modernistic solitude on worn-out grass lawns.

The plan never came about, and the Village and Soho were saved. Also the Lower Manhattan Expressway never materialized, and the soul of New York was saved by a strenuous effort. What would New York have been without the Village and Soho? So thank you, Jane, for your impressive fight for a people-oriented New York as early as the late 1950s and early 1960s.

You had a hard fight and indeed some victories. Fortunately for the city, you helped bury the Lower Manhattan Expressway and a number of drastic urban renewal schemes, but Robert Moses had his way in most other districts in the city. Every New York street was filled from wall to wall with traffic, and as a matter of principle nearly always with one-way traffic, because this makes room for more and faster circulation, and as a byproduct gives the pedestrians a much harder and more risky time crossing the streets.

But, Jane, luckily the winds have at last started to blow from new directions. The leadership of the city is now committed to reduce the noise, the pollution, and foremost the carbon dioxide footprint of the city. New leaders are questioning the wisdom of allowing one million automobiles to enter Manhattan daily by way of bridges and tunnels just to move around and go back later. Some of the traffic brings needed deliveries, but honestly, is this done in the most efficient and sustainable way? Other cities have banned big trucks in their centers and forced merchants to collaborate so that one smaller truck can take the goods from many companies to one district—for example, Coca Cola and Pepsi bottles travel side-by-side and are delivered in the same truck in order to save gasoline, relieve traffic, and create a more pleasant city environment. Furthermore, most deliveries are carried out at nighttime in these pioneer cities. New York might do something along these lines as the Great Streets scheme unfolds.

After all, we are speaking of one of the most concentrated, dense cities in the world, and of a city with a very finely meshed and well-developed public transportation system. A high proportion of people who commute to work in New York (an impressive 82 percent) do this via public transport, but so far only one percent of the city residents use bicycles to go to work (in comparison, 36 percent are now commuting to work on bicycles in Copenhagen, Denmark, and this is a figure which is creeping up all the time, with 50 percent bicycle commuting planned for 2015). In a time in which concerns for pollution, climate deterioration, and the health of the population are rapidly growing, inviting New Yorkers to use bicycles to get around the city would be good policy. The stage appears to be perfectly set for this in a city generally dense and flat, with generously wide avenues and streets.

Bicycling is one important element in the new PlaNYC. Another element is improving public spaces and thereby inviting New Yorkers to not only walk in style on wider and better sidewalks, but also to stop walking, sit down, linger, enjoy the outdoors, play and socialize in the manner good city streets have always been able to accommodate. All this, and quite a few more efforts toward a greener and more people-friendly city, are part of the new NYC World Class Streets plan published on that memorable Thursday evening in November 2008.

It took half a century to get this far with your beloved city of New York. And certainly the visions and the blueprints that have by now been published would indeed have been enough to get Robert Moses to rotate uneasily in his grave. Not only are the blueprints available for all to see, but New Yorkers can watch one project after the other materialize around the city, based on the spirit of your early visions. Bicycle lanes are rapidly being introduced all over. The new lanes are proper ones, not just some token gesture of painted lines next to fast-flowing traffic. In the old line of thought, bicycle lanes were painted on the outside of the parked cars so that the bicyclists, by their mere presence, could protect the parked cars. This is not the case anymore. The new bicycle lanes are, as a matter of principle, placed inside the parked cars, so that the parked cars can protect the bicyclists: a small but crucial difference, which makes it much safer to circulate, and which will result in many more New Yorkers riding bicycles. It will be good for the climate, and certainly good for the general health of the bicyclists.

You did not write much specifically about bicycles, Jane, but you wrote much about life in the city, and one can see pedestrians, public life in general, and people on bicycles as different ways for people to use the city—as people.

I am sure you would have enjoyed the new inviting bicycle lanes on 8th and 9th Avenue, on Grand Street, and everywhere else. And surely you would appreciate that even on Broadway the priorities have been changed in order to make room for an excellent bicycle lane.

Talking of Broadway, it is just now in the process of being transformed from a noisy, polluted car corridor into a much more pleasant Broadway Boulevard, and you would especially enjoy the widened pedestrian areas giving room for flowers, tables, and chairs. You would not be surprised to see that as soon as spaces are converted from traffic space to people space, people come along in thousands and settle down to enjoy the scenery, the city, and city attraction number one—the other people. You were the one who very early pointed out the virtues and potential of lively city streets. On Broadway you can see it all happening almost before the sidewalk extensions are put in place.

Coming down to Madison Square you would, to your great surprise and joy, see waste areas of traffic space recently converted to people space, with planters, benches, chairs, and tables, and you would find that the new opportunities have almost overnight become a major people attractor, a place for hundreds to rest and enjoy. You would see these new people spaces emerging throughout the city, in Bronx, Queens, Brooklyn, and Staten Island, and as of May 2009 you would see Broadway closed to through traffic at Times Square and at Herald Square. If somebody in the future wants to cruise down Broadway, it will be on bicycles. This closing of Broadway to cars will actually assist the smooth and safe running of traffic on avenues and streets; but, most importantly, it will also provide much more space for pedestrians and public life, especially where the overcrowding and disgraceful conditions for people are most prominent—namely at Times Square and Herald Square.

Surely you would rejoice seeing such major improvements in the city where you fought so hard for proper respect for people. And, as if these new projects—and many more to come—were not enough, you would enjoy seeing the intensive work on the transformation process itself. A good city does not only come about by improving the streetscapes: the culture that goes with the new opportunities has to be developed as well. People must discover the new places and realize the new potentials. This work on changing old habits and old-fashioned mindsets takes many forms. One of the most enjoyable is the new Summer Streets initiative introduced in 2008, by which on summer Sundays selected streets are closed to traffic and given over to all kinds of people activities, which can prosper in car-free streets. These streets are found in all parts of the city, the most spectacular being the closing of Park Avenue coming out of Central Park from 72nd Street all the way down to the Brooklyn Bridge. Here you will find bicycle riders of all age groups as well as thousands of people walking, dancing, performing, playing, and generally having a good time. Indeed, New York has come a long way, and more and more is done along this line toward the life rather than death of a great American city.

Almost five decades have passed from the 1961 publishing of your *Great Cities* book, before New York started in earnest to turn around. In a wider, global perspective it has for most of these fifty years been a slow uphill battle to spread and implement the ideas pioneered in the book. In 1961, the background was the sterile modernistic planning principles originating from Europe in the late 1920s and early 1930s and expressively staked out in the 1933 CIAM/Athens charter of city planning. For reasons of health and rationality, the general rule was to always separate residences, work places, recreation, and transportation. These ideologies even expressively banned public spaces and streets as unhealthy and politically suspicious. They were seen as the breeding grounds for street boys, street girls, street fighting, and "parliaments of the street." Grass and parklands were much cleaner. This led to the ideation of freestanding high-rise buildings and towers placed out of city context and to the creation of separated monofunctional city districts, along the lines of what Robert Moses and his contemporaries were pushing for. Sadly, this line of thinking—in spite of everything—has been embraced for five decades by many cities and city planners. Endless modernistic suburbs were created in European and to some extent in American suburbs in the 1960s and 1970s, and these planning principles continued for decades to be used in East Europe and are now prevailing in the contemporary expansions of the cities of China.

These principles did not work for people in 1961, and they do not work today. Unfortunately, these ideologies have also dominated the planning of many downtown areas throughout the world, and are used in alarming scale in new towns such as Dubai, as if no one in these places ever came across your writings, Jane. It is not pleasant either to realize that many schools of architecture and planning still cherish the basic modernistic principles together with a devoted worship of form, rather than the important interaction of life and form you so convincingly advocated in your books. By 1961 the invasion of motorcars and traffic in Western societies really took off, and inaugurated a long period of continuous panic to secure capacity for ever more driving and parking. You saw the beginning of the siege and the panic, Jane, and warned against it. These two movements in the 1961 society—the modernistic planning ideas and the invasion of traffic—were the background for your warnings about the risk of death for great cities. These two threats are still very much present. It can be seen as quite surprising that actually so little progress has been made to master these problems in all these years; nevertheless, if we take a closer look, changes have been introduced here and there.

There is the Copenhagen story of gradually turning a car-oriented city into a quite impressive people-oriented one, with fine conditions for pedestrians and public life and with bicycles becoming more and more widespread. This gradual movement of city improvements actually started by closing the main street Strøget to car traffic in 1962, almost simultaneously with the publishing of *The Death and Life of Great American Cities*. Hardly anyone in Copenhagen would have known about this brand new book from America at that time, but the Copenhageners were reacting against the same pressures that made you write the book. And actually for five decades Copenhagen has become, day-by-day, a little bit better to live in than it was the day before. Surely, here is a city that has understood the spirit of your thoughts—and acted accordingly—almost from day one.

And certainly Copenhagen by now has many sisters and brothers in the family of steadily more livable cities. Cities such as Barcelona, Lyon, Strasbourg, Bordeaux, and Freiburg in Europe, and Vancouver, Portland, Curitiba, and Bogota in North and South America have engaged since the 1980s in similar turnarounds towards more people-oriented city politics. Impressive results have also been accomplished or are presently being carried out in the cities of Australia: Perth has come quite a distance; Sydney is just now in the process of starting up in a big way, wakening up after having slept for four to five decades just like New York. Both cities are in the process of implementing radical improvements for pedestrians, public transport, and bicyclists. First and foremost, miracles have been accomplished in Melbourne, famous in the 1980s for its dull and useless city center. In just ten years, Melbourne's city center has got ten times more residents, many more students, an array of new pedestrian lanes, streets, squares, and parks, which together with thousands of new street trees and a number of other visionary improvements in areas such as art and nighttime illumination, have resulted in an impressive and well-documented increase in city life. A vibrant, almost Parisian atmosphere is now prevailing in the streets that were once very quiet, if not for the noise of much too many cars. Another good news from Melbourne is that the economics of the city has thrived excellently during this process, and the city has been voted the most livable city in the world three times out of ten. Melbourne has by now turned its energy to implementing a full Copenhagen-style bicycle network in order to have even more Australians let go of the steering wheels and turn to the streets—as people.

A strong tailwind towards better cities has definitely started blowing. It is now known that looking carefully after the pedestrians and the bicyclists provides an obvious opportunity to address—with one simple strategy—four important issues in city planning. Pursuing a people-friendly city policy makes the cities more *lively*, *safe*, *sustainable*, and *healthy*, all qualities that are increasingly thought after in city policies. First and foremost, the cities will become more lively. People are universally the greatest urban attraction. Moreover, with more people walking and bicycling, the cities become safer. More eyes are steadily on the street. Walking and bicycling also helps to save energy resources, and further constitutes an important precondition for better quality and more use of public transportation. And finally, seriously inviting people to walk and bicycle more in the cause of their daily doings constitutes a very useful health strategy for modern societies.

These are some obvious virtues of a city planning policy inspired by your principles, Jane, and these virtues are exactly what many cities are by now seeking to provide, driven by their wish to be greener, to address the climate challenge, and to support more healthy lifestyles. New York has taken many years to get around to this point, but by now the city has started to change and is moving with impressive speed toward becoming a valuable and wonderful inspiration for cities around the world.

The ideas are back where they originated. The cities of the world are finally rolling.

Thank you, Jane.

THINK OF A CITY
AND WHAT COMES TO MIND?
ITS STREETS

Janette Sadik-Khan

T HE EPIC BATTLE between Robert Moses and Jane Jacobs over the streets of New York is something even the most casual observer hears about within months of arriving in the city. And while it was half a century ago that this high-stakes battle occurred, the debate over Jacobs' and Moses' diametrically opposed views on transportation and communities lives on today. Just attend any one of the community board meetings on any number of New York City Department of Transportation's (NYCDOT) projects, and you will hear the echoes of those early skirmishes.

The Moses vs. Jacobs debate also resonates in cities beyond New York. There is increasing recognition around the world that the auto-centric policies of the past, in which automobiles ruled the road and pedestrians were mere obstacles interfering with the movement of traffic, are not effective strategies for cities and metropolitan areas. During the twentieth century, many cities redesigned their central areas to better accommodate vehicular traffic and commuters who had moved to the suburbs. Today, many cities have rediscovered the advantages of their dense historic forms, and they are supporting public life through pedestrian, bicycling, and public space improvements.

Shortly after I was appointed Transportation Commissioner by Mayor Bloomberg in April 2007, we began developing a strategic plan that built on the mayor's PlaNYC sustainability initiative. And while "sustainability" was not even in the dictionary twenty years ago, in many ways Jane's vision is epitomized in "Sustainable Streets," the new strategic plan for NYCDOT, and our corollary report, "World Class Streets: Remaking New York City's Public Realm." These documents outline a new direction for the city's transportation system and a new approach to city streets, with the essence of the plan revolving around investing in public transit, bicycling, and walking infrastructure, and bringing a more pedestrian-focused agenda to the streets of New York City. With more transportation choices and more reliable travel—and streets that serve as public places in themselves—we will improve New York's communities, environment, and quality of life.

There is no question that we face major challenges in creating an urban environment that makes our streets and squares more people-friendly. Through new initiatives like Broadway Boulevard—where we transformed two lanes of traffic from 42nd to 35th Street in Manhattan (65,000 square feet of pavement) into a plaza area with tables, chairs, umbrellas, and an accompanying bike lane—we are showing that our streets can do more than move cars as quickly as possible from point A to point B. And that's the point: for far too long we have looked at the city's six thousand miles of streets from behind a windshield, and overlooked what is actually going on in them.

So, what is going on out there on our streets? They are the same streets that Jane Jacobs and Holly Whyte saw in the 1960s and 1970s. Thousands of pedestrians fill the sidewalks, stopping to talk in the midst of the flow and desperately seeking places to sit. We are looking to meet that "latent demand" for public space in this city by reclaiming the one piece of real estate left to work with—streets. We know the demand for lively streets is there because when we put out the bright orange cones that mark off an area for the construction of a pedestrian plaza, people flock to it, even before the work is completed (or sometimes even begun!). In the last year alone, we created forty-nine acres of public space, an area four times the size of the Great Lawn in Central Park. We have created more room for pedestrians, separated lanes for bicycles, and established bus lanes for transit. This effort has the dual advantage of making the streets more accommodating to pedestrians, transit, and bicycles, and less accommodating to private vehicles—an explicit nod to Jacobs' well-formed ideas about attrition.

In *The Death and Life of American Cities*, Jacobs defines attrition as "action taken to diminish vehicular traffic" (1961, 359). Contemporary planners frequently use the term "traffic evaporation" and cite the demolition of the Embarcadero Freeway in San Francisco following the Loma Prieta Earthquake of 1989. Opponents of the freeway's demolition thought that traffic would clog the city's streets, but instead, the thousands of cars that the freeway used to carry every day simply "evaporated" into the network, leaving no discernable effect on congestion. Jacobs uses as an example of this "evaporation" Washington Square: when the road through the park was closed in 1959, after a protracted battle with city planners like Moses, little provision was made for surrounding roads to be widened to accommodate the vehicles that previously went through the park, and no appreciable increase in traffic was evident. Attrition had occurred.

Now it is the "powers that be" who are advocating for attrition, and for several reasons: not just because we want the city to be more accommodating for pedestrians, cyclists, and transit, but also because we know that the only way this city can grow successfully over the next decades is by growing sustainably.

The sustainability initiative that Mayor Bloomberg launched in 2007 grew from a planning exercise to see how the city could continue to grow and thrive. The plan concluded that reducing environmental impacts and improving the quality of life were the only ways to secure the city's future. In fact, PlaNYC showed that continuing population growth in New York City carried a big national and global environmental benefit, because bringing another million people here, where we live transit-oriented, energy-efficient lives, has far less impact than spreading a million people out anywhere else in the U.S. Our challenge at NYCDOT is to make a nine-million people New York better and more livable than it is with fewer people today.

That requires a new transportation policy. PlaNYC emphasized mass transit expansion as well as other mobility strategies such as more bike lanes and, of course, congestion pricing, to both decrease the number of private vehicles on the streets of Manhattan and fund mass transit improvements that encourage people to switch modes of transportation.

Jacobs says that "attrition of automobiles operates by making conditions less convenient for cars… If properly carried out, attrition would decrease the need for cars simultaneously with decreasing convenience for cars" (1961, 363).

While we were unsuccessful in implementing congestion pricing in 2007, we have continued to use both mass transit expansion and pricing strategies to achieve a similar (if not as dramatic) result. Three examples of this are our Bus Rapid Transit program, which we piloted in 2008 on Fordham Road in the Bronx; variable parking pricing, which we piloted in Greenwich Village the same year; and expanded ferry service on the East River.

Our BRT program (called "Select Bus Service," or SBS) uses our streets more efficiently and cleanly—since our streets are the tracks for the city's massive bus system. Working with a new leadership at the MTA, we have implemented some ambitious initiatives to speed up buses that were previously considered "undoable." These innovations include off-board fare collection, special dedicated lanes, and traffic signals that give buses priority and longer green time at intersections. The Fordham Road SBS service, which operates on separated bus lanes along both the southern and northern curbs of Fordham Road in the Bronx, has attracted over 5,000 new riders by speeding travel times for the Bx12 service across the borough by over 20 percent.

The city is also moving forward with a new ferry service on the East River and will underwrite its operating costs. The new East River ferry network will be tied into the surface transportation system, notably to an exclusive busway we created on 34th Street which connects the ferry terminals on both the Hudson and East rivers.

And while congestion pricing remains on hiatus, we have begun a pilot program to test the effectiveness of charging higher parking meter rates during times of peak parking demand. The idea is that higher prices will lead to less meter feeding and more turnover of parking spaces, and the greater availability of parking spaces should mean less cruising for parking, less double-parking, and less congestion.

When I look back at the Moses-Jacobs battles, it seems that they clashed over not only their vision for the city, but also their approach to change. Moses was a big-thinker—he promoted massive projects, from Flushing Meadows Park to the Cross Bronx Expressway. Jacobs approved of a more incremental approach to change. And while she fought (and won) a few battles over the large-scale projects that threatened the city (like the Lower Manhattan Expressway), she saw the small, everyday decisions that planners and engineers made to speed trips for cars on city streets as more destructive:

> Erosion proceeds as a kind of nibbling, small nibbles at first, but eventually hefty bites. Because of vehicular congestion, a street is widened here, another is straightened there, a wide avenue is converted to one-way flow, staggered-signal systems are installed for faster movement... More and more land goes into parking, to accommodate the ever increasing numbers of vehicles while they are idle. No one step in this process is, in itself crucial. But cumulatively the effect is enormous. (Jacobs 1961, 349)

For decades, New York City has been a victim of this phenomenon and has restricted itself to a narrow approach to our streets. We have added left-turn lanes, removed medians, and built slip lanes all over the city in the name of furthering traffic flow. Signal timing and one-way conversions to favor vehicular mobility abounded over the last decades. As a result, we have much less interesting streets than NYC deserves. But now we are beginning to bite back.

Consider 9th Avenue between 14th and 31st Street on the West Side of Manhattan, where we have removed a travel lane through Chelsea in favor of a protected bicycle track. At the terminus of that bike lane, we converted two blocks of extra north-bound lanes (which provided access to a now dormant facility) into 4,500 square feet of new public space. Further south, in Gansevoort Street in the Meatpacking District, a neighborhood largely starved of public space, we transformed a riotous, chaotic roadbed of speeding traffic into a public plaza.

We've also built over two hundred miles of new bike lanes in the last three years. They are a particularly quick and simple way to reclaim street space without reconstructing roads and significantly impacting traffic. But still, even as thousands of new bike commuters take to the new lanes, citizens feel threatened by the reorganization of the streets.

It's not easy to bite back given the mindset of citizens who view our streets as car-only conveyances. In fact, we have to present many of our public realm improvements to community and business groups as traffic improvement plans. The plans have the benefit of better organizing our streets and generally improving, or having no discernable effect, on traffic flow. However, community groups, many of them bearing the scars of battles with the city over their neighborhoods, do not easily embrace change and are typically wary of government officials bearing plans presented as "good for them." When we develop a plan, such as the recent plan to downsize Broadway through Midtown Manhattan and turn its intersections with Times and Herald Squares into pedestrian areas, it takes months of work with community and business stakeholders to refine and explain the plan and garner their support.

For the Broadway project we have developed a long list of stakeholders, and worked hard to address their concerns while keeping the major principles of the project intact. The list of interested parties we've met with goes well beyond residents and elected officials—it includes tour bus operators, parking garage owners, Broadway theater groups, hoteliers, landlords and property managers, billboard and sign leasing agents, taxi and livery drivers, truck drivers, public sanitation and private carters, police and fire departments, street vendors, retailers, and event producers. Even a street performer like Times Square's famous Naked Cowboy has had his say (he likes the plan). It is quite clear to me that the quality of public outreach and communication on this project is as important as the public space and transportation benefits of the plan itself.

Reclaiming the streets is not an easy business, but the consequences of not acting are quite clear. I recently visited the city of São Paulo and witnessed almost constant gridlock and bumper-to-bumper traffic throughout the city. In an ironic twist, it turns out that the city had adopted a plan written by Robert Moses—and the results could not be clearer about what happens when you design streets to maximize the throughput of automobiles. It was eerie to see what a city looked like without the counterweight of a Jane Jacobs (the business community got around by helicopter, and all the major buildings and hotels had heliports on top.) The ghost of Moses lives on in cities like São Paulo—though the latter is moving forward with ambitious plans for an extensive subway, bus, and bike network.

In so many ways, the intellectual DNA of our work to create more sustainable streets can be found in *The Death and Life of American Cities*. When I read Jane's writing today, I'm struck by the "flair for the obvious" nature of her findings, which shows how far we have come since 1961. I think that's because there has been a slow but growing realization that we cannot build vital, exuberant, and healthy cities with a business-as-usual approach to our streets and streetscapes. We can't accommodate the million more people expected in NYC by 2030 by double-decking the West Side Highway or the FDR Drive, nor can we expect to create in this way the kind of economic growth and quality of life we need to continue to attract families and visitors. Many things have changed in this great city in the past fifty years, but our streets are not one of them. We are addressing this now, using the building blocks of Mayor Bloomberg's PlaNYC to create more sustainable streets and implement a new approach to transportation programs which contains many of Jane's deeply held principles.

Streets that help create and strengthen communities and business, in addition to connecting neighborhoods to one another, are an essential component of New York City's overall sustainability strategy. Quality-of-life policies will enable the city to continue to grow its economy and retain more residents as they raise families and grow older, and will even lead New Yorkers to spend more leisure time in the city.

It is no accident that NYC's business districts focus heavily on streetscape quality. Welcoming, attractive streets can spell the difference between growth and just getting by. NYC has the most famous streets in the world. Now we're working to make them the most attractive streets in the world for walking and cycling—and that other great NY sport, people-watching. I like to think that somewhere, Jane Jacobs is smiling.

REFERENCES

Jacobs, Jane. 1961. *The Death and Life of Great American Cities*. New York: Random House.

THE NEEDS OF CHILDREN
IN CONTEMPORARY CITIES

*Clare Cooper Marcus**

I ARRIVED IN THE United States from England in 1961, the year that *The Death and Life of Great American Cities* was published. Jane Jacobs experienced New York City as a lively and engaging place. As an immigrant knowing no one, and living there just long enough to earn the money to travel across the U.S. to Berkeley, I found it a miserably lonely city.

When I started my graduate program in city planning at the University of California, Berkeley, I joined a group of feisty students, itching to challenge old myths. In that heady time of peace marches and civil rights protests, one of my most eye-opening classes was a seminar with Jesse Reicheck where we read *The Death and Life of Great American Cities*, one or two chapters a week for a whole semester. That was all we read; that was all we needed to read. It changed my life and that of many of my classmates.

My whole career henceforth revolved around promoting the needs of those for whom we plan and design, who are often not consulted. A new field began to emerge, variously known as "environment and behavior,"

*Portions of this essay appeared in Robin Moore and Clare Cooper Marcus, "Healthy Planet, Healthy Children: Designing Nature into the Daily Spaces of Childhood," in *Biophilic Design: The Theory, Science and Practice of Bringing Buildings to Life*, edited by Stephen R. Kellert, Judith H Heerwagen, and Martin L. Mador, New York, John Wiley & Sons, 2008; and in "Shared Outdoor Space and Children's Play," in *A Place for Play: A Companion Volume to the Michigan Television Film, Where Do the Children Play?*, edited by Elizabeth Goodenough, National Institute for Play, 2008.

"man [*sic*] environment systems," "the social implications of design," or "environmental psychology." Since little had been published on the topic in the 1960s, I learned by observing the world around me and taking to heart Jacobs' words: "Cities are thoroughly physical places. In seeking understanding of their behavior, we get useful information by observing what occurs tangibly and physically, instead of sailing off on metaphysical fancies" (Jacobs 1961, 95-96).

I became a faculty member in the departments of architecture and landscape architecture at Berkeley, and from the mid-1970s to the mid-1990s, among a variety of assignments, I asked students to write what I called an "environmental autobiography." An important component of this exercise was to draw and describe their most fondly remembered childhood places. After reading hundreds of these papers over many years, it became clear that the places most often remembered were predominantly outdoors and nearly always semi-wild or overgrown areas such as woods, ravines, creeks, ditches, mudflats, trees, vacant lots, leftover urban spaces, and spaces between buildings in public housing or apartment complexes. From among hundreds of students completing this assignment, almost no one remembered a place specifically *designed* for children. Only one remembered a schoolyard as a favorite place, and none remembered a park.

I began to discern that these special places offered qualities supportive of children's self-directed play: they were relatively close to home, sometimes frequented by a small group of close friends, not particularly valued or visible to adults, and they incorporated an abundance of manipulable "loose parts." Remembered activities ranged from girls outlining "houses" with fallen leaves to boys "damming" a creek with stones and mud; from friends creating a secret den under bushes in a housing project to a boy seeking solace from family problems on a platform built in a tall tree.

Such activities are essential to a child's cognitive, social, and emotional development, and we should be concerned that these forms of play have been markedly curtailed in the last few decades. We can point to a number of reasons for this: the erosion of "leftover spaces" where children in middle childhood (about six- to eleven-year-old) can find places for absorbing self-directed play; the compulsion many parents feel to overschedule their children's lives; a focus on competitive sports as an unconscious "training" for life in an increasingly competitive society; the fears many parents harbor over letting their children engage in unsupervised play; and children's increasing absorption in technological tools such as cell phones, text messaging, video games, DVDs, and TV.

While there is clearly not a single way to encourage more self-directed play close to home, one suggestion to counteract some of the impediments described above is "cluster housing"—building dwellings around a shared outdoor space which forms a semiprivate core to a mini neighborhood. In this structure, children have ready access to the outdoors without having to be driven to soccer practice or walked to a park. Parents can see and monitor their children from home, alleviating their fears of traffic and "stranger-danger." The area becomes a large, shared backyard. Since the outdoors is nearby and neighboring children have equal access, those who might be watching TV or playing video games out of boredom or loneliness are more likely to run out to join friends for spontaneous play—no playdates necessary here. Also, children are likely to play there in the odd half hour before they are called in to dinner or during the time between homework and bed. These are precious fragments of time in an often overscheduled day, periods when tired, overworked parents are not likely to walk their children to a nearby park.

The idea of a core of shared outdoor space enclosed by buildings is not a new one: European monastic cloister gardens, Oxford and Cambridge colleges, California 1920s bungalow courts, and 1960s Planned Unit Developments are all examples. Plenty of contemporary examples can be found both in urban and suburban settings. We are not referring here to gated communities. In clustered housing schemes, which might range from ten to several hundred dwellings, the buildings are arranged to create a sense of enclosure around a shared green space, but there is usually nothing to stop non-residents from walking through.

A study of five such clustered housing communities—all in northern California—indicates that 80 percent of the use of shared green outdoor space is by children; most families are highly satisfied, friends who visit want to "move in" (or get on the waiting list), and children spend more time outdoors (Cooper Marcus 2003). In one case study (that of Cherry Hill affordable housing in Petaluma), 50 percent of parents reported that their children watched less TV since moving to the neighborhood. An indication of how much parents value clustered housing is illustrated by the trend toward cohousing, where future residents choose the site and have a say in its design. Each one of the more than a hundred cohousing communities in North America (completed or in the planning stage) features a site plan where units are clustered around shared outdoor space.

Community Greens, a nonprofit based in Arlington, VA, that promotes shared outdoor space in housing, notes that homes in developments that abut shared outdoor space generally sell at prices 5 percent to 15 percent higher than the competition, and the sales rate is also faster.[1] This fact is not lost on Jim Soules, developer of the Cottage Company in Seattle, who creates clusters of homes, termed "pocket neighborhoods." Small, cottage-like houses designed by Ross Chapin Architects are grouped around attractive shared green spaces used for adult socializing and children's play. Soules states that he will never build another project without this shared green space.

A more extensive example of shared outdoor space is provided by the case of Village Homes in Davis, CA. Traffic enters the neighborhood via long narrow cul-de-sacs; an extensive area of interconnected paths and greenways at the heart of the neighborhood, accessed from the backs of the houses, provides a setting where children can play and move around safely away from traffic, amidst creeks, fruit trees, wildlife, and gardens (Corbett, Corbett, and Thayer 2000).

Despite extensive national and international recognition of the innovative neighborhood design of Village Homes, this blueprint has not been replicated. Why? Many developers are understandably leery of attempting something they perceive as innovative in a precarious marketplace. But another barrier is the philosophy of the increasingly influential New Urbanist movement, in particular its belief that *all* green space should be fully public, that shared green space doesn't work (despite many examples to the contrary), and its rigid opposition to the cul-de-sac. Shared (not

---

1. www.communitygreens.org.

public) green space and cul-de-sacs are essential ingredients in the success of places like Village Homes.

In a *Wall Street Journal* article entitled "The Suburbs under Siege," Amir Efrati notes:

> Thanks to a growing chorus of critics ranging from city planners and traffic engineers to snowplow drivers, hundreds of local governments from San Luis Obispo, CA, to Charlotte, NC, have passed zoning ordinances to limit cul-de-sacs or even ban them in the future. In Oregon, about 90 percent of the state's 241 cities have changed their laws to limit cul-de-sacs, while 40 small municipalities outside Philadelphia have adopted restrictions or an outright ban. (Efrati 2006)

Opponents argue that cul-de-sacs exacerbate traffic-load on collector streets, and that reimposing a grid redistributes traffic and encourages people to walk and not get into their car for every errand. While there is certainly some truth about redistributing traffic, people are not going to walk unless there is somewhere to walk *to*, and with the best of intentions, many New Urbanist developments have failed to promote small retail within the neighborhood, so people still have to get into their cars and drive to the supermarket, drop their children off at school, and so on.

All over Davis, CA—a bicycle-oriented university town—there are developments with cul-de-sacs abutting onto greenways enhancing pedestrian and cycle movement. The dead ends of cul-de-sacs facing across a greenway are linked to each other and to pathways, forming an extensive "grid" of bicycle and walking paths. People, including children, walk or cycle to shops, school, parks, and the university campus. If one of the aims of the New Urbanists is to create more walkable neighborhoods, which laudably it is, Davis should be a model to emulate. It is, however, ignored. This is a glaring example of how the dictates of traffic engineering take precedence, and how a set of strict "rules" which are now the core of New Urbanism can become a rigid planning philosophy, the like of which Jane Jacobs argued against fifty years ago. Much anecdotal evidence and some empirical data indicate that homes on cul-de-sacs sell faster and command a higher price than those on through streets, and that children living on cul-de-sacs are more likely to be playing actively outdoors than those living on through streets. With growing evidence of children's lack of activity and weight gain, this fact should give us pause.

Balancing the needs of traffic and of children *can* be achieved, and is done so in a number of countries beyond the U.S. (Despite its assumed self-image, the U.S. is not a particularly child-friendly society.) The *woonerf*, meaning "residential precinct" (sometimes referred to as slow street, shared street, or home zone) was first developed in the Netherlands to curb speeding traffic on inner-city, grid-pattern streets. The street is transformed by means of speed bumps, bulb-outs, planters, trees, benches, and play spaces. Pedestrians and cars share the paved space of the street (with no specific sidewalks), and pedestrians have legal priority. Entrances to the shared zone are clearly marked; through traffic is discouraged, but residents on the street have auto access to their dwellings. The shared-street concept became established through sets of design guidelines in the Netherlands and Germany (1976); England, Denmark, and Sweden (1977); France and Japan (1979); Israel (1981); and Switzerland (1982). Studies of shared streets in Europe, Japan, Australia, and Israel have found reductions in traffic accidents, increased social interaction and play, and a high degree of satisfaction by the residents.

While traffic-calming devices (bulb-outs, chicanes, speed bumps, etc.) are being incorporated on many city streets, there are no fully developed *woonerfen* in the U.S., primarily due to opposition from traffic engineers, road building companies, and fire and police departments. One expert points out that the reintroduction of the grid, as insisted upon by New Urbanism, raises the likelihood of cut-through traffic and of inappropriate speeds in residential neighborhoods—the original impetus for *abandoning* the grid and introducing winding streets and cul-de-sacs in suburbia more than sixty years ago. A carefully planned grid with some through streets and some shared, *woonerf*-type streets could provide for safe traffic movement as well as create safe places for children to play outside, close to home (Ben-Joseph 1995).

It wasn't always the case that children's needs were downplayed compared to the needs of moving traffic. In the 1920s, developments such as Sunnyside Gardens, NY, Radburn, NJ, and Baldwin Hills, CA, were created with inner-block, shared green space, traffic and parking on the periphery, and were motivated in large part by the desire to create safe, close-to-home space for children's play. In the flush of new town planning in the 1950s, particularly in Britain and Sweden, whole towns were created with an emphasis on the preservation of green space, transit connections, and the safe mobility of pedestrians, particularly children, separate from traffic streets. Meanwhile, in the U.S., the postwar demand for housing for returning veterans and the automobile and highway construction lobbies combined to create an explosion of car-dependent suburbs. In the sixty years since, not a lot has changed, rising gas prices and house foreclosures notwithstanding. With the exception of some urban infill projects, the needs of cars (movement and parking) take precedence over the needs of children. Children don't pay taxes, don't vote, and are rarely consulted on environmental decisions that affect their lives. They are a silent minority; in some neighborhoods, a majority. Planners think in terms of master plans and neighborhood layouts, and assume that with a regular scattering of parks and schools, children's needs will be met.

But there is hope in sight. An enlightened Chicago developer, Perry Bigelow, has created an extensive new suburban neighborhood—Home Town, in Aurora, IL—where the needs of children take precedence over traffic engineering. While not as child-pedestrian friendly as postwar Swedish suburbs (or even Village Homes), Bigelow's plan breaks the mold of traditional U.S. suburban design by providing traffic-calming devices such as raised crosswalks and tight corner turns so that cars can only travel comfortably at 15–20 miles per hour. Houses are located facing onto green pedestrian ways, or living courts, completely removed from automobile traffic, where children can play on walks wide enough for two tricycles or Big Wheels to pass, and adults and teens can hang out on shaded benches. A visit to this community on a summer evening in 2008 confirmed everything the developer's website touts as special in this "kid safe neighborhood." There were children playing safely and happily everywhere in the living courts and on attractive playgrounds. It is heartening to learn that in setting the goals for Home Town, Bigelow drew heavily on planning research literature, a step which is not universal among developers and designers. Sources included Christopher

Alexander's *A Pattern Language* (Alexander et al. 1977) and a book co-authored by this author and Wendy Sarkissian, *Housing as if People Mattered: Site Design Guidelines for Medium-Density Family Housing* (Cooper Marcus and Sarkissian 1986). Bigelow and others (including this author) are working on a scheme to rate neighborhoods in terms of their child-friendliness, on the lines of LEED ratings for energy-saving buildings.

How do these arguments to reconsider neighborhood design from the viewpoint of children relate to the work of Jane Jacobs? In *The Death and Life of Great American Cities*, Jacobs pointed out that most gang and antisocial behavior in New York occurred in the outdoor spaces between high-rise buildings in housing projects, and rarely on the sidewalks where there were plenty of adult eyes on the street. She derided the planning beliefs of the time that parks are "good" for children, while sidewalks and streets are "bad." She even found fault with the kinds of clustered housing around green enclaves I have been describing, arguing that after a very early age, children find them boring and want "out," and that buildings turned inwards to enjoy the green outlook inevitably result in blank walls facing the street. There is some truth to both these arguments, but they are the result of poor architectural and landscape design. There are plenty of examples built in the last fifty years where the buildings present equally attractive inward and street-facing façades. Landscape architects—cognizant of the boring green deserts of housing projects and 1960s Planned Unit Developments—have created varied and attractive environments of grassy areas for ball games and running; play equipment for climbing and swinging; shrubbery where children can make dens and club houses; and footpaths wide enough for ride-on toys, roller skating, hopscotch, jump rope, shooting marbles, and writing in chalk—activities Jacobs observed on the sidewalks of New York. Studies of children's play in shared outdoor space such as I have been describing indicate that the far majority of play occurs on paths because the favored activities require a hard surface. If it is carefully planned for, casual, unorganized "sidewalk" play can happen just as easily on the interior pathways of a clustered housing scheme as on the "real" sidewalks of a city, and in a much safer milieu.

In the fifty years since Jane Jacobs wrote, cities have changed. Children do still play on some wide city sidewalks, but there are many fewer small shopkeepers ready to run out and settle a dispute (as Jacobs observed), and many fewer eyes on the street as most adults are (or were, until recently) in the workforce. A high ratio of caring, pedestrian adults to playing children is necessary for informal surveillance to work. Unfortunately, beyond the kind of high-density neighborhood where Jacobs lived and raised her children, this is now a rarity. At the other extreme are the auto-oriented suburbs where often there are no sidewalks, since it is assumed that everyone will move around by car—and they do.

Richard Louv, a perceptive journalist like Jane Jacobs, has brought national attention to the plight of U.S. children in his book, *Last Child in the Woods: Saving Our Children from Nature-Deficit Disorder* (2005). He writes not only of children's lack of access to nature close to home, but also of their diminishing territorial range and independent mobility. Visits to the website generated by his work indicate that this book has touched a nerve among many American parents and teachers.[2]

A recent policy statement by the American Academy of Pediatrics also breaks new ground. In "The Built Environment: Designing Communities to Promote Physical Activity in Children" (2009), doctors who treat children are being urged to consider how decisions regarding the design of our cities may be affecting children's physical activities and health. Various planning solutions are presented, including the one described in this essay. The serious epidemic of childhood obesity and the concomitant rise in the incidence of type 2 diabetes, linked in part to lack of exercise, should prompt us all to reconsider how design and planning decisions are affecting the lives of our most vulnerable citizens.

Beautiful streets, as appealing as they are, are not enough. Coordinated house façades and form-based codes inspired by New Urbanism, as attractive as they are, are not enough. A scattering of neighborhood parks on a master plan is not enough. Just as the ADA turned our attention to how the design of the environment supports or thwarts people with disabilities, every design decision needs to be assessed in terms of how child-friendly it is—i.e., the height of handrails on steps to a subway station; the height at which art is hung in a children's hospital; the provision

---

2. www.childrenandnature.org.

for creative, nature-based play in child-care centers; the design of school-yards and classrooms with views out to nature; the clustering of dwellings to encourage creative, self-directed play close to home; and the design of family neighborhoods so that children's independent mobility is on a par with the needs of moving traffic.

If I were to write a manifesto to support children's needs in an ideal neighborhood, it would state the following requirements:

1. A natural or quasi-natural area away from traffic and within sight and calling distance of homes surrounding the space occupied by families with children. This space needs to provide opportunities for as many different kinds of play as possible: places where digging in dirt or sand is encouraged; semi-wild areas where dens might flourish; trees for climbing; grassy areas for ball games and running; planting beds for gardening; paths for wheeled toys; and equipment for climbing, swinging, sliding, etc.

2. The shared green space needs to be separated from dwellings by a privacy "buffer" such as a fenced yard or patio, with easy access out to the shared space.

3. Access from homes needs to be safe, not requiring a street crossing wherever possible. Studies of children's perceptions of their own neighborhoods repeatedly cite the problem of traffic in limiting mobility and access (Hillman 1993; Davis and Jones 1996; O'Brien 2003; Wheway and Millward 1997).

4. The shared green space needs to be well maintained, but without removing those "loose parts" (leaves, twigs, cones, seeds, etc.) valuable for children's creative play.

5. Adults and children alike need to understand that this area is a legitimate locale for children's play.

6. This space needs to provide for all age groups, from toddlers to late teens, without any one group or gender dominating the use of the space and intimidating others.

7. Where provision of such a space is not possible, houses for families with children should face onto a cul-de-sac or *woonerf*-type street, or back onto an alley with limited traffic access and some play features.

8. Where these street solutions are not possible, sidewalks at least 12–15 feet wide should be provided, separated from parking lanes and moving traffic by a planting strip of street trees or, in particularly rainy environments, by bioswales.

9. Where possible, spaces for children's outdoor play (shared green areas, cul-de-sacs, traffic-limited streets, alleys, or streets with wide sidewalks) should link via a greenway bike and path system to natural areas, public parks, schools, local shops, library, etc., to facilitate children's safe and healthy mobility within the neighborhood.

10. Above all, we need to protect and enhance children's access to nature, whether to a large, semi-wild space or something as simple as a single tree growing in an "island" in the middle of a cul-de-sac. Research indicates that today's environmental activists all had access as children to wild or semi-wild nature and at least one caring adult who encouraged that access. It is critical that we promote such access for children in contemporary cities in order to educate and inspire the next generation of earth stewards.

REFERENCES

Alexander, Cristopher, Sara Ishikawa, Murray Silverstein et al. 1977. *A Pattern Language*. New York: Oxford University Press.

American Academy of Pediatrics, Committee on Environmental Health. 2009. "The Built Environment: Designing Communities to Promote Physical Activity in Children." *Pediatrics* 123, no. 6: 1591-1598.

Ben-Joseph, Eran. 1995. "Changing the Residential Street Scene: Adapting the Shared Street (*Woonerf*) Concept to the Suburban Environment." *Journal of the American Planning Association* 61, no. 4: 504-515.

Cooper Marcus, Clare and Wendy Sarkissian. 1986. *Housing as if People Mattered: Site Design Guidelines for Medium-Density Family Housing*. Berkeley, CA: University of California Press.

Cooper Marcus, Clare. 1993. "Post-occupancy evaluation of Cherry Hill affordable housing, Petaluma, CA" (unpublished manuscript).

———. 2003. "Shared Outdoor Space and Community Life." *Places: Quarterly Journal of Environmental Design* 15, no. 2: 32-34.

Corbett, Michael, Judy Corbett, and Robert L. Thayer. 2000. *Designing Sustainable Communities: Learning from Village Homes*. Washington, DC: Island Press.

Davis, Adrian and Linda Jones. 1996. "Children in the Urban Environment: An Issue for the New Public Health Agenda." *Health and Place* 2, no. 2: 107-113.

Efrati, Amir. 2006. "The Suburbs under Siege: Homeowners Love Cul-de-Sacs, Planner Say They're Perils; Taking Sides in Minnesota." *Wall Street Journal Online*, June 2.

Hillman, Mayer. 1993. *Children, Transport and the Quality of Life*. London: Policy Studies Institute.

Jacobs, Jane. 1961. *The Death and Life of Great American Cities*. New York: Vintage Books.

Louv, Richard. 2005. *Last Child in the Woods: Saving Our Children from Nature-Deficit Disorder*. Chapel Hill: Algonquin Books.

O'Brien, Margaret. 2003. "Regenerating Children's Neighborhoods: What Do Children Want?" In *Children in the City: Home, Neighborhood and Community*, edited by Pia Christensen and Margaret O'Brien. London: Routledge Falmer.

Wheway, Rob and Alison Millward. 1997. *Child's Play: Facilitating Play on Housing Estates*. Coventry, UK: Chartered Institute of Housing.

SECTION 6

Economic Instincts

WHEN PLACES HAVE
DEEP ECONOMIC HISTORIES

Saskia Sassen

T HE RELATIONSHIP BETWEEN older material economies—
manufacturing, mining, agriculture—and today's knowledge economy needs to be recovered.[1] The idea that such a relationship exists has
been lost in academic research and in more general commentaries about
the knowledge economy. The latter is seen as new and non-material,
whence it is easy to assume that its existence is predicated on the overcoming of the older material economies of a place, a city, a region. The
contemporary understanding of the knowledge economy is that it is about
abstract knowledge and the talent of the so-called "creative classes" and
"symbolic knowledge workers." I will argue that we have overvalued this
class of workers: one consequence is a devaluing of material economies,
notably manufacturing, and of workers who deal with materials. Such a
devaluing of manual work holds even when it is part of new and state-
of-the-art economic sectors.

Two links are lost in analyses that conceive of the knowledge economy as a sort of opposite, radically different economy from the older
material economies. The first break is between the knowledge embedded
in older material economies of craftworkers and skilled manual work;
often this rupture also holds for knowledge workers directly involved in
material economies, such as high-tech.

---

1. For data and bibliography on the issues discussed in this brief article, please see Sassen
(2006); see also Birch and Wachter (2009).

The other link that is lost is with the city. Particular types of material economies, including those I will refer to as urban manufacturing, are today a critical component of multiple knowledge sectors. These kinds of urban material economies matter enormously for cities and vice versa, as Jane Jacobs described so brilliantly. They are one component in Jane Jacobs' proposition that cities are creative.[2] Urban manufacturing thrives in cities and contributes to create a more distributed type of economy— producing more mid-level jobs and firms with mid-level rather than hyper profits. This kind of urban production is mostly highly specialized, but in ways that the "knowledge economy" analysis simply overlooks. Unlike mass manufacturing, it needs to be in cities or urban areas because it is networked, is based on multiple supplier and contractor links, and needs direct contact with customers. Moreover, it varies enormously across cities, thereby reflecting the particularity of a city's economic history. Urban manufacturing is often unrecognized by economic development experts and planners, or misunderstood as an anachronism because its connection to the advanced knowledge sectors is not noticed.

THE DEEP ECONOMIC HISTORY
OF A CITY AND ITS CONSEQUENCES

Recognizing the link between older material economies and current components of the knowledge economy helps us understand why these components can vary sharply across cities, and why these specialized differences keep getting reproduced. New York and Chicago, for instance, are the two leading financial centers in the U.S., and both are among the top ten global centers. It is often assumed that they compete with each other, but they actually compete far less than is generally assumed. Why? Because the extreme complexity of their financial sectors is rooted in very diverse material economies: one city developed its finance sector from trading and banking, while the other city's financial center grew

---

2. I take this insight a step further in my global city analysis and argue that even highly abstract economic activities that would seem to have little connection with a city actually need urban environments for their most complex activities.

from the specialized servicing of huge steel mills and vast industrial scale farming. The result was a set of highly specialized differences, beyond the range of more routinized activities evident in all cities.

What is usually understood as coming out of the head of talented professionals turns out to have profound links with the economic histories of cities. By this I mean those histories, inevitably mostly material, that forged a city's (modern) economy. This holds for cities with somewhat complex and diverse economies; it does not hold for towns that emerged around one single industry or firm, such as a mine or steel mill whose death meant the death of the town itself.

The argument I am making here is twofold. On the one hand, I suggest that major components of today's knowledge economy started with the knowledge embedded in the material practices of older economies, which eventually fed more abstract forms of knowledge. On the other, I argue that insofar as these older material economies of cities were diverse, each city wound up with a specific type of specialized knowledge economy. Cities that lack a complex economic history can eventually buy into the knowledge economies; thus the strategy adopted by some cities to attract "creative classes" will work for more routinized knowledge economies, which can be standardized and easily sold. Ultimately, however, that highly diversified entity we refer to as "the knowledge economy" could not simply emerge from the heads of the creative classes, no matter how brilliant they might be. Cities are complex systems and, as Jane Jacobs explained, enablers of creative activities. Why would these original economic histories in the making not extend into our present? This approach also helps us recognize how our major cities have each made their economic history.

Recognizing that the deep economic history of a place feeds its specialized knowledge economy carries various political implications. One consequence is that it returns value to earlier material economic practices—the craft and the mental work embedded in those practices.[3]

---

3. Richard Sennett (2008) examines the complex connection between mind and hand in a broad range of activities, well beyond the basic notion of craftwork and specialized manufacturing.

The other is that cities actually compete with each other far less than is typically argued in the mainstream discussion.[4] Thus a city's leadership can, for instance, make a far tougher bargain with large corporations that aim at setting up offices, and make far fewer concessions than has been typical over the last twenty years. Urban governments should also work much harder at collaborating with other cities—for instance, the cities where a given firm also has set up offices. This need for collaboration among cities will be critical as we begin to confront our major environmental challenges. Effective greening of our economies will require active participation of all actors in and across cities, and much exchange of best practices and just plain communication of what works.[5]

How much the specificity of a city and an urban region matters can vary considerably depending on multiple factors, including the city's positioning in local and global markets. This specificity matters more than is usually assumed, and in ways that are not generally recognized. The policy implication of my argument is that there is too great a focus on competition and not enough on specialized differences among cities—and on the resulting possibility of greater bargaining power vis-à-vis global firms and of coalitions among cities worldwide confronting those same corporations.

The increasingly homogenized landscapes and built environments tend to obscure the fact of regional or urban specificity. Part of the confusion and the difficulty in capturing the importance of the specialized differences of cities is due to the globalizing of production standards for

---

4. The key frame for policy recommendations that emerged over the last twenty years is that cities need to be competitive in a global world. Part of the influence of the creative classes concept is that it is seen as making cities more competitive. However, in this vast literature there is little elaboration of the significant difference between being competitive and competing.

5. For instance, we now have considerable knowledge of how to use nature's capacities to do what we now do via factory-made chemicals. However, applying this awareness to the complex and fast-moving space of large cities will require much trial and error. Communication among the leaderships of cities will become a must. There is already a rapidly expanding network of cities for this type of environmental work.

the built environment. Thus the state-of-the-art office district, luxury consumption space, and high-income neighborhood all need to meet certain requirements. However, while the office buildings may look the same, this does not mean that the work that gets done in them is necessarily the same. To recognize these economic differences in similar office buildings, we need to use a lens that can capture high levels of specialization. I argue that this kind of built environment is more akin to an infrastructure: necessary but indeterminate. That is to say, if the state-of-the-art built environment that produces a homogenized urban visual order is actually an indeterminate infrastructure, it can accommodate enormous economic differences. It becomes critical to establish what are the particular specialized sectors that might inhabit that uniform landscape.

SWITCHING FROM A MATERIAL
TO A KNOWLEDGE ECONOMY

The case of Chicago helps to illustrate some of the issues discussed so far. It is common to see Chicago as a latecomer to the knowledge economy (and thus to global city status). Why did it happen so late—almost fifteen years later than in New York and London? Typically the answer is that Chicago had to *overcome* its agro-industrial and heavy manufacturing past, and that this economic history put it at a disadvantage compared to old trading and financial centers such as New York and London.

Yet Chicago's past was not a disadvantage to the city. It was one key source of its specialized difference among major cities worldwide. The particular specialized corporate services that had to be developed to handle the needs of its agricultural and heavy manufacturing regional economy gave Chicago a key component of its current specialized advantage in the global economy. The complexity, scale, and international character of Chicago's economy required highly specialized financial, accounting, legal, and other kinds of expert services quite different from those required to handle, for instance, New York's key sectors—service exports, finance on trade, and finance on finance.

Chicago became the leading global financial center for commodities futures through a process that started with the growers who knew about corn and about pigs, and who were growing at such vast scales that the Adam Smith market of the farming village—that is to say, the market where sellers see each other's products and prices during the process of selling and buying—was not an option. They had to establish a future price on the basis of their knowledge of corn and pigs—what the quality and price of the corn and the pigs would be at maturity—rather than an amount simply based on the going price at the time of sale. Out of this embedded knowledge came a complex financial instrument: commodities futures, which are a type of derivative. More generally, out of this came a very specific capacity to serve the advanced service needs of particular types of firms, particularly firms in highly speculative sectors such as finance.

For this specialized advantage to materialize, it is necessary for past knowledge to get repositioned in a different set of economic circuits. This entails, then, disembedding that expertise from an agro-industrial economy and re-embedding it in a "knowledge" economy—an economy where expertise can increasingly be commodified, function as a key input, and thereby constitute a new type of intermediate economy (that is, the firm-to-firm economy). Having a past as a major agro-industrial complex makes that switch more difficult for a city than having a past as a trading and financial center would. This partly explains Chicago's "lateness" in bringing that switch about. That switch, however, is not a matter of overcoming that past, but rather of using it in a sharply different way. It requires a new organizing logic that can reposition, and thereby revalue, the capabilities developed in an earlier era.[6]

São Paulo, Tokyo, Seoul, and Shanghai, along with Chicago, are today the major global cities with particularly strong histories in heavy

---

6. Elsewhere I develop this notion of switching (existing capabilities switching to novel organizing logics) in order to understand the formation of today's global economy as well as today's partial denationalizing of state capacities: see Sassen (2008, chapters 1, 8). Here I extend this notion to a specific case: the switch from knowledge embedded in material practices to the commodification of that knowledge.

manufacturing and a specialized services sector that can service the needs of firms in material economies. In the U.S. we can see the same phenomenon occurring in several minor ways in smaller cities that have lost much of their old manufacturing base. For instance, when Austin, Texas, and Toledo, Ohio, both sought to attract photovoltaics manufacturing, a key sector for a greener economy, Toledo won because of its established base of skilled labor and knowledge in glass manufacturing (Fitzgerald 2009). The sophisticated industrial knowledge that grew around Pittsburgh's metals industries allowed it to become a global player in aluminum (Alcoa), copper (Koppers), and steel (U.S. Steel); this kept money flowing back to the city even when the mining and manufacturing sites moved to other countries. More generally, the widespread pattern of having industrial research and design operations under the same roof as the actual manufacturing is a key indication of the dynamic interaction between actual fabricating and knowledge economy components.[7]

A second issue raised by the Chicago case is that while there are a number of global cities today with heavy manufacturing origins, many once-important manufacturing cities have not made the switch into a knowledge economy based on that older industrial past. This is the case of Detroit and of several English manufacturing cities.[8] They were too dominated by a single or a few industries and shaped up more like monocultures—not unlike the plantation economies of colonial empires, which also have had great difficulty switching into more complex knowledge economies. This points to the importance of thresholds in the scale and diversity of a city's manufacturing past—diversity being a key tenant of

---

7. Today, knowledge economy and actual fabricating have been separated in standardized sectors, but not in advanced high-tech manufacturing, as is evident in Silicon Valley or in car manufacturing in Germany and Japan, which make some of the best cars in the world.
8. Carl Taylor, from Michigan State University, has developed the Taylor Report (www.thetaylorreport.org). It addresses post-industrial Detroit citizens' efforts to redevelop Detroit through urban gardening and youth development at the YouthVille center (www.youthvilledetroit.com). These are the types of activities and projects that can feed rebirth in the face of socioeconomic decline and devastation. See also www.thirdcity.org for an overall description of what is taking place in Detroit as the city is trying to redefine itself, moving beyond the almost absolute dependence on the three big auto manufacturing companies.

Jane Jacobs in characterizing the urban economy. When such thresholds are not reached, it becomes difficult to secure the components of knowledge production I identify in Chicago's case—specialized servicing capabilities that could be dislodged from the organizational logic of heavy manufacturing and relocated in the organizational logic of today's so-called knowledge economy.

The specialized economic histories of major cities and regions matter in today's global economy because they are the main way in which national economies are inserted in multiple global circuits. It never was "the" national economy that positioned a country within the international division of functions. But today it is even less so, because the global economy consists of a vast number of particular circuits connecting particular components of cities and regions across borders.

URBAN MANUFACTURING: A HISTORIC INVERSION

A very different way in which the deep economic history of a place shapes its present-day specialized advantages is through urban manufacturing. There are two aspects often overlooked in discussions about urban economies—whether small or large, global or local. One of these aspects is the fact that there are actually multiple articulations between "backward" and advanced sectors in these cities. The second, a critical instance of the first, is that a particular type of manufacturing is very much part of today's urban service economies, including the most advanced ones. When we started our research about this in the 1990s, we chose to call this "urban manufacturing."[9]

Urban manufacturing is geared to design sectors of all sorts (from jewelry to furniture design, architecture, and interior decoration), cultural industries (theaters and opera houses need sets and costumes, museums and galleries need display settings for their collections), building trades

---

9. See Mitchell and Sassen (1996) and Loomis (1995). See also Matthew T. Mitchell, "Urban Manufacturing in New York City" (master's thesis, Department of Urban Planning, Columbia University, 1996).

(customiz10ed woodwork and metalwork), and to other sectors that are very much part of advanced service-based economies (the staging in luxury shops and restaurants, displays in corporate headquarters, and so forth).[10]

Urban manufacturing has several characteristics: 1) it needs an urban location because it is deeply networked and operates in contracting and subcontracting chains; 2) it is often fairly customized and hence needs to be in close proximity to its customers and to a diverse pool of first-rate craftworkers; 3) it inverts the historic relation between services and manufacturing (historically, services developed to serve the needs of manufacturers) in that it serves service industries.

A very advanced and rapidly growing type of urban manufacturing is emerging out of the diversity of projects to green our economies. It is a mix of more standard manufacturing and the features of urban manufacturing I described above. For instance, an intense initiative to use the manufacturing knowledge base of Chicago is the Chicago Manufacturing Renaissance Council's work on a new type of education of manufacturing workers that combines knowledge economy and fabrication. Its aim is to use advanced knowledge to manufacture the new types of products that the greening of our economy will require. Thus its Wind Turbine Supply Chain Project seeks to link local manufacturing companies to the emerging wind turbine sector, a cutting-edge field that requires complex machined inputs. This is the type of advanced manufacturing at which Europe (e.g., wind power) and Japan (e.g., hydrogen car batteries) have excelled. It is interesting to note that of the nearly 16,000 factories employing 660,000 workers in Illinois, three quarters are in the Chicago metro area (Swinney 2009). This is urban manufacturing at a grand scale.

For much of the 1980s and 1990s, most policy analysts and government economic development agencies in New York, for instance, did not recognize the existence of a specifically urban manufacturing sector. Policy was oriented towards retaining the large, standardized factories, as

---

10. In this regard see also Gratz (2010), in particular her chapter on manufacturing in New York City and its links to top-level design sectors—e.g., making classic-style furniture to be sold through the Museum of Modern Art.

these were far more visible and known, and had more sizable workforces. But these were precisely the ones for whom it made no sense to stay in the city: they did not need the urban economy with its multiple supplier and contracting chains and diverse craft talent pools. Finally, these were the decades in which government policy makers easily fell under the spell of powerful corporate services and finance, with their rapidly increasing numbers of very high-income employees and extremely high profits. Eventually, the cultural sector and tourism joined the list of glamorous and desirable sectors.

What was not clear was the extent to which urban manufacturing was growing partly as a result of the expansion of these advanced service sectors, including cultural industries. For this reason, perhaps, urban governments generally did not support the sector, which was often extremely vulnerable, given the sharp rise in the costs of manufacturing in cities dominated by high-profit-making corporate services. Indeed in the case of New York City we see that the more dynamic the advanced corporate services and the cultural sector, a) the more dynamic the urban manufacturing sector,[11] and b) the more difficult it becomes for the latter to meet its basic needs (space, reasonable energy costs, technical and banking support, and so on).

One way of capturing these somewhat invisible dynamics is to think of the urban economy as traversed by multiple specialized circuits. An analysis of the diverse circuits that connect a given sector to various urban activities shows us that even finance, when disaggregated into such circuits, is linked to urban manufacturing suppliers, often through the design and building trades element, including the installation of advanced security devices throughout corporate office buildings.

Many smaller cities nowadays have the talent pools and the potential for a small-scale urban manufacturing sector. This is due to the

---

11. Just as urban manufacturing is intimately connected with—not opposed to—an advanced corporate services sector, so is much of the economic informalization that has appeared in major global cities in North America, Western Europe, Latin America, and to a lesser extent Japan (see Sassen 2006, chapters 6, 7). This in turn helps to explain a mostly overlooked development: the proliferation of an informal economy of creative professional work in cities worldwide—artists, architects, designers, and software developers (Sassen 2009).

earlier mentioned trend toward the urbanization of economic activities, so that even a mining- or manufacturing-based regional economy feeds the growth of specialized corporate services in cities: firms in all economic sectors nowadays are buying more insurance, and legal and accounting services. The specialized services needed by more routinized economic sectors (heavy manufacturing, mining, industrial agriculture, transportation) are also more routinized, and hence can be produced in smaller and more provincial cities—they do not need a global city. The presence of a growing advanced services sector, along with the resultant growth of a high-income workforce with a strong preference for urban living, generates the conditions for a demand for urban manufacturing. Such urban living today entails a bundle of demands: for elegant restaurants and shops, for museums and cultural events, for customized furniture and metalwork, and for the rehabilitation of older buildings to new high-end uses. This potential, however, is easily killed due to little or no recognition and support from policy makers, and even from analysts and researchers.

In the 1980s there were multiple initiatives to get policy makers to recognize the presence of urban manufacturing in New York, Los Angeles, Boston, Philadelphia, and Pittsburgh, all cities with strong manufacturing histories.[12] But the 1980s were also the period in which large factories were leaving the cities, and policy makers and analysts did not capture the distinctiveness of urban manufacturing. The focus was exclusively on the advanced services sector as such, and not on the demand it engendered indirectly for urban manufacturing. This left many firms struggling even though there was demand for their products. The privileging of advanced services easily misses the opportunity to articulate the multiple components of urban economies more strongly and effectively. One can reach a multiplier effect whereby the whole is more than the sum of its parts—that is, the network effect that lies at the heart of urban manufacturing. It is not only finance and high-tech sectors that are networked. Further, in this networked urban manufacturing, there is a collective action dilemma that can work to the advantage of the city:

---

12. See Loomis (1995), Mitchell and Sassen (1996). See also Gsis and Zeltsman (1994).

a single firm cannot move out without losing the network effect. Thus, individual firms are more likely to stay in the town. This dilemma would be solved if the whole network had to move together, but individual firms tend to be small factories managed by independently minded owners.[13] A central plan to move together is not an easy option for these owners. Therefore, a town that puts in the effort and resources necessary to develop urban manufacturing is likely to be in a win-win situation if there is a demand for these products, which means that it needs some type of dynamic service economy. This would then be a very different angle from which to look at the service economy: ensuring a dynamic advanced services sector is a condition for having a dynamic urban manufacturing sector, but only if the latter is supported in sustaining the added costs of operating in a city with a vigorous service economy.

REFERENCES

Birch, Eugénie L. and Susan M. Wachter, eds. 2009. *The Shape of the New American City*. Special issue, *The Annals of the American Academy of Political and Social Science* 626, no. 1.

Fitzgerald, Joan. 2009. "Cities on the Front Line." *The American Prospect*, April 13.

Gratz, Roberta Brandes. 2010. *The Battle for Gotham: New York in the Shadow of Robert Moses and Jane Jacobs*. New York: Nation Books.

Gsis, Tamar and Jon Zeltsman. 1994. *The Wood Research and Action Project: Project Report, Findings, and Analysis*. New York: Industrial Technology Assistance Corporation.

13. I have made a parallel analysis for the advanced service sector: its highly networked character creates a similar collective action problem. For instance, São Paulo is the leading global city in Latin America, and hence a critical platform for global firms from around the world interested in Latin America. But it is a city with vast stretches of poor and miserably housed populations, much violence (including by the police), and generally inadequate basic services, except in very high-income urban spaces. Surveys of advanced services firms and high-income professionals showed over and over that both had a strong preference for moving to Buenos Aires. But this was not an option except if the whole networked sector moved, which was of course not quite feasible.

Loomis, John. 1995. "Manufacturing Communities." *Places: Forum of Design for the Public Realm* 10, no. 1: 48-57.

Mitchell, Matthew and Saskia Sassen. 1996. "Can Cities like New York Bet on Manufacturing?" In *Manufacturing Cities: Competitive Advantage and the Urban Industrial Community*. Conference sponsored by the Harvard University Graduate School of Design and the Loeb Fellowship, March 8.

Sassen, Saskia. 2006. *Cities in a World Economy*. Thousand Oaks, CA: Pine Forge Press.

———. 2008. *Territory, Authority, Rights*. Princeton, NJ: Princeton University Press.

Sennet, Richard. 2008. *The Craftsman*. New Haven, CT: Yale University Press.

Swinney, Dan. 2009. "Illinois Future: The Global Leader in Manufacturing the Products of the Future." Chicago: Center for Labor and Community Research, www.clcr.org.

THE GRACE OF
IMPORT REPLACEMENT

Susan Witt

> Economic life develops by grace of innovating; it expands by
> grace of import replacement.
> —Jane Jacobs, *Cities and the Wealth of Nations: Principles of Economic Life*

WHAT I FIRST noticed about Jane Jacobs was the power, breadth, and mobility of her intellect. Only later did I recognize the equally great warmth of spirit that informed her thinking and turned into a force of change. She stands as one of the most visionary economic thinkers of the last part of the twentieth century.

Her intellect was breathtaking. I first heard her speak at the Annual E. F. Schumacher Lecture she gave in 1983 on "The Economy of Regions." From the podium at Mount Holyoke College she painted an image of regional economies in which myriad small industries produce for regional markets—small industries that depend on local materials, local labor, local capital, local transport systems, and appropriately scaled technology to conduct business. She pictured the fruits of this regional industry spilling over to support a rich cultural life in the city at the hub of the region. This bustling creative energy would then foster new innovation and industry, filling in the "niches" of the economy.

The products of a regional economy would be particular to it, using the woods and stones found there—cherry tables, white cedar decks, and granite steps. The choices in the marketplace would vary with the seasons—eagerly anticipated summer berries, autumn apples, the new maple syrup in February, and spring garlic and parsnips.

The diversity of products would require a diversity of workers with a diversity of skills, all part of a face-to-face economy of place with the multiple sidewalk contacts "from which a city's wealth of public life may grow." Citizens would have direct knowledge of working conditions in offices, factories, and home industries; they would see the results of manufacturing practices on hillsides, fields, and rivers. Landowner, banker, shopkeeper, entrepreneur, laborer, secretary, teacher, craftsman, and government official would sing together in the community choir, carpool one another's children to school, and meet at the farmers' market. They would see the complexity that shapes the regional economy, understand its various elements, and remain accountable to each other in maintaining the web of connections that sustains it. Practiced conservationists, they would recognize the necessity of protecting and renewing the natural resources that form the basis of economy.

Yes, there would be products exported to other regions—but only the excess, and in moderation. Yes, there would be imports for their variety, exoticness, their sweet breath of other cultures and places. But at the core of these robust and vital regional economies would be the capacity to meet the economic, social, and cultural needs of the people of the region from within the region itself, not in a spirit of isolationism but in a spirit of self-determination and with the hope that other regions will achieve similar economic independence. In such a scenario, the wealth of one region would not depend on exploiting the natural and human wealth of other regions.

Jacobs believed that the best way to achieve such sustainable economies is to examine what is currently imported into a region and develop the conditions to produce those goods from local resources with local labor. She referred to this process as "import replacing."

By contrast, the typical economic development model for a city is to use tax credits and other incentives to lure the branch of a multinational corporation into its environs. Yet without deep roots in the local economy and local community, the same corporation might suddenly leave the area, driven by moody fluctuations in the global economy, and abandon workers and families.

Building a regional economic development strategy based on import replacement will require appropriately scaled economic institutions to meet the needs of local businesses. The elements of any economic system are land, labor, and capital. Land and other natural resources are the basis of all production; labor transforms the raw materials into products; capital organizes the labor and facilitates distribution of the goods.

New import replacement businesses will require:

- Affordable access to land on which to locate the enterprise and gather the raw materials used in production;
- Capital in amounts and on terms tailored to the business;
- A trained, engaged, and supported workforce.

How a society shapes its institutions for land, labor, and capital will determine if it can meet these requirements. These regionally based economic institutions will not be government driven. Rather, they will be undertaken by free associations of consumers and producers working cooperatively, sharing the risk of building an economy that reflects a shared culture and shared values. Small in scale, transparent in structure, designed to profit the community rather than to profit from it, they can help facilitate a community's desire for safe and fair working conditions; for production practices that keep air, soil, and water clean, and renew natural resources rather than deplete them; for innovation in the making and distribution of food, clothing, shelter, and energy; and for a more equitable distribution of wealth.

Many models for such new economic institutions have already been developed, and more are being pioneered.

ACCESS TO LAND

Aldo Leopold, the great American ecologist and environmentalist, argued in *A Sand County Almanac* that "land should be a community to which we belong, not a commodity that is bought and sold." The commodification of land and other natural resources means that those who control ownership can benefit unfairly from the universal need for land to build homes, maintain a healthy environment, and produce the goods needed by all members of a cooperative society. Land prices increase simply because land is in demand, not necessarily because of a deliberate effort by the owner. The nineteenth-century political scientist Henry George referred to this increase as a speculative gain, an "unearned increment," and noted that it distorts the economic system, placing value where no real value has been created and transferring wealth unfairly.

To address this problem, Robert Swann, the founding president of the E. F. Schumacher Society, was inspired by Henry George and his intellectual descendants Leo Tolstoy and spiritual leader Vinoba Bhave, to develop a new approach to land tenure for North America: the community land trust, a regional nonprofit corporation with open membership and a democratically elected board of directors. A community land trust acquires land by gift or purchase, develops a land-use plan according to local need, and then leases the sites for residential or commerical uses. Individuals own the buildings on the land but not the land itself. At resale the buildings must be offered back to the land trust at no more than the replacement value of improvements adjusted for deterioration, thus keeping the land out of the speculative market. The owner is able to reap the fruits of labor applied to natural resources but not the land value itself, which is held for the community.

An example is Indian Line Farm in South Egremont, Massachusetts—the first Community Supported Agriculture (CSA) farm in North America. In 1997 its owner and CSA pioneer, Robyn Van En, met an untimely death. In the popular vacation region of the Berkshires the farm could have easily been sold as a site of an imposing second home. But the fertile soils were good for growing quality vegetables, and the citizens of the region wanted to maintain Indian Line as a working farm.

Two farmers, Alex Thorp and Elizabeth Keen, joined the Community Land Trust in the Southern Berkshires and the Nature Conservancy in an innovative partnership. The Community Land Trust raised the money to buy the land, the Nature Conservancy acquired a conservation easement on the land, and the two farmers purchased the buildings and entered into a 99-year lease on the land. The lease and attached land-use plan stipulated organic farming methods and ecological care of abutting wetlands, and set a minimum standard for the amount of crops raised per year to ensure that the land be kept in active production. Addressing the critical connections between ecology, economy, and community, this model project is protecting habitat, preserving agricultural property, and keeping small-scale, organic farming viable, so that the farmers can practice wise stewardship without having to use unsustainable growing methods to pay off land debt. There are now over two hundred community land trusts in the United States. They stand as a vehicle for citizens to make land in their communities available for appropriate productive purposes, including renewable energy production, agriculture, sustainable timber practices, new industries, recreation, and cultural activities. They also serve as one of the major providers of affordable homeownership opportunities throughout the United States.

If a significant amount of land in a region is held by a community land trust, the economic role of land is transformed. Access to land will be by social contract rather than by market forces. Citizens of a region, working together, can determine specific priorities for land use, such as identifying a site for a cannery that would extend the capacity of the region to produce its own food. The land trust can then offer favorable terms in a lease if those priorities are met. Funds once tied up in land purchase and financing are then freed and can be invested in equipment and product innovation, thus facilitating new import-replacement activity.

CAPITAL TAILORED TO REGIONAL NEEDS

The function of money is to serve as an abstraction for real economic exchange. This is both its almost mystical power and its flaw. If we did not have the tool of money, we would be left with direct barter, limited to what we could trade at a particular place and time—such as carrots for cordwood. Without the carrots I could not acquire the cordwood. Money stands for a value created at an earlier time, stored, and used in exchange for goods needed in the present time. Money allows values to be gathered together and applied to an entirely new type of venture in the future. This accumulation allows the entrepreneur to organize human initiative and raw materials, using them to create some previously unrealized product for healing the sick, producing energy, or transporting goods. Quite wonderful.

This property of money to serve as an abstraction for actual exchange can, however, rapidly escalate unchecked, so that ultimately money begets money through sheer movement of capital. The real living consequences of the workings of capital—the labor conditions, the manufacturing process, the effect on ecosystems of obtaining raw materials, the use of fossil fuels to transport goods, the pockets of accumulation—all tend to be obscured. Our private discussions and public debates, by consequence, become limited to the cost of goods and return on investments, resulting in a global economic system unimpeded by environmental, social, or cultural concerns.

Placing control of monetary issue in a centralized coalition of national governments and for-profit banks is to choose a system that intrinsically favors the biggest borrowers. Creating a tool appropriate for financing import replacement by regional businesses will require a democratization and decentralization of the monetary issue.

In the question period following her 1983 E. F. Schumacher Lecture, Jane Jacobs was asked how best to foster the robust regional economies she called for in her talk. Her answer was "regional currencies." She called a regional currency one of the most elegant tools for stimulating and regulating production and trade.

Encouraged by her remarks, E. F. Schumacher Society staff took up the challenge to launch a regional currency. In 2006 it incorporated a new nonprofit, BerkShares, Inc., serving the Berkshires of western Massachusetts. BerkShares' local currency was issued that September. The notes are beautifully designed, printed on high-quality security paper, and honor the values of community, economy, ecology, and sustainability. Each of the five denominations of notes (1, 5, 10, 20, and 50) carries the picture of a local historic figure: the Stockbridge Mohegans, the Berkshires' first people; W.E.B. Du Bois, the great civil rights leader

and author; Robyn Van En, CSA pioneer; Herman Melville, author of
Moby Dick; and Norman Rockwell, who captured small-town America
in his paintings and illustrations.

The currency is placed in circulation when citizens exchange federal
dollars for BerkShares at any of the thirteen participating branches of
five regional banks. The federal dollars remain on deposit in anticipation
of any future redemption. During the first three years of issue, 2.5 million BerkShares went out in circulation from the banks. In a region of
19,000 residents, over 400 businesses have formally signed on to accept
BerkShares, and another 300 do so informally and on occasion.

The use of BerkShares, a paper currency, requires face-to-face economic exchange. The citizen/buyer must meet the merchant/owner
and enter into conversation. In the course of multiple transactions, an
understanding begins to grow of the nature of the business, how it fits
in the streetscape of the town, the working conditions of its employees,
the availability of locally made goods, the impact of new regulations, the
necessity to respond to the changing tastes of consumers, the hurdles
to prosperity, and the many roles the merchant plays in the community—as volunteer ambulance squad member, school board official, or
community theater player.

When using BerkShares to purchase directly from a *producer*, the
information shared may be even more deeply sourced in the local landscape. The conversation may turn to how to detect the first signs of a
tree blight plaguing the maple syrup industry, or how the heavy spring
rains kept the bees from pollinating the apples, resulting in a smaller crop.

BerkShares are a "slow money," to borrow a term coined by author
and investor Woody Tasch. It takes more time to process a transaction:
time for courteousness, time for building a connection with a community
of place. "Inconvenient," some will say. Yes, when compared to the hasti-
ness and anonymity of an internet purchase; but rich with information
needed for public life. A democracy thrives only when its citizens are
informed and engaged by public issues.

Slow money is not sleepy money: it is awake to the flow of economic
life pulsing through a region, shaping its future, providing warning signs,
and creating options for public policy and private initiative. Slow money

makes us conscious again of the impact of our economic transactions, not just as purchasers but as taxpayers, investors, and philanthropists.

BerkShares circulate in the Berkshire economy from tree pruner to lawyer to auto mechanic to potter; from low-powered community radio station to theater to printer to doctor to grocery store. Whenever a business cannot recirculate all of the BerkShares in its till, it returns them to one of the banks to convert to federal dollars. That return to the bank, taking the notes out of circulation, means that a merchant or craftsman or service provider cannot find products he or she needs in the local economy. There is a leak in the system. Every leak identifies the potential for a new import-replacing business to stop the leak and keep the wealth in the community. The identification of new locally sourced products to meet local demand is the first step in transforming a local currency from a simple medium of exchange to a tool for financing new manufacturing.

From its initial role as manager of the flow of the currency, a non-profit issuer such as BerkShares, Inc. could convene a process for setting community priorities for loans made in the local currency. Loan applications should meet economic, ecological, and social criteria, and could be weighted according to the type of business. For instance, lending policies might favor loans to producers of basic necessities, rather than luxury goods. Through favorable financial terms, citizens of the region, working with the nonprofit issuer and local banks, could help direct the nature of economic development.

BerkShares, Inc. is planning to develop such a loan program, and ultimately to untie BerkShares from their federal dollar backing and turn them into a more independent regional currency. The value of the currency could be linked to a local standard, such as a basket of agricultural goods—maple syrup and field greens and goat cheese and apples. In this way the currency would hold a constant local buying power independent of the fluctuations in the federal dollar. Rather than an abstract concept, the value of exchanges between citizens would be linked to the actual goods produced locally.

During the current period of precipitous global financial collapse, communities are quickly learning to be flexible and creative, and local currency experiments are proliferating. From Philadelphia to Ithaca, across Michigan to Wisconsin and out to Oregon, as well as in small towns in England, Germany, France, and the former Soviet Union, in Thai villages, and in Australian cities, citizens are designing their own currency systems to help shape their unique economies.

ENGAGED WORKERS

Workers who have affordable access to land through community land trusts enabling them to create import-replacement businesses, and who have access to financing opportunities through a developed local currency program, have more opportunity to become owners of the means of production rather than being only dependent laborers. Such ownership means a more equitable distribution of wealth in the regional economy and a healthier, more engaged social life.

The most praised example of a region that has expanded its economic development with the creation of worker-owned and worker-managed businesses is the city of Mondragon, in the Basque region of Spain. In the 1950s, inspired by the social teachings of the parish priest, Father José María Arizmendi, the youth of the town organized worker cooperatives to produce industrial goods.

Ownership in each of the Mondragon cooperatives is limited to workers. Capital is borrowed, rather than raised through stock sales to outside investors. The highest paid worker/owner earns no more than seven times the income of beginning worker/owners. Thirty percent of profits is kept for reinvestment in the business, and another 10 percent is given away to support cultural and educational activities.

Because of the success of the cooperatives and their generous donations, the Mondragon region has seen a renewal of Basque language, dance, and music programs. Education is free to all age groups. The technical schools provide a steady stream of newly trained workers for the growing cooperatives. The specific capital needs of cooperatives requiring loans, not stock investment, led to the creation of a unique bank. One arm of the bank serves as a "social entrepreneur" researching new business opportunities for future cooperatives.

When the Mondragon Cooperatives became convinced of the importance of ecologically responsible products and production practices, they placed the full force of their research and development team to the task. They are becoming leaders in Europe in wind and solar energy production. A related group of consumer cooperatives have begun their own canneries and greenhouse production to ensure quality food over extended seasons.

There are now over 125 cooperatives in the Mondragon system and another 125 related businesses (www.mcc.es). Together, they generate over 16 billion euros in revenue on an annual basis and employ over 100,000 people, the majority of which are worker/owners. Of these jobs, 45,000 are in the once-economically-depressed Mondragon region.

We can draw many lessons from Mondragon: the cooperative structure that makes owners of workers; the reinvestment in the cultural life of the region; the health-care and pension plans, also run cooperatively, providing a social safety net without depending on government programs; and the significant role of the research and development arm of the bank, which reduces risk in business startups, maximizing community investment and entrepreneurial capacity. Mondragon's social entrepreneur section has generally focused on products that fill niches in the global marketplace, leading to several successes, but also creating dependencies on the stability of the global economy. If the same capacity were turned to creating business plans for import-replacement enterprises that meet social, ecological, and cultural priorities, the combination could be a powerful additional force for generating the vital and diverse regional economies envisioned by Jane Jacobs.

EXUBERANT EPISODES OF IMPORT REPLACEMENT

Building new regional economies is hard work: most of us rest complacently in our role as passive consumers instead of co-producers and co-shapers of our own economies. Yet the work is being done in small towns and cities around the country and around the world, sparked by the urgency of the times and motivated by affection for neighbors and neighborhoods; for the fields, forests, mountains, and rivers of specific landscapes; for the local history and culture that bind all these together; and for a common future.

Still I hear the cautionary voice of Jane Jacobs. Yes, citizens working in partnership can and should create conditions that foster regional economies, such as the ones described so far. But these initiatives cannot by themselves determine the shape of new economies: "Nobody commands an economy that has vitality and potential. It springs surprise upon surprise instead of knuckling down and doing what's expected of it, or wished for it," Jane Jacobs wrote in *The Nature of Economies*.

In the end, it is the diversity and spontaneity of regional economies that is the measure of their strength—an exuberance that engages entrepreneurial skills and leads to unpredictable and unplanned "repeated episodes of import replacement," that mighty fountain of community economic regeneration.

RETHINKING "JACOBS SPILLOVERS,"

OR HOW DIVERSE CITIES ACTUALLY MAKE INDIVIDUALS MORE CREATIVE AND ECONOMICALLY SUCCESSFUL

Pierre Desrochers & Samuli Leppälä

> Specialization of economic activity in a city can be a starter, a transitory starting point. If the city doesn't diversify rapidly, specializing is a dead end. No specialty is safe. All become either obsolete or outgrown...so forget it as an economic strategy, except as a very transitory phase.
>
> (Chavez et al., Interview with Jane Jacobs, 2002)

INTRODUCTION

ALTHOUGH BETTER KNOWN for her writings and struggles against "highway men" and modernist planners, Jane Jacobs' own favorite book was *The Economy of Cities* (1969), and she considered her economic writings to be her most significant legacy. Despite the work of a few heterodox scholars who built on her ideas, however, her contribution in this area initially failed to generate much interest among well-established academics. Then, in the 1990s, a string of papers written by prominent economists tried to compare her core insights with those of highly respected scholars. Unfortunately, these researchers essentially reinterpreted her writings in light of their own agenda, and ultimately reduced her framework to so-called "Jacobs spillovers," i.e., how skills and know-how developed to solve problems in one line of work end up being used to solve problems in other lines of work, a process that is assumed to be greatly facilitated in a local economy where numerous and different industries stand side by side (Desrochers and Hospers 2007).

Our goal in this chapter is to first review and expand briefly on the "Jacobs spillovers" literature. We then briefly discuss our own attempt to address the latter's shortcomings through case-study research.

I. JANE JACOBS ON THE BENEFITS OF LOCAL ECONOMIC DIVERSITY

From the moment she left Architectural Forum for good in 1962, Jane Jacobs devoted most of her writing to issues related to economic development. Keeping up with the approach and themes she had elaborated upon in *The Death and Life of Great American Cities* (1961), she argued that urban economic diversity is absolutely crucial to economic development because it offers a wide range of resources to deal with the numerous challenges of a city's economy.

Jacobs' case for local economic diversity is grounded in the study of past and present entrepreneurs, inventors, businesses and economic institutions, but also in the evolutionary biology's tenet that greater biodiversity facilitates the emergence of different niche-seeking species (Jacobs 1980, 113). In the context of local economies, this analogy suggests that a city dominated by one industry is similar to a one-crop ecosystem in terms of vulnerability, lack of resilience, and incapacity to generate new differentiations (Jacobs 2004). As mathematician and philosopher David Ellerman (2005) points out, the evolutionary biology/ Jacobsian perspective contradicts mainstream economists' long-standing emphasis on static efficiency[1] and comparative advantage—the principle according to which regional economies should specialize in what they do best. As another Jacobs enthusiast, the clinical biochemist and historian of technology Terence Kealey observes, "large markets are more

---

1. By "static efficiency," Ellerman refers to mainstream economists' habit of studying how existing resources are allocated between competing uses as opposed to how new resources and products are created through entrepreneurship and innovation.

efficient than thin ones [because they] create a greater diversity of goods and companies and consumers" (2008, 353).

Of course, Jacobs was far from being the first individual to view local economic diversity as more desirable than a poorly diversified industrial structure. Traditional arguments in this respect fall within three categories. The first is the idea of "urbanization economies," in which diverse firms are in close geographical proximity from one another and benefit from better and more affordable services—ranging from shared transportation infrastructures to services provided by specialized firms (for example, accounting, manpower, and catering firms)—than would otherwise be the case. A diversified economic structure also results in more jobs being created when a new productive activity is added to the local mix because of the presence of a larger number of local suppliers that can be called upon. Finally, diversified local economies are more stable and resilient than regional economies, whose fate ultimately rests on the temporary demand for a particular type of good or service (Desrochers and Sautet 2008).

Jacobs' writings, however, went beyond these arguments and further emphasized the importance of local economic diversity for entrepreneurial and innovative activities. While Jacobs' discussion of the issue is complex, the key insight that drew economists to her work is that innovations are the result of new combinations and are thus facilitated by local economic diversity. "The greater the sheer numbers and varieties of divisions of labor already achieved in an economy," Jacobs explained, "the greater the economy's inherent capacity for adding still more kinds of goods and services. Also the possibilities increase for combining the existing divisions of labor in new ways" (1969, 59).

While Jacobs gave numerous illustrations of the result of these processes, such as firms branching out into new types of production or existing materials put to new uses, she did not write much about how these things actually occur through individuals' actions and interactions. One exception is a case in which she describes how old skills were preserved by "combining them with new goods or services or new purposes":

Some artists of my acquaintance who were fighting a proposed expressway in New York decided, as part of the campaign, to paint a huge street banner. A banner of the weight and opacity desired, capable of withstanding the wind without being torn from its ropes, turned out to be impossible to construct until someone remembered an old-fashioned sailmaker in the second story of a loft nearby. He had never made a street banner before, but he made one now, and a good one. Here was a case in which the practitioner of the old work (to which a new purpose was, for the moment, added) was not the one who took the initiative. His work, rather, was seen—by somebody who had a problem—as appropriate work upon which to add something more. In this instance, since the sailmaker produced only this one banner, the addition of new work was ephemeral. But much the same thing can happen on a more permanent basis. (Jacobs 1969, 69-70)

2. ON THE BIRTH AND LIMITATIONS OF "JACOBS SPILLOVERS"

The current popularity of Jacobs' writings among well-established economists can be traced back to the work of the "new growth theorists" and their emphasis on the importance of knowledge accumulation and diffusion between individuals (Romer 1994). The first influential paper that looked at Jacobs' work in this light was a discussion by Robert Lucas (1988) of various ways to incorporate human knowledge or skill levels in mathematical growth models. Among other things, Lucas speculated on the importance of the "external effects" of human capital—i.e., the ways by which improvement in one individual's skills raises the productivity of other individuals. The economist, however, was at a loss to explain how these externalities worked in practice and directed his readers to Jacobs' "remarkable" *Economy of Cities*, which he reinterpreted in this light without really discussing its content.

The second paper to refer to Jacobs' economic writings was an attempt by Edward L. Glaeser and three colleagues (1992) to assess the respective importance of various types of knowledge spillovers from one person or group to another. The economists distinguished between three different perspectives, named after important contributors to the field: "MAR" (after the economists Alfred Marshall, Kenneth Arrow, and

Paul Romer), "Porter" (after the management scholar Michael Porter), and "Jacobs" spillovers. The first two approaches analyze the effect of spillovers within a sector (*intraindustrial spillovers*) and the importance of geographical economic specialization, whereas Jacobs spillovers occur between sectors (*interindustrial spillovers*) and will therefore be more abundant in a more diversified local economy. In addition, the MAR perspective favors local monopolies, whereas the other two see strong local competition as a better incubator for innovative behavior. Although much debate surrounds the issue, it seems fair to say that Jacobs' perspective has gathered more support from econometricians (see Beaudry and Schiffauerova 2009).

According to critics, however, these studies rely on measures of industrial concentration or diversity in a local economy—i.e., the importance of one line of work in relation to the total local economic mix—that are then correlated (or not) with general "outputs" such as innovations, new products, patent data, or employment, income, and productivity growth. Researchers invoke the existence of localized knowledge spillovers, but these studies *do not* document or even prove it. As such, localized knowledge spillovers are "no more than a 'black box'" that "provides the researcher with an escape route to avoid studying the specific mechanisms through which [geography and innovation] are linked" (Breschi and Lissoni 2001, 976).

What follows is a summary of our own attempt to document what "Jacobs spillovers" actually are and how they occur in practice.

3. "JACOBS SPILLOVERS" IN PRACTICE

Perhaps the main reason for the paucity of detailed studies of "Jacobs spillovers" is the difficulty of tracking large numbers of individuals who move frequently between different lines of work and/or regularly borrow ideas from fields other than the one they are working in. We tried to address these issues through two rounds of semistructured interviews with Canadian inventors. The first interviews took place between 1997 and 1999 and involved almost exclusively individuals of French-Canadian origins who were somewhat evenly distributed between urban and rural locations in southern Quebec. The second series of interviews was conducted between 2006 and 2009 among English-speaking individuals of diverse geographical origins and cultural backgrounds who were then located in the Greater Toronto Area. Individual inventors were considered good candidates for our purpose because they typically have very diverse professional and educational backgrounds and do not limit their activities to one type of problem or industry. They also frequently move between different lines of work.

Our interviews quickly revealed recurring patterns. The first concerned the nature of the inventive process. As observed by Jacobs and countless other students of human creativity, inventors either applied a familiar solution to a novel task or a novel solution to a familiar problem. Secondly, we identified three broad types of individual actions conducive to an exchange of ideas across industries: 1) switching or moving some types of know-how or materials between different lines of work; 2) observing know-how and materials in one context and incorporating them in a different production setting; and 3) collaborating, formally or informally, with individuals possessing different skills, which results in the development of new or improved products or processes. All inventors who had experienced both diversified urban environments and rural and/or less diversified ones strongly emphasized that the former provided a much better setting for the discovery and development of new combinations of ideas and know-how.

It was also frequently mentioned that urban diversity further improves the chances of switching between different lines of work, especially if an individual is reluctant to move his or her family or separate from well-established social networks. The collaboration of individuals and firms across industries is also much easier when they are in close geographical proximity, as face-to-face interaction greatly facilitates communication between individuals with different types of expertise and jargon. Local diversity further facilitates the observation (whether deliberate or serendipitous) of something useful outside one's core competencies. Finally, as inventors combined ideas from different fields or areas of expertise, arbitrary divisions among "industrial sectors" were constantly crossed.

These processes seemed to remain constant even as other local circumstances and backgrounds varied significantly—for example, linguistic differences, professional trainings, countries of origins, or the technological complexity of an invention/innovation. Our evidence illustrates both the universality of fundamental human creative processes and the recurring problems faced by most individual inventors, such as gathering useful knowledge, finding potentially helpful collaborators, and securing financial resources. Furthermore, our findings support Glaeser's contention that the primary role of cities may not be the creation of cutting-edge technologies, but rather the provision of learning opportunities for "everyday people" (Glaeser 1999, 255). Creative individuals such as the inventors we talked to can develop over a hundred innovations during their lifetime, the near totality of which, of course, remain confined to their places of employment or living. Their main economic impact is therefore overwhelmingly embodied in undocumented innovations created and used in specific factories or plants.

Another significant conclusion of our work is that, as Thomas Edison reportedly observed, genius is one percent inspiration and 99 percent perspiration, meaning that an idea for a new marketable device is only the beginning of a lengthy process, most of which is entrepreneurial in nature. All the creative activities aimed at the development of a final product that we observed required much improvisation, prototyping, trial-and-error, and production and marketing efforts. Access to diverse resources and people proved crucial at each stage of the process. While Jane Jacobs acknowledged the importance of local economic diversity for entrepreneurial activities, this aspect is in our opinion insufficiently appreciated by academics who are naturally inclined to emphasize knowledge creation above all else.

One case which illustrates most of the issues discussed so far is that of an experienced entrepreneur/inventor based in Jacobs' adoptive hometown of Toronto. A chemical engineer by training, he first worked for the oil refining industry, but soon struck out on his own as he felt that this would give him more freedom to use his creative capabilities. His first business was in plastic molding, where he constantly developed new products such as bottle openers, sophisticated key holders, travel mugs, and acrylic wine goblets. His inspiration for that last item came as a result of meeting glassmakers in various trade shows and of seeing the advantages of acrylic for some segments of this market. Acrylic was strong, safe, and much more versatile in terms of using colors, attachments, and printed text or figures. Interestingly, the product turned out to be a commercial success in the U.S. market, but not in Europe.

Later on, the inventor/entrepreneur moved to the glassware industry, where, after some research, he was eventually able to build on technologies used in windshield production to create a compound that drastically improved the resistance of glassware. While learning and experimenting, he had observed the difficulties of decorating glass and learned about safety issues related to the use of lead. To overcome these problems, he developed a plastic coating for glassware on which ink could be sprayed. He further refined his ideas after seeing a demonstration of digital ink-jet printing at a graphics show in Toronto. He looked for a specialist in this area and is now developing the product together with a digital ink-jet printing company. According to him, digital printing will make the production faster and less costly than traditional methods would allow, while the resulting product will be durable, non-toxic, and visually much more appealing. In the course of the interview, the inventor/entrepreneur strongly emphasized the importance of locating his main operation in Toronto, which provided him over time with, among other things, easy access to suppliers and specialized workers of all kinds who had themselves had clients and experiences in a large array of industries.

CONCLUSION

As the economist Sanford Ikeda observed, Jacobs' dynamic vision has much to offer to mainstream economists who, long ago, "stopped thinking about markets as urban" and replaced them with a "plantation model" that disregarded the importance of time, changing preferences, and creativity. In Ikeda's opinion, Jacobs offers a way out of the economists' fixation on the notion of efficiency, "where today is basically the same as yesterday and tomorrow the same as today, and nothing can be made to work better than it already is." We could not agree more and hope that in the future more academic researchers will be willing to venture out of their offices to gain a greater appreciation of Jacobs' economic insights and of human creativity in general.

REFERENCES

Beaudry, Catherine and Andrea Schiffauerova. 2009. "Who's Right, Marshall or Jacobs? The Localization versus Urbanization Debate." *Research Policy* 38, no. 2: 318-337.

Breschi, Stefano and Francesco Lissoni. 2001. "Knowledge Spillovers and Local Innovation Systems: A Critical Survey." *Industrial and Corporate Change* 10, no. 4: 975-1005.

Chavez, Roberto, Tia Duer and Ke Fang. 2002. *Urban Economy and Development. Interview of Jane Jacobs.* Interview on behalf of Urban Forum 2002. Washington, DC: The World Bank. www.worldbank.org/urban/forum2002/docs/jj-full.pdf.

Desrochers, Pierre and Gert-Jan Hospers. 2007. "Cities and the Economic Development of Nations: An Essay on Jane Jacobs' Contribution to Economic Theory." *Canadian Journal of Regional Science* 30, no. 1: 115-130.

Desrochers, Pierre and Frederic Sautet. 2008. "Policy Environments that Best Enable Entrepreneurship: The Case of Regional Specialization vs. Spontaneous Industrial Diversity." *Entrepreneurship: Theory & Practice* 32, no. 5: 813-832.

Ellerman, David. 2005. "How Do We Grow? Jane Jacobs on Diversification and Specialization." *Challenge* 48: 50-83.

Glaeser, Edward L. 1999. "Learning in Cities." *Journal of Urban Economics* 46, no. 2: 254-277.

Glaeser, Edward, Hedi Kallal, Jose Scheinkman and Adrei Shleifer. 1992. "Growth in Cities." *Journal of Political Economy* 100, no. 6: 1126-1152.

Jacobs, Jane. 1961. *The Death and Life of Great American Cities.* New York: Random House.

——. 1969. *The Economy of Cities.* New York: Random House.

——. 1980. *The Question of Separatism. Quebec and the Struggle over Sovereignty.* New York: Random House.

——. 2004. *The Nature of Economies.* New York: Random House.

Kealey, Terence. 2008. *Sex, Science & Profits*. London: William Heinemann.

Lucas, Robert E. 1988. "On the Mechanics of Economic Development." *Journal of Monetary Economics* 22, no. 1: 3-42.

Romer, Paul M. 1994. "The Origins of Endogenous Growth." *Journal of Economic Perspectives* 8, no. 1: 3-22.

BEYOND GREEN JOBS:

SEEKING A NEW PARADIGM

Ron Shiffman

A S A CHILD, I often accompanied my father to the factory in the Bronx where he worked. Everyone in my family—indeed everyone I knew, including my uncle, who owned the factory—referred to it as "The Place." It was during those visits to "The Place" that I learned about manufacturing and what it meant to the people who worked there—both the exploited and the exploiters, although the line between the two was often blurred. I also learned about the interrelationship between what went on in "The Place" and the city's various specialty districts that enhanced and nurtured it and so many other "Places" like it. In essence, I learned through osmosis the importance of location on production activities and the impact of agglomeration on our local economy.

Those visits, many of which occurred on the weekend, exposed me to the internal operations of "The Place" and taught me about machinery and assembly lines—albeit short ones, since the business was of a modest size. I discovered the tool-making activities of skilled craftspeople, some of whom moonlighted at my uncle's place and were employed by others during the regular workweek. Their presence in turn enhanced the production activities that took place during the week at my uncle's factory and expanded the product line that was offered. I sat by, watching my father conceive and build machines aimed at improving productivity that looked like they had been designed by a cartoonist, but still made the production process far more efficient. I saw my father forming an idea for a machine, awkwardly designing it, and then cobbling it together with parts he would search out and purchase during our meanders through the machine-part shops of Lower Manhattan. I often accompanied him and my uncle on trips to the inner suburbs, where they would visit with an industrial engineer. They took with them ideas, hastily drafted plans, and, at times, working models of machines, which were assembled by my father based on his intimate knowledge of the production process. On these visits, "Bennie the Engineer" would refine my dad's ideas and eventually produce the plans for a more efficient version of my dad's creative efforts. Observing the process, I learned to draw, to draft, and eventually to become an architect. Along the way, I also learned that more often than not, we work in teams to accomplish our goals, and that the synergy that results from interaction of people with varied skills and insights is critically important.

More significantly, because of my exposure to the social conditions of the workers, I gained an understanding of what work meant to people and the importance of having a job. I also learned about the relationship of "The Place" to other "Places"—the impact of the city on the manufacturing process and the impact of manufacturing on both the city and its residents. All of this contributed to fuel my interest in cities, with their concentrations of interrelated and synergistic functions. Years later, when I became a planner and a member of the New York City Planning Commission, these memories re-emerged. I visited a number of factories—real "Places," for those who worked there. I remember, for example, visiting with Donald Gratz, of Gratz Industries, in Long Island City, Queens, and seeing his custom metal fabrication business. I was struck by the diversity of the people who worked there and of the products he crafted, from sculpture and high-end furniture to Pilates exercise machines. Most of all, I remember the pride he and his workers took as they toured me through their "Place." I remember his discussion about the suppliers, finishers, and upholsterers he purchased parts from—his entire supply chain. He discussed how, one by one, they were being displaced, and how this had an adverse affect on his business. He discussed his own displacement history and the importance of location. Location to him was not theory: it was time and dollars saved or lost. He and others whom I visited taught me the cumulative impact that ad hoc

decisions and the absence of a manufacturing policy had on our economy. While working on a community-initiated plan for West Harlem, I
became acquainted with a portion of the community between Broadway
and the Hudson River running from 125th Street to 133rd Street. The
area had been selected by Columbia University to build a second campus
to address their perceived expansion needs. The planners and architects
hired by the university described the area as vacant and underutilized.
Indeed, when viewed from the air and from afar, it looked that way.
However, when you walked through this "terrain vague" and entered the
building, you found scores of new and emerging enterprises—furniture
makers, restorers, sculptors, painters, musicians engaging in rehearsals,
ethnic art dealers who had rented small storage spaces to sell their wares,
and interior designers who used the area's storage facilities as swing
space for their efforts further downtown. They were the incubators of
new enterprise development, the nurturers of new cultural institutions,
and the silent partners of dozens of flourishing activities that made up a
diverse and dynamic urban fabric.

Earlier on, while working in the Williamsburg and Greenpoint
communities on a community-initiated plan, I and my colleagues at the
Pratt Center encountered similar enterprises as well as a sprinkling of
larger manufacturers. We also encountered cases of high respiratory illness, many of them rooted in the industrial past of the area. The concentration of poorly regulated businesses, highways, and waste transfer
stations that had replaced former industrial sites all contributed to create
one of the city's most polluted areas. At the same time, the area still
generated a significant number of jobs. The planning challenge, as we
defined it, was to avoid eliminating manufacturing and the desperately
needed jobs it created, while at the same time addressing the pollution
and the high rates of respiratory illness associated with it. We learned
that the two major causes of respiratory illness were air pollution and
poverty. Based on those findings, and the realization that many of those
victimized by the pollution were also dependent on those unhealthy jobs
for a livelihood, we developed a plan for the area that sought, and continues to seek out, ways of cleaning up manufacturing processes and
producing green products. Out of that effort we built alliances between

manufacturers and environmental justice activists, believing that by cleaning up the environment we could, as Paul Hawken, Amory Lovins, and Hunter Lovins declared in their book *Natural Capitalism*, kick-start the next Industrial Revolution.

As we end the first decade of the twenty-first century, whenever we discuss the state of the economy, our attention is drawn to the necessity of mitigating the pervasive threat of global warming and respecting our natural environment, while at the same time stimulating sustained growth. This is a paradigm shift from the conventional wisdom that addressing issues of the environment and global warming will only weaken and destroy our economy, a belief that has long mired us in the policies of the past and continues to plague the present. This new paradigm urges us to recognize that we must create new economic models that move us far beyond the mere creation of green jobs towards the creation of an entire green economy based on a new view of the relationship between financial, natural, and human capital. This view is predicated on the belief that equity, environment, and economy are integrally linked and synergistically interdependent—something every person who ever worked in an urban factory (a "Place"), or whose child, as in my case, visited a factory, experienced and learned firsthand. It is a concept often espoused of late, but rarely understood and almost never practiced. It embraces, as a fundamental principle of sustainable development, that our focus should be on *qualitative* concepts of development rather than *quantitative* growth.

This sea change in thinking is partly the outgrowth of the advocacy work of people like Van Jones of Green For All, The Apollo Project, and countless other activists in the Environmental Justice movement. Many of them followed in the footsteps of Yolanda Garcia of Nos Quedamos, a group that organized to save their neighborhood from the ravages of abandonment and redevelopment; or took inspiration from Peggy Shepard of WeACT in West Harlem and Elizabeth Yeampierre of UPROSE in Sunset Park, Brooklyn, who organized their respective communities and addressed the interconnected issues that affect environmental quality of life, such as air, water and indoor pollution, land use, sanitation, transportation, and historic preservation.[1] Just as importantly, they acknowledged the need for clean and well-paying jobs for those that reside in the community.

I cite the names above not only to honor the role they played, but also to make the point that this movement emerged from people who are rooted in our neighborhoods and work hand in hand with the members of their community. Their efforts have birthed ideas that are astonishingly timely and pertinent. These visions are often nurtured by necessity and are not the brainchild of any one group, person, or charismatic leader, the way the press and/or the dominant power structure often portrays it, but rather the result of local ingenuity that first and foremost struggles to survive, and over time yields to the instinctive desire to build community. Local experiences coupled with innate observational skills have resulted in a highly sophisticated group of self-educated individuals that in turn are educating a new generation of activists and community developers. The broad and fertile base that birthed the green economic revolution is reflected in region after region throughout the country, and throughout the world.

Indeed, green economic development concepts have emerged in a manner similar to the processes of economic development described in Jane Jacobs' classic book, *The Economy of Cities,* albeit tempered by

---

1. The list goes on and on. Each of us can and should add names to this list, because it is a great indicator of the many successful social change movements that Jane Jacobs and her neighbors in Greenwich Village, and her counterparts like Fran Goldin in the Lower East Side and Elsie Richardson of Bedford-Stuyvesant, epitomized. People like Alexis Torres-Fleming of Youth Ministries and Luis Garden Acosta of El Puente, who have organized and engaged their communities in environmental justice issues, formulated and affected public policy and helped to educate legions of young people. The same did my former colleague at the Pratt Center, Joan Byron, who helped to translate many of these visions into plans for community and economic development. I should mention as well Omar Freilla of the Green Workers Cooperatives and Majora Carter, formerly of Sustainable South Bronx, who turned their talents to build institutions in their communities to foster green economic development and to communicate the message to countless others, and Eddie Bautista, organizer and advocate, who left the New York Lawyers for the Public Interest to become a staff member of the Mayor of New York, Michael Bloomberg, moving environmental economic development concepts from idea and advocacy to policy and action.

today's technologies and our increased awareness of global warming and the ever-increasing environmental—i.e., natural capital—deficit. This is a deficit far more onerous and threatening than any financial shortage: it cannot be easily corrected, and definitely not in a timely manner.

Building on these community-based initiatives, and in partnership with other environmental justice organizations, think tanks, and some innovative local government agencies, nonprofit organizations like the New York Industrial Retention Network (NYIRN) have embarked on programs to link green jobs with green manufacturing. Others, like the Center for Social Inclusion (CSI), are focusing on the closely related issue of racial equity to make sure that the "green economy" does not exclude women, new immigrants, and people of color. In essence, it was people of color who took the lead in dispelling the myth that the environment and the economy are in conflict. If "green jobs" bypass communities of color, they will by definition cease to be "green," in that they would fail to launch sustainable livelihoods for those who need them most. The work of groups like CSI is essential if we are truly to see our economy thrive both domestically and internationally. Like a three-legged stool, if any of the three Es—Economy, Environment, and Equity—is not there, the stool will not stand.

Earlier, I alluded to the fact that as citizens of the world we cannot afford to keep increasing our natural capital deficit by depleting our natural resources. Similarly, we cannot afford to further increase our human and social capital deficits by subjecting any sector of our society to poverty and inequality. Simply stated, we have the means to replenish our financial resources within a discreet period of time, but lack the political will and the capacity to replenish our social or human capital deficits within a similar period. We have even less capacity, and far less time, to replenish our natural capital. If we succumb to a policy of investing too little in people, in our natural environment, and in a green and sustainable infrastructure, we are doomed to a world of increased chaos and economic and social disintegration.

Our challenge, therefore, is to see how we can bring about a more sustainable system of wealth creation while also promoting a higher quality of life for a greater and more diversified number of people. Diversifying our economy to respond to the diverse interests and capabilities of our population is fundamental to meeting this challenge. The development of green industries provides this opportunity: by creating well-paying jobs, supporting a local, green economy, and building upon a renewed infrastructure and available renewable resources, green industries have the potential for creating sustainable economic growth and reducing adverse impacts on the environment. Sustainable industries encompass diverse products, processes, and supply chains, such as energy-efficient devices and their components; products made from recycled, recyclable, and sustainable materials; non-toxic products; and traditional products made at factories through new, more energy-efficient, and environmentally appropriate processes. Furthermore, sustainable industries are founded on "high road principles," which include standards for job equity and fair living wages.

Given the extraordinary financial challenges this generation is facing, the private sector and governments at every level must invest wisely to get as much return as possible for the scarce resources available. Sustainable industrial development has emerged as an overarching winning strategy for urban metropolitan regions dealing with an array of complex challenges, from stagnant tax bases, suburban sprawl, global warming, and increasing energy and transportation costs, to deteriorating infrastructure and growing un- and underemployment.

The market demand for more energy-efficient, environmentally friendly products, and for local sourcing of materials and goods is already growing. Connecting this demand to supply chains in urban areas can create considerable economic and environmental benefits for cities. Moreover, these urban industries are often connected to regional supply chains that could be further developed to create more competitive economies and reduce the carbon footprint of metropolitan regions.

In 2006, New York City Mayor Michael Bloomberg launched PlaNYC 2030, a major initiative to address the issue of global warming. At the time I wrote that "PlaNYC 2030 is one of the most exciting initiatives I've seen [in my 40-plus years as a practicing planner]."[2] While

---

2. Jeff Byles and Olympia Kazi (eds.), *The New York 2030 Notebook. Institute for Urban Design, Notebook#01.* New York: Urban Center Books, 2008.

some significant progress has been made, particularly by the city's Department of Transportation, much remains to be done. Some innovative initiatives, such as restricting auto access to the central business district by adopting a congestion pricing strategy, were unfortunately politically rejected. However, more disturbing to this observer is that while some mayoral agencies have honed their activities to achieve the goals outlined in PlaNYC 2030, others seem to have ignored them completely. Ironically, every major development plan supported by or initiated by the city ignores PlaNYC 2030: Willets Point in Queens; Columbia University's Expansion into West Harlem, Manhattan; and Atlantic Yards and the Broadway Triangle in Brooklyn, New York. All of these significant developments planned for the next ten or twenty years are on the whole devoid of any sustainable strategies.

Over the past nine months, a group of Pratt graduate planning students have been working with me on an alternative plan to the city's proposed rezoning of the Broadway Triangle, a predominantly underdeveloped, former manufacturing area that lies between the largely Hassidic and Latino South Side of Williamsburg, the predominantly Latino community of Bushwick, and the largely African-American community of Bedford-Stuyvesant.[3] This highly contested area, which was designated an urban renewal zone decades ago, is slated to be rezoned by the City from a mixed-use manufacturing and residential area to a low- to mid-rise residential community. The zoning proposal is devoid of any sustainable development requirements and would allow the reuse of city-owned property for affordable housing, while the private landowners would be free to build market-rate housing to serve the rapidly growing Hassidic community. If the past is any indicator of what will happen, we will see a rapid development of slipshod six- to eight-story residential structures through the area, exploiting every available property and taking advantage of the

---

3. The extraordinary Pratt Graduate Planning Team that worked on the Broadway Triangle included Alisa Drooker, Ryan Grew, Simon Kawitzky, Scott Lyon, and Anusha Venkataraman. All have continued their involvement in the project to this day and are working on finding ways to implement the recommendations put forth in this innovative and sustainable effort.

families that will eventually occupy the housing. Community facilities, open space, and parks have all been ignored in the city's rezoning proposal.

The alternative plan that the Pratt students developed increased the density and heights of the buildings to make them compatible with the surroundings, and targeted housing to low-, moderate-, and middle-income families. This retains the existing job base, and creates opportunities for green enterprise development and green jobs. The plan calls for space for parks and a range of community facilities—the building blocks upon which a sense of community can emerge. The students also proposed closing selected streets to create pedestrian pathways, creatively using the roofs of buildings, and retaining and improving manufacturing uses. Most importantly, they called for all of the new buildings to produce more energy than they consume by taking advantage of new green technologies such as biofuels, geothermal energy, wind, and solar. To tap the full potential of this new source of energy, they proposed the establishment of a community-owned energy company to help design, develop, distribute, maintain, and "sell" these distributive forms of energy production. In other words, they put forth a twenty-first century strategy that truly met the objectives of PlaNYC 2030, and that I believe will eventually become an accepted model for sustainable development. Unfortunately, as of this writing the city has chosen to ignore innovation and pursue instead a familiar and politically comfortable path, one that ignores the needs and imperatives of our time.

The locational advantages and the opportunities described above are similar to those I observed in the visits with my father, with Donald Gratz, and in the community planning studies that my colleagues and I have engaged in over the years. Those observations have led me to believe that addressing issues such as environmental justice, sustainable livelihoods, and global warming in a holistic way will rekindle our local economies. I often feel like the child watching the parade go by in the fable "The Emperor's New Clothes." But like that child I feel obligated, and I hope all of us feel obligated, to point out what we observe and believe—actually to shout it out loudly in the same way that Jane Jacobs did in her writing and in her actions.

Epilogue

JANE'S CUP OF TEA

Mary Rowe

> [T]ruth is made up of many bits and pieces of reality. The flux
> and change in itself is of the essence. Change is so major a
> truth that we understand process to be the essence of things.
>
> Kate, protagonist of Systems of Survival (1992)

I FIRST MET JANE JACOBS in the fall of 1996. She greeted me
at her front door with a bright smile and took me into her house,
where we settled at one end of her dining table. Behind me was a bank
of windows, in front of which the Jacobses had created a well to support
various houseplants. Over the subsequent years, I watched that well grow,
as plants arrived as gifts and were given a home there. Along the other
wall of the dining room were high bookshelves that ran the whole length
of the area. I now know that there was no single room in the Jacobs
house that didn't have stacks of books, placed on homemade shelves: her
own and a wide range of others, spanning topics from micro- and macro
economics, ancient history, metallurgy, microbiology, botany, and quantum physics to philosophy. Oh, and a few about cities.

At our first meeting we shared a pot of herbal tea. I had approached
this encounter with trepidation. My host notoriously resented intrusion
and had been cautiously hospitable to my request to meet, reminding
me she was eager to get back to work and did not want any distractions.
Jane was ambivalent about making herself available to others, suspicious
of requests from groups simply wishing for her endorsement or too

lazy to develop their own campaigns. She did not suffer fools well, and arriving at her house or taking any of her precious time unprepared was not met with a grandmotherly sympathy. But once you survived the gauntlet, and proved to her you were dedicated and well-informed, she was extremely generous with her time and counsel. As I got to know her better, I became aware of the many, many mentoring relationships (she would never have called them that) she had formed with students, activists, aspiring planners, and architects wanting to reclaim the virtues of their professions that Jane had so rightly critiqued.

My hesitation to contact her was also partly due to my own insecurity: I had arrived in Toronto at eighteen for university and had stayed, but recently decamped to an old schoolhouse in a rural county, commuting in to Toronto a few days a week. I worried I'd lost my urban "cred." I remember standing on her porch after I had rapped on her door, feeling guilty about having driven to her house. Why hadn't I parked the car at a remote lot on my way in from the country and at least taken public transit part of the way? I fessed up that I thought she might view me as some sort of traitor, having moved to the country, or worse, ill-equipped to be managing a project with cities (and their economies) as its focus. I like cities, I really do, I assured her. She matter-of-factly responded: country folk have always enjoyed coming to the city.

My unease was quickly calmed by Jane's quirkiness. I'd brought her some strawberry jam I'd put up earlier that year. She would accept it only if we negotiated a trade from her larder of handmade things, which included her special peach jam. We sat for an hour conversing about the events of the day (Jane read the daily newspaper religiously first thing in the morning, and worked on the cryptic crosswords throughout the day), and I began my tentative inquiry into the ideas that mattered to Jane Jacobs.

What occasioned my visit was the job I had been hired to do—coordinating a complex series of events and initiatives in celebration of Jane's work. Eventually this programming would come to be called Ideas That Matter: Jane Jacobs. After my first few months of creating some infrastructure to support it, I was pretty much directed by the founder and funder of it, Canadian businessman and philanthropist Alan Broadbent, to *go meet Jane*. Up until that point, John Sewell, who had been Mayor of Toronto when I was an undergraduate and had since evolved into a skilled journalist and often strident city activist, had been the project's main connection to Jane. It was Sewell who had cooked the idea up with Broadbent to mobilize a series of events in Toronto to focus local and national attention on Jacobs' ideas. He had then convinced Jane to let it happen. Sewell would leave brainstorming meetings at which various speakers and topics would be proposed, warily saying, "Well, now I have to run this by *Jane*..." Jane had consented to the initiative with two conditions: that she did not have to do anything in preparation for it, and that her friends and family could come for free. Sewell proposed a public "conversation," and she consented. The planning of the event reflected a concept Jane had identified early as the key underpinning of city vitality: self-organization. So groups and individuals and institutions across Toronto were invited to develop for the fall of 1997 their own programming in connection to Jacobs' ideas—and hundreds did.

During one of those public conversations, Jane chose to highlight in her discussion with the venerable Canadian journalist Peter Gzowski a project some young people had conceived in their contribution to the fest. They had imagined their city and what was at the heart of it: a candy factory. A bemused Gzowksi probed Jane about the young people's choice, and what followed was a vintage Jacobsean explanation, with appreciative chuckling, of how local economies develop—and flourish—by initially reflecting local needs. Of *course* the children embedded a candy factory at the center of their city: it met their needs. Jane went on to explain how the children's city economy could grow, and if it began to replace whatever it was importing with locally sourced materials, then it could sell its candy to other children's cities, who needed and wanted candy too.

One of the outgrowths of the Ideas That Matter program was the creation of an annual Jane Jacobs Prize, which Alan Broadbent continues to fund. Part of the deal of the award was an annual dinner at Jane's house with her and previous recipients of the award. The event at Jane's house evolved into a raucous potluck to which recipients brought their favorite food. Each year I would hear from the kitchen a rite of passage, when the newest recipient, flush with excitement, would launch confidently into laying out some generalized learning from his or her work. A rebuke from Jane would abruptly follow, with her characteristic adamancy: "No, no, you've got that all wrong..." Humbled, the new recipient would then be challenged by Jane's formidable reaction to not overdraw conclusions from a particular experience, but to appreciate better what else was taking place, what other details were there to pick up, and what was to be learnt about how things actually work in their particular, unique and specific sphere.

Jane valued invention, experimentation, and new approaches. She also valued old ideas and old ways, observing that if they were useful once, they might well come back into fashion or necessity. Long before "diversity" became the new urban buzz word (which has become code for racial and ethnic variety), Jane was pointing out how diversities of all kinds—in work, in language, in currency, in custom and practice—strengthen the capacity of a culture to adapt and evolve. She was particularly appreciative of new ideas that came out of the old, that built upon what was already in place. As Jane aged, her hearing failed and efforts to find hearing aids that were easily manageable by an older person's level of manual dexterity proved fruitless. Jane's daughter, Burgin, lived on the West Coast, where, among other things, she had made bags and purses from recycled materials. During one of her visits, Burgin developed an ear trumpet for Jane—a molded piece of shellacked paper shaped to funnel the sound into Jane's ear. After making a few prototypes, Burgin perfected the ear trumpet, and Jane proceeded to carry at least one (she had alternates in different colors) in the blue cloth bag that she toted around. It helped her hear, and she was fiercely proud of her daughter's device.

Jane was thrifty. Her thriftiness was born not simply of economic necessity, but from instincts of resourcefulness and curiosity. In addition to her own jams and jellies, the roof garden atop the third story of her house was an urban legend in Toronto that proved to be true. She bragged about a particular year's abundance of tomatoes they had brought down (to put up) for canning. The tea stash that I would routinely ferret around was full of samples from outings to small Asian groceries—not name brands of hyped caffeine-free products. She kept in the freezer an open can of frozen orange juice (next to the bottle of gin for her famed West

Village martinis), scooping out just the right amount that was needed for the number of glasses required. Jane's seemingly homespun practices were not based on some sentimentalized notion of rural self-sufficiency. She did what she did because she took pleasure in doing it, and because the fruits of her labors were a superior product. Her Loring peach jam really *was* much better than anything you could ever purchase.

Jane was playful. Although she did not see herself as religious, she delighted in certain festive rituals, such as Easter egg decorating and Christmas cookie making. The ever-present jigsaw puzzle, the small toys, the bits of foil wrapping she would crunch into tiny-sized goblets: Jane had an enjoyment of whimsy, rooted in a frugal basic-ness. She did not like flash, was not attracted to only fine or expensive things: she fundamentally enjoyed simple, plain fun. Once, when she was ailing a bit, I asked if there was something I could prepare her to eat. An egg? A piece of toast? "Chocolate sundae," was the reply, "the Hershey's is on the counter." She had an impish grin and matching giggle, which I saw surface usually in response to something mischievous, fun, or playful. I never heard Jane laugh at another's expense. It's not that she was always charitable towards others—I'm not sure she was. But I don't think she saw other people's weaknesses or errors as funny; the ones she noticed were too serious to be joked about.

Jane was exceptional. She was a fierce intellect, but not a predictable one. One of the infuriating ways in which some of those who valued her work have coped with her death (and their attempt to define, or even capture, her legacy) has been to invoke a kitschy adaptation from the evangelical movement, and propose it as a useful question: What Would Jane Say? Well, one of the most salient attributes of Jane Jacobs was that you never had a *clue* what Jane might say, or how she might say it. Her scope was so broad and her knowledge so varied, that she saw and heard in events and circumstances things no one else noticed or considered. We have much to learn from *how* she arrived at her conclusions, making the observations she did. When you read something of Jacobs with which you agree, it's easy to assume she arrived at that assessment the same way you did. But that was not necessarily so. Jane was ruthlessly rigorous in arriving at her positions, but her route to a conclusion was rarely straightforward. I remember when she told me she had decided on one of the themes for her next book: "It's about the demise of the nuclear family," she offered. Although initially taken aback that this topic figured at all in her thinking, I assumed that her position would stem from her observation of rising divorce rates, and that we shared a socially progressive understanding that families configure in different ways. But a draft of *Dark Age Ahead* (2004) showed me that her path to this conclusion was nothing like my own. Instead, Jane's view was derived from her observation of rising house prices necessitating two working incomes to meet the economic needs of households. The impact on the nuclear family was collateral damage.

It took Jane a very long time—years and years—to develop her ideas, and any suggestion that you could just drop a question into the JJ machine and out would pop the Jacobsean answer tells us much more about our own ill-fated desire for easy answers than it does about her. This was one truly unique and original mind, a person who spurned academia for its rigidity, arrogance, and artificial segregation of disciplines, and whose ideas were shaped by her own observations and the inputs she sought out. Her work reflects directly what she saw (hence the title of this book) in the world, what she heard from others, and what she read in the myriad books she acquired, or the reports and articles and leaflets she was sent, and the often obscure magazines she perused. Jane asked every question when she was figuring something. If you happened to participate mid-inquiry and offer some superficial reading of it, a harsh rebuke was forthcoming. Jane had a tenacity in the pursuit of her ideas that was verging on ruthless. She divided her work time between two phases. The first was for seeking input, a time when she would read widely and seek stimulation and interaction. Following that, there would be extended periods of output, when her writing occupied her completely and she would confine her energy to that and that alone. No phone calls. No visits. No form of output other than that which supported her work.

In *Systems of Survival* (1992), a sort of treatise on the value systems that underpin Western culture, Jane described two moral "syndromes"— a *guardian* one concerned with order, and a *trader* one concerned with commerce—that existed in a dynamic balance permitting a society to survive and thrive. It occurs to me that for most of Jane's time she was very much the trader, living the attributes of the commercial syndrome she described. She was open to inventiveness and novelty, used initiative and enterprise, was industrious and thrifty, dissented for the sake of the task (indeed), and in her activism she collaborated easily with strangers and invested for productive purposes. But when it came time to write, the guardian traits emerged and she shunned trading, exerted prowess, was obedient and disciplined, adhered to her own tradition, was certainly exclusive, and showed great fortitude.

Jane *saw*. This commitment to observation—seeing what really *is*—may be Jane's most significant attribute, because it meant she noticed real things that ideologues, looking for symptoms to support their own theories, missed. She was fundamentally curious. Unlike many of us, though, Jane had a temperament that supported her inquiry; she didn't seem to need things to be predictable or to always "make sense." Surprise and serendipity were her stock and trade: she once told me she was eager to live a long time "to see how things turn out." Because for Jane there was no prescription, therefore no prediction. Things just happened, and she spent a career looking closely to see if she could see how. Jane shunned rules (particularly ones that had become archaic, overly bureaucratic, or ineffective). Perhaps a better way to negate any association of her ideas with the rigidity of an ideology would be to suggest she rejected moving from the general to the particular. Her method was inductive: observe what is actually happening, and see how that can inform our understanding of how things actually work (as opposed to how any theory suggests they should work).

Jane was a pragmatist: societies with a lot of rules are dull, inflexible, and they die; the ones that thrive are constantly finding new ways to self-organize in sustainable ways. She rejected draconian municipal zoning ordinances that sought to control people's behavior. Instead she advocated for performance-based zoning, as a way of reconciling, on a case-by-case basis, conflicting uses. Similarly, for many years Jane sat on the board of a non-governmental organization in Toronto called Energy Probe, and there she kept company with several other outliers to the traditional environmental movement. Rejecting the time-honored (and failed) measures of regulation and control of "bad" behavior, Jane and others favored a system more closely tagged to the dynamics of the market, of use and consumption. They advocated for measures that created accountability and incentive for innovation, which often involved deregulation and decentralization, but brought about a strengthening of the direct relationship between the producer and the consumer.

Jane was not sentimental. I had always understood the word to describe a kind of saccharine-sweet, cloying fondness for something in the past, but Jane corrected my misunderstanding of the term. To be sentimental was to remember something in an idealized way, which was anathema to her. Many of Jane's reflections about why government policies (and their makers) were often so anti-city were rooted in her observations of this culture's penchant for rural sentimentality. To Jane even the White House lawn reflected a misplaced hearkening back to gamboling sheep in pastures-gone-by, when in fact agricultural life was dispatched from the city to begin with and was hard, punishing work with often meager returns. It is important to remember this about Jane as we watch mistaken efforts by some to mimic her observations about neighborhoods and streetscapes and create tidy, stylized communities with front porches and town squares. These are sentimentalized scenes of old towns, and Jane was not interested in anything artificial or disconnected from its surroundings. What she saw was how communities—of people, of businesses—that were allowed to form organically, step by step, connecting with what was already there, were the communities that could adapt and thrive, constantly able to adjust and transform as needed. The idea is not to recreate in new what is old: it is to use the old and add on, in innovative ways that meet current needs and opportunities, to create the new.

Some of us learn the hard way. My work took me to New Orleans in 2005 in the months immediately following the levee failures. I would visit Jane and report what I was seeing. In a weak moment I lamented, "What are we going to do about New Orleans? It's below sea level, people can't get back, and everything's a mess." Jane, with a steely stare, said, "YOU are not going to do anything about New Orleans. You're thinking like a bureaucrat. The people of New Orleans will decide what to do about their city—not you." For many, many months that harsh moniker remained. Jane would greet me with "Are you still thinking like a bureaucrat?" Although stung by it at the time, her brusque rebuke remains with me, daily, as I watch New Orleans (where my wife and I now live) piece itself together organically, idea by idea, block by block. No grand solutions have emerged here. No czar, with one singular vision, has been able to perform (thank goodness). Instead, what we are witnessing are the small and steady efforts of individuals and self-organized groups they form and organize, who build upon what is here, and what can be added. Collectively they are making a city that supports diverse interests and pursuits, that is the crucible for innovation and creative responses to change, and that celebrates what great cities have done for millennia: create multiple forms of wealth and culture.

REFERENCES

Jacobs, Jane. 1992. *Systems of Survival: A Dialogue on the Moral Foundations of Commerce and Politics*. New York: Random House.
——. 2004. *Dark Age Ahead*. New York: Random House.

STUDY GUIDE

THE PURPOSE OF this guide is to spark meaningful discussions about your own community. Using our authors' unique points of view about cities and economies, we offer the following questions to catalyze open-ended conversations. Feel free to create new questions and tailor the ones that follow to the circumstances of your local environment.

1.1. Between Utopias *(Deanne Taylor)*

a. Taylor describes a fundamental difference between the Utopian vision of Toronto held by its officials and the Citizen vision held by Torontonians. Does the same dichotomy exist in your community? If so, what might be done to bridge these differences?

b. Taylor writes about how "the mirror of the local mass media" reflects a city's image. Do the local media in your community faithfully mirror your experience of place? Do you agree with Taylor that much remains "hidden" by the media discourse? If so, what is missing that you would like to expose?

1.2. Jane Jacobs and the "Battle for the Street" *(Ray Suarez)*

a. Do you know what the conditions were like in your community directly following World War II? Were the changes that ensued similar to what Suarez describes? Which senior citizens can you talk with to get an idea of how your community changed after the war?

b. What do you see in your community that would illustrate Suarez' notion of "design for fashion and convenience, not utility and success"?

1.3. **The Mirage of the Efficient City** *(Sanford Ikeda)*

a. Jacobs and Ikeda argue that the sometimes messy inefficiencies of a city are fundamental to a strong urban economy, and that these strengths cannot be achieved in a planned, rational way. Do you agree with this observation? Can you identify "messy inefficiencies" in your community that are also a sign of your city's strengths?

b. Ikeda notes that new entrepreneurial opportunities arise from the mistakes and failures of preceding actions—particularly during a recession. Do you see any new businesses emerging from the detritus of the economic collapse of 2008?

1.4. **The Intelligence of Informality** *(Nabeel Hamdi)*

a. Are there influential civic organizations in your community that started as small, informal grassroots efforts?

b. Hamdi concludes his essay with a list of what he calls "codes of conduct." How do you feel about the following codes?

Imagine first: reason later

Challenge consensus

1.5. **Integrating Observation and Action: The Tao of Urbanism** *(Nan Ellin)*

a. How do you think the concept of "integral urbanism" could add value to your community? Are there examples of integrated urbanism emerging in your city?

b. Ellin identifies the "problem" of too much sun in Phoenix as an opportunity for that community to be a leader in solar energy. Are there any so-called "problems" in your community that could be turned into opportunities?

2.1. Nine Ways of Looking at Ourselves (Looking at Cities) *(Arlene Goldbard)*

a. One of the lenses Goldbard asks us to use as we look at ourselves is the "lens of the uncolonized mind." What do you think about her description of those whose minds are "colonized" in comparison to those whose minds are "uncolonized"?

b. Another lens Goldbard suggests we use is "the lens of common fate." What decisions have policy makers in your community made that might have been made differently if they had used this lens?

2.2. The Logic of Small Places: A Story in Three Ballets *(Mindy Thompson Fullilove)*

a. What does Dr. Alexander Leighton mean by breakdown and repair happening simultaneously, as exhibited in the Japanese internment story?

b. Fullilove presents three very different stories to underline the importance of understanding the human relationships and interactions of a neighborhood. Which story relates more to your experience, and why?

2.3. Of Things Seen and Unseen *(Alexie Torres-Fleming)*

a. Do you know people in your community who spontaneously led a regeneration effort as Alexie Torres-Fleming did? Describe some of these people and the impact of their actions.

b. What assets might be in your community that, as Alexie notes, are not easily "seen" or recognized? Are there "unseen" elements of your community that you believe should be exposed?

2.4. The Fine Arts of Seeing: Professions, Places, Art, and Urban Design *(Rob Cowan)*

a. Cowan created a tool available at www.placecheck.info. If you have computer access, try exploring this tool and see if it offers you and your community ways to convert your observations into action.

b. Find visuals of your city that depict the area and its people in its earliest days. Are there familiar landscapes, historic buildings, or other features that appear similar today? Are there elements missing that you wish were still in place today, or that you are happy not to see anymore?

3.1. Cities and the Wealth of Places *(Daniel Kemmis)*

a. In Kemmis' imagined conversation with Jacobs, she asks him "to take a closer, harder look at what we both see as this inherently valuable phenomenon of the good city." What would you identify as the inherently valuable phenomena of your city?

b. Jacobs also asks Kemmis how these values could contribute to a larger economic system. How could the phenomena you identified strengthen your local and regional economy?

3.2. Queen Street *(Elizabeth Macdonald and Allan Jacobs)*

a. If you were to close your eyes and imagine walking along a street in a city you know well, what details of that street can you see in your mind's eye? What constitutes the "greatness" of that street?

b. How does a streetcar line maintain the diversity and strength of the iconic Queen Street?

3.3. The Interconnectedness of Things *(Ken Greenberg)*

a. Greenberg writes about a city's ability to be "self-organizing" and the importance of "organized complexity." Can you identify a self-organizing system in your home, neighborhood or community?

b. The author presents Jane Jacobs' way of seeing the city as "a perpetually unfinished, intensely interactive web of relationships." How is this way of understanding relationships within a city similar to the interconnected relationships of ecosystems?

3.4. **Jane Jacobs: The Toronto Experience** *(David Crombie)*

    a. The author describes a "civic ethos." Can you describe the civic ethos of your community? What role does it play?

    b. The author writes about Toronto as a "global village" and reiterates the importance of diversity. In what ways does cultural diversity contribute to the fabric of your city? How does diversity in the economy and land use shape your city?

3.5. **The Village Inside** *(Matias Echanove and Rahul Srivastava)*

    a. Srivastava and Echanove write that "Gandhi's most architecturally relevant pronouncement was that any construction must be built with material solicited from an area of approximately five miles radius around the site." If you were to apply this dictum to your community, how do you imagine your city might look today?

    b. Srivastava and Echanove report that one of the keys to the success of informal communities is the "tool house," a live/work structure in which space is used in multiple productive ways. Can you identify any areas in your community where a version of the "tool house" exists?

4.1. **Listen, Learn, and Teach—Patiently** *(James Stockard)*

    a. How can the different perspectives of professionals and non-professional citizens contribute to preserving and shaping vital urban places?

    b. Stockard emphasizes that a planner's role is not to convince but instead to listen, learn, teach, and be patient. Are these components part of planning practice in your community?

4.2. **Built Form and the Metaphor of Storytelling** *(Robert Sirman)*

    a. Discuss Sirman's point that design became political in the 1960s. What changes does he refer to? How did these changes affect your community?

b. Robert Sirman incorporated Jane Jacobs' wisdom into the design and planning of the National Ballet School Building. Are there any buildings in your community where Jacobs' insights seem to be consciously or unconsciously incorporated? What do they contribute to the experience of the building?

4.3. Steps Toward a Just Metropolis *(Chester Hartman)*

a. Hartman challenges the traditional role of the planning profession as being dominated by the physical dimension and stresses the importance of interdisciplinary collaboration. Can you describe an instance in which collaboration has strengthened a specific planning decision in your community?

b. What are your impressions of "The Right to the City" movement?

4.4. Illuminating German Urban Planning Policies in the Light of Jane Jacobs *(Peter Zlonicky)*

a. Zlonicky asks us to consider whose voices remind us of "human values in our cities." Who (person or organization) can you identify in your community who champions the values of people and "knows how to overcome social and economic polarization"?

b. Zlonicky writes about cities being in "constant transformation," and that evolving change and adaptive reuse are what give European cities their "inner strength." Do you see transformation in your community? If so, does it provide an "inner strength"?

4.5. Reviving Cities *(Jaime Lerner)*

a. Lerner maintains that "to innovate is to start. Hence, it is necessary to begin. Imagine the ideal but do what is possible today." Do you agree? What first step would you take to improve your community?

b. What do you think of Lerner's concept of "urban acupuncture"? Where in your community could urban acupuncture be used? What are the neglected areas or "scar marks" in your community?

5.1. Recognizing What Works: A Conscious Emulation of Life's Genius *(Janine Benyus)*

a. Benyus describes the "ecological story" of a place. What ecological stories can be told of your community, town, or city?

b. Benyus suggests that "nature is our partner, our mentor in answering the question, 'How shall we live here?'" Based on the ecological story of your community, how could you alter the way you live there, and how do you see this affecting your environment?

5.2. Codevelopment as a Principle for Next Generation Infrastructure *(Hillary Brown)*

a. Brown refers to the "biophilia hypothesis," a theory suggesting that "humans are psychologically, aesthetically, and ultimately spiritually predisposed to affiliate with nature." Does this theory resonate with you? What natural elements do you feel the strongest affinity with?

b. Brown writes about the elegance of "codevelopment." What codevelopment processes can you imagine that could benefit your home, your neighborhood, and your community?

5.3. Jane Jacobs Basics *(Richard Register)*

a. Register gives some very specific reasons for not designing cities around the car. Can you identify additional reasons specific to your community?

b. How is your community moving in the direction of becoming an "eco-city," if at all? Would you like your city to become the eco-city described by Register?

5.4. **Jane Jacobs: Environmental Preservationist** *(Roberta Brandes Gratz)*

   a. Gratz writes that "conservation, localism, and recycling are essential to true green building and sustainable development." How might this holistic approach be applied to future standards for green building? How can it address the question of measuring sustainability?

   b. How might recognizing the importance of preservation in existing built environments shape a broader purpose for the environmentalist movement? What specific overlapping objectives do you see the environmental movement and preservation movement sharing?

5.5. **For You Jane** *(Jan Gehl)*

   a. Gehl describes how the new NYC World Class Streets plan is beginning to incorporate elements of Jacobs' vision. Which of these elements do you think might be implemented in your own community to help foster better relationships between people and with the built environment?

   b. What does the author mean by "city attraction number one—the other people"?

5.6. **Think of a City and What Comes to Mind? Its Streets** *(Janette Sadik-Khan)*

   a. Sadik-Khan illustrates the decisions New York City leaders are now making in order to remind people that streets are more than places for cars. If you could restore streets in your community as places for people, where would these places be, and how could it be done?

   b. Under Sadik-Khan's leadership, New York City has been converting portions of streets into plazas and adding bike lanes. Who rides bicycles in your community? What are the difficulties bicyclists encounter there?

6.1. **When Places Have Deep Economic Histories** *(Saskia Sassen)*

 a. Sassen discusses the impact of local economic history on a city's current economic character. Does this observation relate to your city? Do you know the "embedded" economic history of your community?

 b. Sassen notes that most people think of the knowledge economy as distinct from the material or manufacturing economy. Name other examples of how the actual fabrication of material goods is necessary to foster the creative process.

6.2. **The Grace of Import Replacement** *(Susan Witt)*

 a. Witt writes that "the elements of any economic system are land, labor, and capital." What role does each of these factors play in sustaining a healthy, local economy?

 b. Witt gives the example of cooperatives as successful tools for invigorating local economies while empowering and democratizing the labor force. How might such an idea apply to a local industry in your own community? What would be the benefits of such a cooperative to both the individual workers and the community as a whole?

6.3. **Rethinking "Jacobs Spillovers," or How Diverse Cities Actually Make Individuals More Creative and Economically Successful** *(Pierre Desrochers and Samuli Leppälä)*

 a. Can you identify any "spillover" businesses in your community?

 b. Do you know of any entrepreneurs in your community who applied their knowledge from another industry to initiate a new business?

6.4. **Beyond Green Jobs: Seeking a New Paradigm** *(Ron Shiffman)*

 a. Shiffman remembers the visits he made to the factory in the Bronx where his father worked. Do you recall taking similar walks in your city? Are there people and businesses that you remember as having magical qualities?

b. The author describes "programs to link green jobs with green production, focusing on green manufacturing and the potential for new enterprise development." What examples in your community show that a green economy is emerging? If you were an entrepreneur in your city, what new green enterprises would you like to launch?

CONTRIBUTORS

Janine Benyus is a natural sciences writer, an innovation consultant, and author of six books. In *Biomimicry: Innovation Inspired by Nature* (1997) she names an emerging discipline that seeks sustainable solutions by emulating nature's designs and processes. She co-founded an education and innovation company called Biomimicry Guild, which consults with business, academic, and government leaders, and conducts seminars about nature-inspired processes. Ms. Benyus teaches interpretive writing, lectures at the University of Montana, and is active in wildlands restoration. She has received several awards, including the Rachel Carson Environmental Ethics Award, the Lud Browman Award for Science Writing, and the Science Writing in Society Journalism Award.

Hillary Brown is a Fellow of the American Institute of Architects and the founding principal of the firm New Civic Works. Clients she has helped adopt environmental guidelines include the Governors Island Education and Preservation Corporation, the City of New Haven, the State University of New York at Buffalo, and the Battery Park City Authority. She established the City of New York's initial Office of Sustainable Design. Ms. Brown has served on both the national and the New York Board of Directors for the U.S. Green Building Council. As a professor at the Bernard and Anne Spitzer School of Architecture, she directs the new interdisciplinary Master of Science in Urban Sustainability program.

Robert Cowan is Director of Urban Design Skills, a London-based consulting and training provider. He is the author of *The Dictionary of Urbanism* (2005) and the editor of *Context*, the journal of the Institute of Historic Building Conservation. His publications include *Urban Design Guidance* (2002), *Re:urbanism* (with Kelvin Campbell, 2002), *The Connected City* (1997), and *The Cities Design Forgot* (1995). Mr. Cowan has written design policy and guidance for the governments of England, Wales and Scotland. He devised the community audit method Placecheck and the urban design skills appraisal method Capacitycheck. He is an illustrator and his weekly cartoon appeared in *Planning* for twenty years.

The Honorable David Crombie, PC, OC, has served as Mayor of Toronto, Member of Parliament, and Federal Cabinet Minister. He is the former President and CEO of the Canadian Urban Institute, former Chair of the Ontario Place Corporation, founding Chair of the Waterfront Regeneration Trust, and President of David Crombie and Associates Inc. He currently serves as Chair of the Advisory Council for the Nuclear Waste Management Organization (NWMO) and as Chair of the Toronto Lands Corporation. Mr. Crombie is also a Chancellor Emeritus at Ryerson University and an Honorary Fellow of the Royal Architectural Institute of Canada. He has been appointed Officer to the Order of Canada.

Pierre Desrochers is Associate Professor of Geography at the University of Toronto. His research interests focus primarily on economic development, technological innovation, and corporate sustainability. His publications have appeared in the *Business History Review, Canadian Journal of Regional Science*, and *Economic Development Quarterly*. He was recently awarded a position as Senior Research Fellow at Duke University's Center for the History of Political Economy in Durham, NC.

Samuli Leppälä is Research Associate in the Department of Economics at the Turku School of Economics in Finland. His research findings have appeared in several prominent publications, including the *Chicago Journal of Law and Economics* and the book series *Advances in Austrian*

Economics. Currently, Mr. Leppälä is writing a dissertation on the economics of knowledge.

Matias Sendoa Echanove studied economics at the London School of Economics and urban planning at Columbia University in New York. He has published several articles and essays on urbanism, informal economy, unplanned settlements, participatory politics, and information technology. His project-oriented research investigates the potential of high-tech and low-tech information systems for participatory planning in four cities: Tokyo, New York, Bombay, and Bogotá. He is a co-founder of urbz.net in Mumbai and The Institute of Urbanology in Goa. Mr. Echanove is now a PhD scholar researching information technology and participatory urban planning at the University of Tokyo.

Lynne Elizabeth is founder of New Village Press and past President of Architects/Designers/Planners for Social Responsibility (ADPSR). She is co-editor of *Works of Heart: Building Village through the Arts* (2006) and *Alternative Construction: Contemporary Natural Building Methods* (2000, 2005), and a contributing author for *Ecovillage Living* (2002) and *Sustainable Architecture White Papers* (2000). Ms. Elizabeth previously produced periodicals on sustainable community development, *New Village Journal* and *Earthword Journal*. She founded the former Eos Institute for the Study of Sustainable Living and has served since 1998 as committee member and former juror for the Berkeley Prize for Architectural Design Excellence.

Nan Ellin is Planning Program Director and Associate Professor in the School of Geographical Sciences and Urban Planning at Arizona State University. Ms. Ellin is a former Fulbright Scholar, the author of *Integral Urbanism* (2006) and *Postmodern Urbanism* (1996), and the editor of *Architecture of Fear* (1997). Most recently, she collaborated with Edward Booth-Clibborn on *Phoenix: 21st Century City* (2006). She is a popular essayist and lecturer on urban revitalization, sustainable urbanism, regional planning, and the creative city.

Mindy Thompson Fullilove, MD, is Research Psychiatrist at the New York State Psychiatric Institute and Professor of Clinical Psychiatry and Clinical Sociomedical Sciences at Columbia University. She has conducted research on AIDS and other epidemics of poor communities. She co-authored Rodrick Wallace's *Collective Consciousness and Its Discontents: Institutional Distributed Cognition, Racial Policy and Public Health in the United States* (2008), and is the author of *Root Shock: How Tearing Up City Neighborhoods Hurts America and What We Can Do About It* (2004) and *The House of Joshua: Meditations on Family and Place* (1999). Dr. Fullilove's current work focuses on the connection between urban function and mental health.

Jan Gehl is Professor of Urban Design at the School of Architecture at the Royal Danish Academy of Fine Arts in Copenhagen and the founding partner of Gehl Architects. The findings of his research on Copenhagen have been applied to several cities in Europe, North America, Asia, and Australia. Mr. Gehl's publications include *New City Spaces* (2001) and *Public Spaces, Public Life* (1996). His works present a method for evaluating city quality, the effect of sensory ability on the use of space, and the use of design techniques to encourage active use of outdoor space.

Arlene Goldbard is a writer, social activist, and consultant. Her books include *New Creative Community: The Art of Cultural Development* (2006), *Community, Culture and Globalization* (2002), and the novel *Clarity* (2004). Ms. Goldbard's essays have been published in *The Arts Politic, In Motion Magazine, Theatre, Tikkun*, and others. Her work focuses on the intersection of culture, politics, and spirituality, and she has addressed academic and community audiences on topics ranging from the ethics of community arts to the need for a new cultural policy.

Stephen Goldsmith has worked as an artist, educator, and activist for affordable housing and community development. He was the founder and director of Artspace in Salt Lake City and led the development of live/work, mixed-use space through the adaptive reuse of historic buildings. He was a Loeb Fellow at the Harvard Design School, and served as Planning Director in Salt Lake City before becoming the Director of the Enterprise Rose Architectural Fellowship. He is the Director of the Center for the Living City and an Associate Professor at the College of Architecture and Planning at the University of Utah.

Roberta Brandes Gratz is an award-winning journalist, author, and New York City Landmarks Preservation Commissioner. Her work focuses on historic preservation and community development based on organic, incremental processes. Ms. Gratz's published works include *The Battle for Gotham: New York in the Shadow of Robert Moses and Jane Jacobs* (2010), *Cities Back from the Edge: New Life for Downtown* (2000), and *The Living City: Thinking Small in a Big Way* (1994).

Ken Greenberg is an architect, urban designer, teacher, writer, and principal of Greenberg Consultants. His consensus-building approach has led to coordinated planning and a renewed focus on urban design in cities like Toronto, Hartford, Amsterdam, New York, Boston, Montréal, Washington, DC, Paris, Detroit, Saint Paul, and San Juan. He is the recipient of the 2010 American Institute of Architects Thomas Jefferson Award for public design excellence. He is currently working on a book about cities.

Nabeel Hamdi is a Professor Emeritus of Housing and Urban Development at Oxford Brookes University, a teaching Fellow at the University College in London, and a consultant on participatory action planning and slum redevelopment in cities worldwide. Mr. Hamdi is the author of *Small Change* (2004), *Housing Without Houses* (1991), co-author of *Action Planning for Cities* (1997) and *Making Micro Plans* (1988), and editor of the collected volumes *Educating for Real and Urban Futures*. Among other distinguished honors, he was awarded an Honorary Doctorate from the University of Pretoria, South Africa, in 2008.

Chester Hartman, PhD, is the Director of Research and founding Executive Director of the Poverty & Race Research Action Council in Washington, DC. He is currently serving as an Adjunct Professor of

Sociology at George Washington University. Additionally, Dr. Hartman is the founder and former Chair of the Planners Network and has been a consultant to numerous public and private agencies. He has nearly two dozen books to his name, including *Poverty & Race in America: The Emerging Agendas* (2006), and *There is No Such Thing as a Natural Disaster: Race, Class & Hurricane Katrina* (2006).

Sanford (Sandy) Ikeda, PhD, is Associate Professor of Economics at the State University New York at Purchase and a visiting scholar at New York University. His work emphasizes the impact of governmental institutions on urban areas. Dr. Ikeda's published works include *The Role of Social Capital in the Market Process* (2008), *The Career of Robert Moses: City Planning as a Microcosm of Socialism* (2004), and *Dynamics of the Mixed Economy: Toward a Theory of Interventionism* (1996). He has recently published scholarly articles on social capital, urbanizing economics, and the economic impact of Hurricane Katrina on New Orleans.

Allan Jacobs is Professor Emeritus, Department of City & Regional Planning, at the University of California, Berkeley. He has formerly served as Director of Planning for the City of San Francisco, and as a consultant in city planning and urban design for the cities of Curitiba, Berkeley, Los Angeles, Portland, and several others. His publications include *Great Streets* (1995), *Looking at Cities* (1985), *and Making City Planning Work* (1980). He has won a number of honors and awards, including the Resident in Architecture Fellowship from the American Academy in Rome, the American Institute of Architects Excellence in Education Award, California Chapter, and a Guggenheim Fellowship.

Daniel Kemmis is former Mayor of Missoula, Montana, and Speaker and Minority Leader of the Montana House of Representatives. He is the author of *The Good City and the Good Life* (1995), *Community and the Politics of Place* (1992), and several articles on community building and Western politics. In 1997 he was awarded the Center of the American West Wallace Stegner Award for uniquely articulating a Western brand of community-based politics. In 1996, Mr. Kemmis was awarded the Charles Frankel Prize for outstanding contributions to the field of humanities.

Jaime Lerner is an architect and urban planner, and the founder of the Instituto Jaime Lerner. As the former President of the International Union of Architects and three-time Mayor of Curitiba, Brazil, Mr. Lerner led the urban revolution that made the city renowned for its innovative approach to public transportation, environment, and social programs. He also served two terms as Governor of the State of Paraná. His international awards include the Sir Robert Matthew Prize for the Improvement of Quality of Human Settlements, the World Technology Award for Transportation, the Child and Peace Award from UNICEF, and the United Nations Environmental Award.

Elizabeth Macdonald, PhD, is Associate Professor of City Planning at the University of California, Berkeley. A registered architect and member of the Berkeley Landscape Architecture Department, she is co-editor, with Michael Larice, of *The Urban Design Reader* (2006) and co-author with Allan Jacobs and Yodan Rofé of *The Boulevard Book* (2002). Her most recent research on Olmsted's Brooklyn parkways has been accepted for publication. As a partner in the firm Jacobs Macdonald Cityworks, she was instrumental in the design of Octavia Boulevard in San Francisco and Pacific Boulevard in Vancouver, among other projects.

Clare Cooper Marcus is Professor Emerita in the departments of Architecture and Landscape Architecture at the University of California, Berkeley. She is internationally recognized for her research on the social and psychological implications of design, which focuses on urban open space, affordable housing, and environments for children and for the elderly. She has authored, co-authored, and edited numerous publications, including *Healing Gardens* (1999), *House as a Mirror of Self* (1995), and *People Places* (1990). She has received awards from the American Institute of Architects, the American Society of Landscape Architects, The National Endowment for the Arts, and the Guggenheim Foundation.

Richard Register is an educator and Director of EcoCity Builders, a non-profit organization working on ecological city design, planning, and policy development. He is the author of several books, including *Ecocities: Rebuilding Cities in Balance with Nature* (2006), which features more than 120 of his illustrations. Mr. Register is frequently invited as a speaker at international conferences for designers, architects, planners, environmentalists, government officials, and concerned citizens.

Mary Rowe is a civic and social organizer currently serving at the New Orleans Institute for Resilience and Innovation. She manages projects in the areas of health, governance, environment, and housing and social services. Ms. Rowe was previously Vice President of Urban Programs and Senior Urban Fellow at the blue moon fund. She was also Director of the Toronto-based Ideas That Matter, a convening and publishing program based on the work of Jane Jacobs. Ms. Rowe was a close personal friend and colleague of Jane Jacobs.

Janette Sadik-Khan was appointed Commissioner of the New York City Department of Transportation by Mayor Michael R. Bloomberg in 2007. She is internationally recognized for her expertise in transportation issues, public policy development, and innovative finance. Previously, she has served as Deputy Administrator at the Federal Transit Administration (FTA), where she managed the capital construction budget and was responsible for developing an innovative finance program. Ms. Sadik-Khan holds a law degree from Columbia University School of Law and is a member of the New York State Bar. She was a Rockefeller Fellow and a former visiting scholar at New York University.

Saskia Sassen is an American sociologist internationally renowned for her analyses of globalization, cities, and international human migration. She is a member of the Council on Foreign Relations and of the National Academy of Sciences Panel on Cities. Her most recent publications include *Territory, Authority, Rights* (2008), *A Sociology of Globalization* (2007), and *Cities in a World Economy* (2006). Ms. Sassen has also contributed articles to *The Guardian*, *The New York Times*, *Le Monde Diplomatique*, the

International Herald Tribune, Newsweek International, Vanguardia, Clarin, and the *Financial Times,* among others.

Ron Shiffman is Fellow of the American Institute of Certified Planners, Professor at Pratt's Graduate Center for Planning and the Environment, and former Director of the Pratt Center for Community Development, which he co-founded in 1964. He has authored several articles on urban planning, social justice, and community economic development. Mr. Shiffman has received numerous awards from community-based organizations and national advocacy groups including Architects/Designers/Planners for Social Responsibility (ADPSR), the local chapters of the American Institute of Architects (AIA), the American Institute of Certified Planners (AICP), and the Municipal Art Society.

Robert Sirman is Director and CEO of the Canada Council for the Arts based in Ottawa, Canada. As co-CEO of Canada's National Ballet School in Toronto he spearheaded a massive expansion program that tripled the school's physical plant and revitalized the surrounding inner-city neighborhood. Mr. Sirman served for ten years as Director of Operations and Director of Research and Policy Planning at the Ontario Arts Council. In 2005 he was honored by having a Toronto street—Sirman Lane—named after him. In 2004, he was featured by the Toronto Star as one of the city's top ten "leading lights" in arts and culture.

Michael Sorkin is Distinguished Professor of Architecture and Director of the Graduate Program in Urban Design at the City College of New York. His most recent publications include *Twenty Minutes in Manhattan* (2009), *Indefensible Space* (2007), and *Against the Wall* (2005). He is the author of several hundred articles on architectural and urban subjects. For ten years, he was the architectural critic of *The Village Voice.* He is currently a contributing editor for *Architectural Record.*

Rahul Srivastava, co-founder of urbz.net, studied social and urban anthropology in Mumbai and Delhi, India, and Cambridge, England. He has done research in Georgetown, Malaysia; Kolkata, West Bengal India;

Tokyo and Nara, Japan; and New York City. His previous publications include *Tribal Identity and Minority Status: An Ethnography of Urbanized Nomads Around Mumbai* (1994) as well as several essays on urban anthropology and popular culture.

James Stockard is Curator of the Loeb Fellowship at the Harvard Graduate School of Design. In this role, he directs the nation's only program of independent study for mid-career practitioners in fields related to the built and natural environment. He is a founding trustee of the Cambridge Affordable Housing Trust. He also served as a commissioner of the Cambridge Housing Authority for thirty years. Mr. Stockard was a Rockefeller Fellow at the Union Theological Seminary and a Loeb Fellow at the Harvard Design School.

Ray Suarez is a broadcast journalist who has covered for over thirty years some of the largest urban areas in the world, including New York, Los Angeles, London, Rome, and Chicago. He is currently a Washington-based Senior Correspondent for the NewsHour on PBS. His books include *The Holy Vote: The Politics of Faith in America* (2006) and *The Old Neighborhood: What We Lost in the Great Suburban Migration* (1999). His next book, on demographic change in the U.S., has the working title *Life in the Next America*.

Deanne Taylor is a playwright and co-founder of the award-winning theater company VideoCabaret in Toronto, Canada. Her repertoire includes video effects for plays, operettas, and mock-news cabarets satirizing mass-media politics. Her interest in city planning dates back to the 1980s, when her seminal theatre troupe, The Hummer Sisters, ran for Mayor of Toronto with the help of hundreds of artists and musicians. Ms. Taylor has written and directed many election cabarets and the recent play *City For Sale*. She has also produced twenty plays by VideoCabaret co-founder Michael Hollingsworth, dramatizing the entire history of Canada.

Alexie M. Torres-Fleming is the founder and Executive Director of Youth Ministries for Peace and Justice (YMPJ), a faith-based organization located in New York City. Since its founding in 1994, YMPJ has helped a generation of Bronx youth utilize advocacy, community organizing, environmentalism, and the arts to actively re-imagine and reconstruct their neighborhoods. Ms. Torres-Fleming, who lives in the South Bronx with her husband and two children, is a recipient of the 2008 Jane Jacobs Medal.

Susan Witt has served as Executive Director of the E. F. Schumacher Society since its founding in 1980. She founded the Community Land Trust in the Southern Berkshires and the newly formed BerkShares local currency program. Ms. Witt is a frequent guest speaker on the topics of citizen responsibility and local economies. Her essays appeared, among others, in *The Essential Agrarian Reader* (2004), *The Money Changers: Currency Reform from Aristotle to E-cash* (2003), and *Environmental Activists* (2001).

Peter Zlonicky is a German architect. He studied urban design and renewal in Darmstadt, and in 1963 established the Büro für Stadtplanung und Stadtforschung (Urban Planning and Research Office) in Darmstadt, Essen, and Dortmund. Professor Zlonicky has been a full-time professor at the Technical University in Aachen, then in Dortmund and Hamburg. He has held guest professorships at universities in Venice, Trent, Zurich, and Vienna.

INDEX

ABOUT THE CENTER FOR THE LIVING CITY

Inspired by the work of Jane Jacobs and established with her encouragement prior to her death in 2006, the Center for the Living City aims at enhancing our understanding of the complexity of contemporary urban life and promoting the civic engagement of citizens who care deeply for their communities. Through generative portals including symposia, exhibitions, fellowships, and publications, we work to empower individuals and organizations endeavoring to address the interrelated issues of economies, ecologies, society, and city building.

The Center's work includes coordinating the Jane's Walk program throughout the United States. This annual event, held in honor of Jane Jacobs on the weekend closest to her birthday on May 4th, is designed to connect people with their environments and each other. These informal walking and bicycling tours are part of a self-organized, international movement to discover, explore and celebrate one's own neighborhood.

Further information can be found at **www.janeswalkusa.org** and **www .centerforthelivingcity.org.**

ABOUT NEW VILLAGE PRESS

The book you are holding was brought to you by New Village Press, the first publisher to serve the emerging field of community building. Communities are the cauldrons of social transformation, and the healthiest changes rise from the grassroots. New Village publications focus on creative, citizen-initiated projects—good news and useful tools for growth. Subjects we cover include social justice, urban ecology, and community-based arts and culture. Our core mission has been deeply influenced by Jane Jacobs, so it is indeed an honor to publish *What We See*.

New Village Press is a public-benefit project of Architects/Designers/ Planners for Social Responsibility, an educational nonprofit working since 1983 for peace, environmental protection, social justice, and the development of healthy communities (www.adpsr.org).

See our catalog at **www.newvillagepress.net.**

Learn more about *What We See* and join in the public dialog and other activities related to this book at **www.whatwesee.org.**